airy

ter · Cream
ELIVERY

f Milk

'arm,

Down 603

BOOK NOW FOR CHRISTMAS PARTIES –
DINNERS – OTHER CELEBRATIONS

PARTIES UNLIMITED

*Christmas table decorations
to order*

Tel: HADLOW DOWN 541 or
BUXTED 3442
'AILSA'
Waghorn Lane,
Hadlow Lane

STORES
WN
EVENS

S

OS

VISIONS
Phone: 297

Snip and Stitch

Soft Toys, Pyjama Cases,
Draught Excluders etc.
Made to order

Phone Hadlow Down 375

Anne Purser

"IRVIN"

HADLOW DOWN

ANTIQUES, DECORATIVE PIECES

· · · · · · · · · · · ·

Combining

ultivation
NG
N G H A M

low Down 324

· · · · · · · · · · · ·

THE NEW INN

Beers and Spirits

Cars for Hire
Phone
Hadlow Down 209

G. Standen

DANCES, SOCIALS & WEDDINGS
CATERED FOR

TUROG, HOVIS & WHEATMEAL
BREAD

J. J. ASHDOWN

Baker & Confectioner

'Phone HADLOW DOWN 243

Y HERD

m,

reen

336

n Cream

otatoes

Family Butcher

G. A. HENTON & SON
(S. G. HENTON)

Tel. HADLOW DOWN 213

HADLOW
DOWN
DUPLICATING
DETAILS
AND PRICE LIST
from
"LAWTON"
HADLOW DOWN 504

SPECIAL RATES TO
VILLAGE ORGANISATIONS

Hadlow Down

An Autobiography

A Mile post in the journey of a Wealden Parish

Incorporating

Alice Catherine Day's

Glimpses of Rural Life in Sussex

Published by Hadlow Down Millennium Book Committee

First Published October 1999

© Hadlow Down Book Committee
Published by: Hadlow Down Millennium Book Committee,
Spoods Farm, Tinkers Lane, Hadlow Down TN22 4ET
ISBN 0 9537125 0 8

Drawings and Maps by John Wiltshire
All Rights Reserved

Typeset by David Brown, Maynards Green, Tel. 01435 812506
Using Garamond 12pt on 11 pt leading.

Printed By Ashford Colour Press, Portsmouth.
In conjunction with Windmill Press, Tel. 01825 830319
Using Sovereign Classical Matt 115gsm and Cream Book Wove 80gsm Vol 18

I was very pleased and honoured to be asked to write the foreword for the Hadlow Down Millennium Book as it is an imaginative and creative way to mark the millennium.

My connection with the village goes back to my great grandfather, he was Charles Lang Huggins, he lived at The Grange, Hadlow Down. My grandmother [Dorothy] who was one of his nine children, was brought up there. My father spent much of his childhood in the village and talked about it often, so when I was 18 years of age, on my way to work my passage around the world I called in on Ulric and Pat Huggins who lived at the Wilderness. My life was interrupted for six years. Within days of arriving I must have been introduced to at least three quarters of the villagers who seemed the most friendly and helpful people in England.

Hadlow Down was meant to be just a brief stop over, but the New Inn, the local farmers and the hospitality of the village changed my overall big plan. I feel I must have stayed at nearly all the houses in the village at one time or another. I worked on most of the surrounding farms doing seasonal and relief work. I was forgiven for many misdeeds, including, getting my instructions wrong and mowing the hay in our neighbour's paddock at Stocklands Farm, leaving the pipe out of the bulk tank and spilling the whole morning's milk down the drain . Worst of all leaving a gate open and having the bull charge up and around the village. On that occasion I was on my own. Everyone shut their gates and doors and let me get on with it myself. Even the local policeman turned his van around and drove off in the other direction.

While living in Hadlow Down I had the good fortune to meet and marry my wife Anne Hale. She came from that far off village in Kent called Chidingstone. We have just celebrated our silver wedding anniversary this year. Of all the places we have lived, none has been as friendly as Hadlow Down.

I wish the book every success, and who knows, it could be on the shelves out selling Jeffery Archer.

Lord Rugby

AUTHORS

Sarah Welbourn

Sarah and husband Tom moved into Loudwell Farm in Tinkers Lane soon after the Great Storm of 1987. Recognizing her position as a newcomer, even after twelve years, she rejoices in the beauty and history of the area.

Meg Rostron.

Meg Rostron nee Greenwood, was born and brought up at Fairlight Glen Farm in the south of the parish. She attended Hadlow Down school during the forties and has remained in the shadow of St Mark's, spending most of her married life at Scocus Farm.

Chris Purser

Chris and family moved into Hadlow Down in 1969 living in School House as Headmaster at our school. They then left the district returning after an absence of 18 years. Now living at Stobcross Lodge he is still engaged in education and extremely active in village affairs.

Gerald Standen

Gerald, born, raised and educated in the village as a single minded and resolute character. He was fortunate to be able to attend Lewes Grammer School. His working life shared between the Pub and Garage, only leaving the village when he joined the R.A.F. to do his bit. Fiercely independent he can be described as a true Sussex Man.

Peter Gillies

Peter and his wife Delia moved into the Parish in 1966 and farmed for the first 20 years at Brookside Farm. Now he lives at Spoods Farm and continues his working life as a printer. With his agricultural roots and love of the countryside he is proud to be called a peasant.

Marjorie Jarvis

Marjorie moved into the village with her parents Herbert and Minnie Richards in 1913,at the age of five. She attended Hadlow Down school and has always lived in the County; Buxted, Eastbourne or here in Hadlow Down.Today she enjoys life in Marlowe House.

David Skinner

David better known as 'Woody' narrowly missed Hadlow Down when he moved into Latch Cottage in Blackboys during 1992. Keeping him company now is Henry a six nominal horsepower steam agricultural tractor and his hyper-active collie, Jess.

Mavis Farrar

Mavis has lived in the village for the last seventeen years since she retired with her husband John who had been the head master of an independent school. Not surprisingly she has been very closely associated with St Mark's school in Hadlow Down, both as a school governor and as a drama teacher. Amongst her other activities within the parish she co-edits the parish magazine and has been an enthusiastic member of the Variety Club.

John Wiltshire

John was born here in Hadlow Down and has lived all his life at 'Lawton' in the centre of the village. Educated at the local school and finally obtaining a fine arts degree at Canterbury University. Today he enjoys a reputation as an artist in many mediums and his work is frequently seen around the village.

Rosemary Alexander

Rosemary has lived in the area for 31 years, the last 15 in Howbourne Lane. When she moved in it was to the Parish of Hadlow Down but then a quirk of fate moved the parish boundary and placed her in Buxted. For nearly nine years she has written a regular Parish Pump feature for the Kent and Sussex Courier. A staunch supporter of her local area.

Joan Wiltshire

Joan moved here in 1968 and raised her family of four boys all of whom attended the village school. Always active in supporting village life, being a Parish councillor, P.T.A. member, Village Hall representative and Variety Club founder.

Cecil Godley

Cecil,was born in Lockes Cottage and has lived and worked on various farms ever since. A familiar sight on his trusty bicycle, he has always been a staunch supporter of Providence Chapel and Hadlow Down.

ACKNOWLEDGEMENTS

The committee would like to pay tribute to all those who have helped with the production of this book. Everybody has been so generous not only in lending original material but also with their time and patience. Strenuous efforts have been made to include all our benefactors, if anybody has been inadvertantly missed please accept our sincere apologies for the oversight.

Tom Bridges
Simon Wright
Mickey Barden
Ron Barden
Julia Emsden
Bob Spencer
Charles Smith
Des Thomas
Joy and Gordon Long
Den and Isa Coates
Alan Cheale
John Mckenzie
Cecil Fry
John Booth [deceased]
Joyce Jessett
Joan Walker
Ulric and Pat Huggins
Gloria Roberts
Sue Andrews
Jane Seabrook
Misses Nelson
Graham Cook
Tony and Brenda Honess
Lord Rugby
Mary Dufore
David Waddington
Robert Harrison
Sonia Edwards
Mick Harker
Brian Gregory

Richard Warriner
Harold Royce
Barbara Ball
Pamela Abdelnoor
Graham Ealy
Bertha Mitchell [deceased]
Mike Ford
Fred Barden
Chris and Pam Greenwood
Chris Mitchell
Faith Lee
Phyliss Foster
Tom Godfrey Faussett
Hazel Pickthall
Arthur Locke
Ralph Walters
John Warner
Geoffrey Sheard
Anne Yarrow
Jane Stockdale
Ray Jarvis
John Ward
Steve Biggs
Norman Edwards
Ray Dennett
Joyce Ashdown
Nicholas Ashdown
Jo Dummer
Robert and Fiona Thorpe
Verity Poole

Joy Collingwood
Betty Turner
Geoffrey Sheard
Kay Phillips
John Murrell
Ron Lees
Lawrence Taylor
Jenniver White
Geoff Humphrey
John Blades
David Waddington
John Warner
Norman Johnson
Reg & Cecily Hunt

Conoco Oil Co
East Sussex Record Office.
Sussex Express Newspapers.
Kent and Sussex Courier.
Sussex Records Society.
Uckfield Historical Society.
Uckfield Library
Ceredigion Museum

Scantech Heathfield
John Wiltshire, Artist
David Brown, Typesetting
Ron Hill, Photography
S & P Printing

CONTENTS

ERRATUM
Page 110 Para. 1&3 Colonel should read Commander.

INTRODUCTION

Glimpses of Rural Life in Sussex was published as far as we can tell around 1927 by The Countryman magazine in Oxfordshire. Identification of the author is more difficult, although expressed on the cover as 'Alice Catherine Day', there is a publisher's note inside thanking Mrs Anderson for putting her records in print. Perhaps Mrs Anderson was using her maiden name. We have had no success in tracing the family. Their residence in Hadlow House is well documented and they were responsible for building South Beacon on the A272 but after that there are no clues.

Today a few copies of this little booklet are known around the village but they are treasured items and jealously guarded. Collectors seeking a copy find it almost impossible to locate and so a gem of local history is in danger of being missed by many interested persons and especially residents. For this reason it was decided to reprint the work here in our book and we trust Mrs Anderson would approve.

Perhaps there is a significance or maybe a good omen, in the fact that the first edition published in 1927 was the last time a total eclipse of the sun was seen in this country, just as there is now in 1999 when we publish it again. In order to try and preserve the Sussex dialect we have reprinted as far as possible exactly according to the original, spelling mistakes as well. The inclusion of John Wiltshires line drawings represent the only changes.

We hope you enjoy reading it as so many have before us.

Copyright claim awaited.

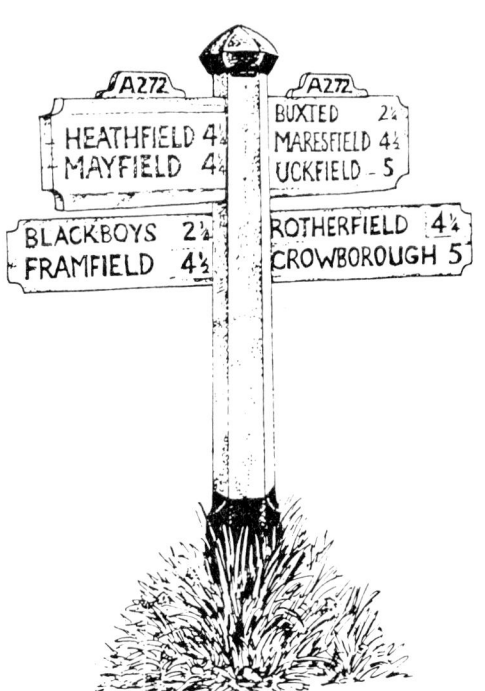

Master and Missus Samuel Sands, of the Boot Cottage, Hadlow Down, who had kept their diamond wedding day when this photograph was taken in 1878. Samuel was born in 1794, Ann in 1793.

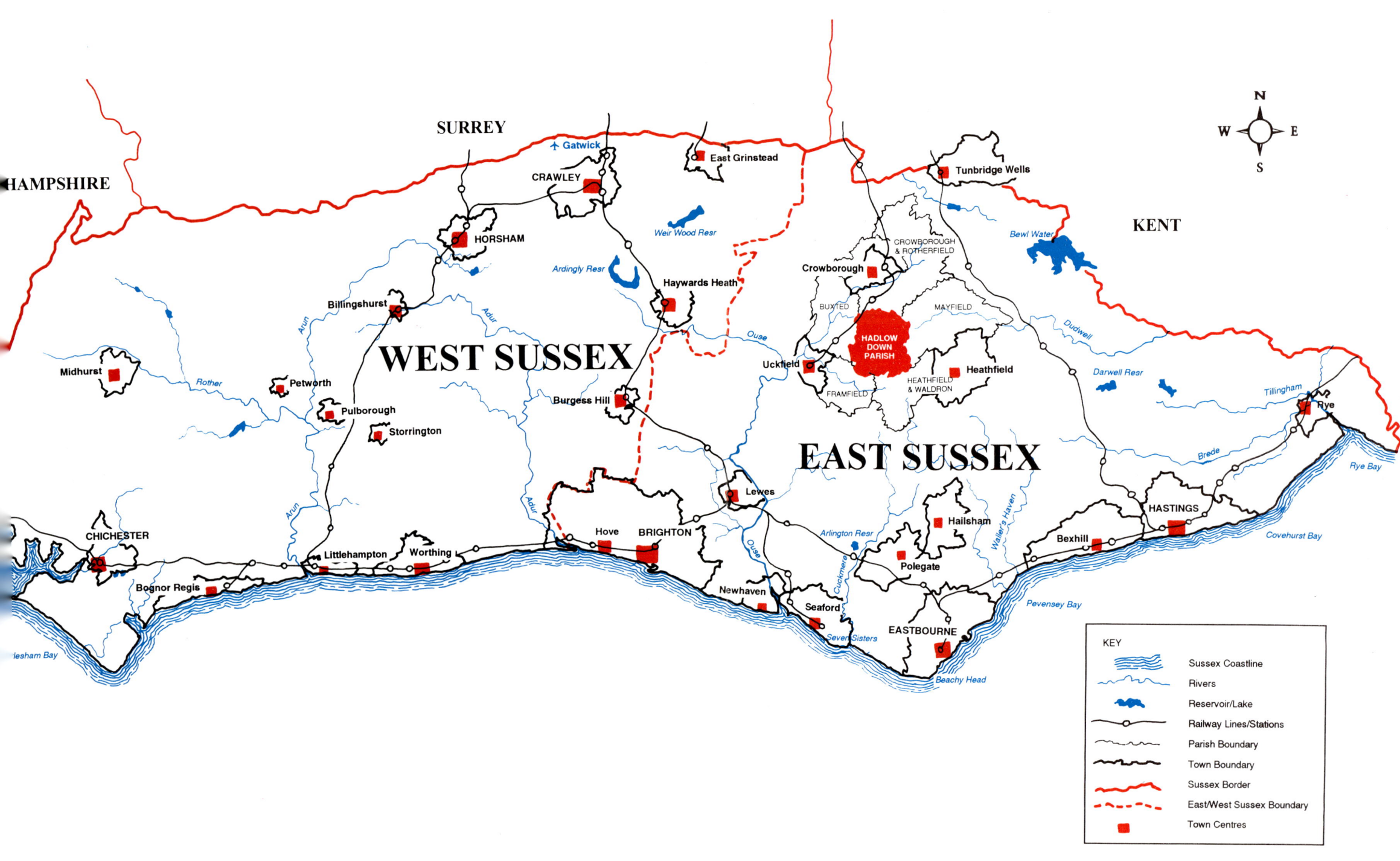

SURREY

HAMPSHIRE

KENT

WEST SUSSEX

EAST SUSSEX

HADLOW DOWN PARISH

Gatwick

East Grinstead

Tunbridge Wells

CRAWLEY

Weir Wood Resr

Bewl Water

HORSHAM

Ardingly Resr

Crowborough

CROWBOROUGH & ROTHERFIELD

BUXTED

MAYFIELD

Billingshurst

Haywards Heath

Ouse

Dudwell

Midhurst

Uckfield

Heathfield

HEATHFIELD & WALDRON

Darwell Resr

Petworth

Rother

Burgess Hill

FRAMFIELD

Pulborough

Storrington

Arun

Adur

Rye

Tillingham

Lewes

Brede

Hailsham

HASTINGS

CHICHESTER

Arlington Resr

Covehurst Bay

Hove

BRIGHTON

Waller's Haven

Bexhill

Littlehampton

Worthing

Polegate

Bognor Regis

Newhaven

Cuckmere

Ouse

Seaford

EASTBOURNE

Pevensey Bay

Seven Sisters

Beachy Head

Rye Bay

lesham Bay

KEY

Sussex Coastline

Rivers

Reservoir/Lake

Railway Lines/Stations

Parish Boundary

Town Boundary

Sussex Border

East/West Sussex Boundary

Town Centres

N
W   E
S

GLIMPSES OF RURAL LIFE
IN SUSSEX

DURING THE LAST
HUNDRED YEARS

BY

ALICE CATHERINE DAY

INTRODUCTION

THE south forest ridge on which Hadlow Down is situated runs parallel to Ashdown Forest, and between it and the South Downs, and lies only about eighteen miles from the sea at Pevensey Bay as the crow flies. The Days have been settled there for several hundred years, and were Lords of the Manor of Hadlow. It was a wild, lawless neighbourhood in old times, and the last gang of smugglers was taken in the Inn at Hadlow Down. As the last survivor born at Hadlow Down of an old Wealden family, I have collected from ancient inhabitants and set down from my own memory a few notes on the village life which has now so completely passed away. Although not, perhaps, of startling interest, they portray a state of things which will be quite strange, and therefore interesting, to the generations which come after us.

PUBLISHER'S NOTE

Need it be said that it is not in the least as a literary performance but rather as a modest act of local patriotism that Mrs. Anderson has thought of putting these unpremeditated records of hers in print?

Some readers may not share the Author's opinions. But every reader in Sussex and outside of it will agree that the story of our countryside would have been richer had more rural residents forgotten their lack of experience of writing and tried to set down as best they could the simple annals of their villages.

CONTENTS

The New Gate and Old George

'PLEASE, Ma'am', said an old farmer who had called on my mother, 'will you be good enough to build me new barn? Mine seems as if it would go to pieces.' 'No', my mother replied, 'I am quite unable to lay out so much money.' A pause. 'Well, Ma'am, have you seen my barnyard gate lately? ' 'No, what is the matter? ' ' It is so broken that the hinges are worn out. In fact, I can hardly open or shut it.

'I think I can promise you a new gate.'

'Thank'ee, Ma'am, that is all I wanted, but thought maybe if I spoke first about the barn I might get the gate.'

Our Sussex folk had much dry humour, as is proved by the primitive arithmetic of a rate collector, whom I will call Mr. George.

The inspector sent his clerk to examine old George's account books.

'What is the meaning of this? 'said the clerk. 'None of the totals are correct at the foot of the pages.'

'Oh! Sir, that don't matter', replied old George, 'you will find the *last* total is right, and *that* is all that mat-

ters. You see I had to copy all the accounts into a new book, and the pages were not the same length. So I made a guess at all the pages except the last. However, I put that down right. You see, I could not be bothered to add up all those figures again.'

The Vicar and the Calf's Head

HADLOW DOWN parochial district was formed about the year 1834. Portions of Mayfield and Buxted parishes were allotted to the district, which was about five miles long by two to three wide, and embraced the hamlets of Hadlow Down and Five Ashes, the desolate region of Spotted Cow, where many squatters had their dwellings, a few houses belonging to gentle-people, many prosperous farms, besides a multitude of small farms worked by 'smock frock' farmers, and probably one hundred and fifty cottages wherein lived labourers. At that time the idea was prevalent that if a man could erect a house in twenty-four hours from the time he start-ed building it, he could claim the piece of unfenced land on which it stood, and hold it in per-petuity. So the squatter to be would call his neighbours together, and, in bee fashion they all would help in building the house. It was in this way that the settlements in the region of Spotted Cow had been made.

Before 1834 a Wesleyan chapel had been built by an earnest working man and services were conducted in it. Meetings were also held in the road by ministers of a sect called Huntingtons, so named after a blacksmith who founded it. Their tenets were High Calvinist. The Huntingtons must not be confounded with the Countess of Huntingdon's denomination. When the chapel was opened in 1834 the remark was made, 'What a number of dissenters this neighbourhood has!' 'Call them not Dissenters', was the reply, 'the Church starved them, and they took the only spiritual aliment that was offered them.'

Centuries of neglect cannot exist without leaving traces behind however, though it is to be hoped that there are few such. But here is a story of a Sussex parson in 1800, as it was told to me.

A young newly-married couple started off on Sunday morning to attend their parish church, five miles distant. As they turned a corner in their gig, they were hailed by someone who called out, 'Where are you going this morning?' 'To church, of course', was the reply. 'Do not trouble, there will be no church to-day.' The voice was that of the vicar. Astounded, the farmer said, 'What do you mean, vicar?' 'Simply this, I learnt last night that twelve miles from where I live a calf was killed yesterday. It was too late then to go so far, so I started off at daybreak, and found the farmer had not disposed of my favourite portion, the head. It was an opportunity too good to miss. I have it here.' And he held up his purchase, wrapped in a blue handkerchief, saying, 'Now I am not going to allow my old housekeeper to spoil in the cooking what has cost me twenty-four miles' riding. I am going back to superintend it's being properly cooked, so you see it is quite impossible for me to have any service to-day.'

'Turned Me Out of His House'

THE first vicar or incumbent of St. Mark's, Hadlow Down, must have been a most devoted shepherd of the sheep. He left London, where he was in comfortable circumstances, and gave up his life to serve his parishioners, and was an indefatigable visitor at all the cottages, an ardent teacher of the young, and a true friend to all. Sometimes in his eagerness to visit all his parishioners, Mr. Edwards allowed his zeal to overstep prudence. One instance of this was told me. A family had sat down to dinner. Mr. Edwards came to call. The master of the house was grumpy at being disturbed; he rose from the table, laid his hands on the clergyman's shoulders, conducted him to the door which he opened, and showed his visitor out! Mr. Edwards went down the path, saying, 'He turned me out of his house, He turned me out of his house.' Ere night he returned and said, 'You did quite right, I apologize.' Result, a lasting friendship between the clergyman and the whole family.

The effects of Mr. Edwards's instruction remain. A man five and forty years old told me that the evening hymn sung regularly at the close of the day school had led to his turning to God. Then, recently, a dear old woman, now ninety-three, told me that Habakkuk, the third chapter, 'Although the fig-tree shall not bloom I will joy in the God of my salvation' was such a comfort to her in hard times, and that the Bible reading in the day school had helped her all her life.

If I mistake not, Mr. Edwards, Mr. Kirby, and Mr. Longland each served St. Mark's for seventeen or eighteen years, being succeeded by Mr. Warner, who came in 1888. There was much to combat in those early days – I remember being shown a cottage in Poundsley Lane which had been used by coiners.

Witchcraft

AND superstition was not dead. 'If you do not tell the bees Mr. Edmund has died in Australia, and bind a piece of crape on the top of their hive, the bees will die', said the Hadlow gardener in 1852. As the bees happened to die, the old man was strengthened in his theory.

'If you expect fine crops of peas and potatoes you must plant them on Good Friday.' At the same time the saying was common, 'Begin a piece of work on a Friday and it will never be finished.' But the most serious thing was the belief in witchcraft, of which I have heard four instances. Mrs. Blackman, who lived near Isenhurst, was dressed in peculiar and rough garments, and people feared to meet her, saying she was a witch, and haunted folk. Old Mrs. Weaver was reputed to have the power of changing her form into that of an animal. At some date between 1851 and 1855 the carter was sent from Hadlow with a wagonload of wheat to deliver at Lewes market. On his return he requested to see Mrs. Day, and I tell the story as she told it to me.

'Last night, the horses and me, we were jogging along, and got just this side of the Dudsland Paygate when they started, and were so fluttered I could hardly get them along. Then something jumped at their heads, and I took my whip and thrashed it. Then it ran under the horses and changed into a big black dog. Didn't I thrash it! Then it yelled and ran away. It had turned into Mrs. Weaver, the witch.'

Some twenty-five years later there was an old woman who lived on the common just beyond Tinker's Lane. Her only companion was her black cat. I do not know her name, nor how long she had held her unenviable character, but she was reputed to be a dangerous witch.

The fourth individual is the only one whom I ever saw. Old Mrs. Jones lived with her son and crippled daughter Ann, near the top of Wilderness Lane. I imagine the date must have been about 1876, when my mother, hearing she was ill, went to see her. The cottage was poorly built, the cold was intense, and the moisture inside the bedroom walls had frozen into a thin sheet of ice. The poor old woman was perfectly clean, so were also all her surroundings, but she had no comforts. Fire there was none in the house because there was no fuel. There was nothing to eat but a piece of stale bread and she had no money. But true to the character of the Hadlow Down people she asked for nothing, and would have scorned to beg. Food was, of course, sent regularly till she was better; but the point of my story is, that my mother was entreated by our local builder to desist from visiting Mrs. Jones lest she should lay her spell on her. He was kindness itself, and sent her a whole load of wood, but told my mother that the neighbours, however ready they were to relieve distress, dared not go in and out of her cottage for fear of consequences.

Remember the gardener's daughter', he said, speaking of an invalid girl, who had become an idiot owing to suffering from fits. 'She was a healthy infant till Mrs. Jones cast her spell on her. Her father is always praying for Mrs. Jones's death, because when that happens she will recover her senses.

Mr. Bridger's Pigtail

I WILL here relate a couple of traditional anecdotes about a well-known and respected farmer. His name was Bridger. He had read much ancient history and some theology, and when he brought his son to be baptized the clergyman was startled by being requested to name the child 'Beelzebub', and refused to do so.

'But Sir, the name is in the Bible, and you are therefore bound to use it.'

The clergyman advised that the baptismal party should adjourn to the graveyard, while he concluded the ordinary afternoon service, and then return to the church where the baptismal service might be completed. In due course Bridger returned, and gave the name Augustus Caesar. Many years afterwards I knew his grandson, Caesar Augustus, a young fellow full of life and energy, with a brother named Mark Antony. His aunt, who passed a useful life teaching the middle-class children of the neighbourhood, was called Venus Pandora.

The Great Exhibition of 1851 made a stir even in these quiet, out-of-the-way parts, and people were anxious to see the 'great glass house'.. Among the crowd of visitors to the Crystal Palace were Mr. and Mrs. Bridger, intent on seeing all they could. Mr. Bridger did not appreciate costumes and other objects dear to the feminine mind, so he left Mrs. Bridger and her friends to wander around, whilst he went in search of the machinery. In course of time a policeman tapped him on the shoulder and said, 'Please, sir, your ladies are asking for you – '

'And pray how came you to have found me among these thousands of people? ' was the reply.

'Well, you see, Sir, you are not dressed just like other people.' And neither was he. Imagine an exceedingly tall man, with fiery red hair plaited in a pigtail, which was tied halfway down his back with white satin ribbon. Further, he was clad in the long, white smock, which the well-to-do farmer affected for Sunday, knee breeches, and gaiters.

He was so proud of his hair that the story went that he chose as his wife the girl of the district who could plait the best. I never saw him but once, when he was sitting in the chimney corner, a very old man, and then he no longer wore the white satin ribbon.

A conversation with Benjamin Austin, aged 77, on 14 March, 1922, throws a light on Mr. Bridger's kindly disposition. He said: 'In eighteen hundred and forty-nine, when I was four, father went to work for Mr. Bridger at Little Cowdens, and we had the cottage just below. Mr. Bridger had lived at Homestalls on the road to Rotherfield. He was a very bookish man and called his sons Virgil and Cicero. I have often seen him with his long hair plaited in a pigtail, and tied with ribbon, looking like a Chinaman. What I remember especially about him was his kindness. He would always help a tramp to a job, and there was a lodge in one of his fields where any man on the road was always welcome to sleep. Once he kept a man half a day polishing up a worn-out wagon shoe, then paid him well for his time and sent him off.

'One day the local policeman saw a ragged man crouching over a fire of sticks near the lodge in which Mr. Bridger allowed the tramps to sleep. The policeman took him in charge, marched him to Mark Cross, and brought him before the magistrates, who, to their surprise, discovered the culprit to be Mr. Bridger himself, who, addressing himself to the policeman, said, "I'll trouble you not to come interfering on *my* land in future."'

Mrs. Samuel Sands

MY mother was very partial to an old couple named Sands who lived in a timber-built thatched cottage called 'The Boot', and she got a travelling photographer to take their portraits just after they had completed sixty years of married life. Notwithstanding his club feet, the old man kept his garden in beautiful order, while the old woman cherished her fuchsias and cacti indoors, as well as her little flower-border out of doors. One day Mrs. Sands produced a patchwork quilt, saying, 'Please, Ma'am, do you remember that when Mr. Ansell[1] was a little boy he had his first shilling, and spent it in buying print to make my Jimmy's frock and this is some of it.'

People sometimes speak as if poor people were ungrateful. How many of us remember little kindnesses shown to us forty years ago?

Questioned about the bringing up of her family, Mrs. Sands said to me: 'Well, Ma'am, I brought up ten children and paid the 1d. a week for their schooling for about two years each. I never sent a girl to service before she was ten years old, could read her book (i.e., the Bible), write a letter, figure out a washing bill, and make a chimmee, and I never had one to disgrace me.'

Samuel and Ann Sands were born in 1793 and married when they were twenty-three. Their

[1]Ansell Day (1826–86).

eldest son worked at Huggett's Furnace for sixty years, always respected and trusted. I have known six generations of the family; little Jimmy is now about five years old.

Norfolk Jack. Self-made Man

IN 1883 I undertook to visit some dozen houses of farmers and labourers in a district called Steep. Not knowing exactly how to introduce myself, I settled to ask for subscriptions to a monthly magazine—*Hand and Heart*. Having been to several of the cottages I turned down a very muddy farm lane to find Rumden, where I was informed Mr. Martin lived. Portfolio under my arm I knocked at the door. No answer. I knocked again. Suddenly the door was thrown back by a man who was standing on a floor, the level of which was much below that on which I was. 'What do you want, where do you come from?' he shouted.

I was startled, but determined not to be taken aback, so replied: 'If you invite me into your kitchen and find me a chair, perhaps I may inform you.' He looked surprised. However, he preceded me into a large kitchen, and when I was seated I said:

'You may have heard of a family named Day, that used to live at Hadlow. I am the youngest daughter.'

Suddenly from the back premises came the old man's housekeeper exclaiming, 'Lor', you must be little Miss Alice. I was cook at Hadlow when you was born.'

The explanation effected, they began to take an interest in me and my movements. I explained that a twelve-month's subscription for *Hand and Heart* would be one shilling, and I could not be troubled to collect pennies; if, therefore, Mr. Martin wished for it, he must pay me the shilling in advance, and I would deliver the magazine monthly.

Money! Is it money you want? Plenty of that! Here is my purse, see gold and notes, beside silver. I've plenty of money.' He gave me the shilling, and some months afterwards amused me by observing, 'Well, considering you have to bring your pony here every month, I do not think you have made much of a bargain! Won't get very rich!'

During 1886 I went to see him, and told him I should like to know about his success in life.

'Well! I suppose you will want to know exactly how many bones I have had broken and accidents I have met with?' 'Oh no, not at all', said I. 'I remember hearing you say that you had risen by your own exertions; and should like to know the steps by which you became a farmer.'

I was born about eighteen miles from Norwich; my father was a sawyer near Diss, who died in 1819, leaving me, a boy of twelve, and my brother of ten quite destitute. The parish took us both, and soon I was put out and bound for three years to a farmer who engaged to find me in clothes and keep me during the time. He was very good to me and I was very happy.

'At fifteen I got myself another place, and I fancied that with wages I should be better off than I was before. A great mistake. I was not well cared for, and my wages were two pounds the first year and three the second. As you may think, I was in rags even before the two years were at an end. At seventeen I got another place at five pounds for the first year. At the end of my first year my master gave me one pound extra, also raised my wages one pound. This kind treatment was repeated the next two years. When about twenty I got another place where I stayed two years, wages ten pounds a year. At twenty-two I was brought from Norfolk into Sussex by a gentleman with whom I stayed four years. I never had any difficulty in getting places because of my good character. That was the thing, my good character did it. If it had been the present day I suppose I should have been taught and got some *larning,* but as it is I have done very well without it. No! I can't read or write a word.

'When I was about twenty-six I went to a gentleman at Withyham who farmed an estate under Lord de la Warr – I was not in the house there – I went with horses, and before long became foreman, being thoroughly trusted, even to taking money to the bank. The average labourer received at that time nine to ten shillings a week I being above the others had twelve. Besides wages I had four loads of dung for my garden and a wood stack worth twenty-eight shillings a year.

'No, I did not save during the first three years; to tell you the truth I got about and amused myself, and the money went. There was a young woman servant at my employer's house. I married her, and then my prosperity began. She was poor – if you reckon having no money to be poor – but, indeed, she was anything but poor to me. She was strong, active, industrious, and a good manager. She would do all kinds of work. We saved and worked till, when my employer gave up farming in Sussex twelve years after I first went to him, we were pretty comfortably off, having saved a nice little bit of money.

'I heard of three drills which were to be sold for sixty-eight pounds, went to a gentleman and borrowed fifty pounds, bought the drills, and before long repaid my loan. Then I heard of a bit of land in the forest, so again went to a gentleman who lent me £150. I bought the piece – it was about four acres – and worked hard with my drills and at other work, besides cultivating my own land.

'When I sold the land I got £350 for it. We lived in the forest about fourteen years, and during that time several children were born – altogether we brought up twelve children. One girl died as an infant, another at nineteen years old. I have only buried one son; he died at forty, but he had saved enough to retire on. He had a milk walk and house property besides. One of his house property investments was worth £1,300. His brother now carries on the milk walk.

'What do I suppose I made while on the forest, besides the purchase of my own land? Well, we put it down four some years and found it averaged £100 a year. What a wife mine was! Brought up chickens? Yes, I should think so. Why, she used to go leasing three miles from home by four o'clock in the morning throughout harvest.

'When I left the forest I took a farm of 130 acres, having saved enough to pay the in-going inventory very comfortably. My next move was to come here in 1862. The farm was forty acres, but last Michaelmas another forty-eight acres was added. I have been here ever since and have mown and thrashed for my neighbours. I still have one of my old drills in the yard, and it has had a great deal of use. I have always made money by hiring out myself and any machine I might have to my neighbours. Why, that pays. Can a man do with only three acres and a cow? No, he cannot do on a small piece of land, unless he earns money in other ways – Massy No!'

Master James Rogers of Rotherfield, 1922

'I WAS born a long time ago. If I live till next June 1 I shall be ninety years old. My sight is very good, and I can take a short walk, but am past going out to work. Most of my life has been passed in Rotherfield, though I have worked in two places in Mayfield besides Huggett's Furnace. I was one of nine; eight were boys, and there was one girl.

'We all grew up, in fact, the one who died youngest of all was forty years old. Our parents brought us up very simply. We knew nothing about the fancy biscuits, tinned salmon, and other delicacies which the grocers offer now to rich and poor. My mother made the bread once a week. She generally kept it three days before we began to eat it, because it lasted so much better if not eaten fresh. But sometimes we had eaten up all last baking too soon. Then, rather than let us go hungry, she would pull out some of the dough and cook it on top of the fire for our breakfast. I cannot tell you about other things, but I mind she used to buy one ounce of tea and two pounds of brown sugar every week regular. And the Brown George turnovers she used to make – how I should like to have one now hot out of the oven! What! you don't know what a Brown George turnover is? I will tell you. It was baked on a flat tin; the paste was filled with apples. You may have seen small apple turnovers on your table, but I doubt if you ever had one of that size. What was the size? Twelve to fourteen inches long by six inches wide and thick, and didn't they just taste good!

'My father was a labourer, but became a farmer. I was a labourer and then I worked on the road for seventeen years.

'Would you like to see me in my round smock frock? Well, here it is, I will put it on, and also my old soft hat. Of course, we always wore corduroy trousers like these I have on. In summer we tied them under the knees in order to shorten them, and in the winter we wore long leather gaiters reaching halfway up our thighs. When I was a young fellow in my 'teens, I went to Huggett's Furnace to work, and lived indoors with three others who all shared the same bed-room. That was in 1853, and I stayed there twelve months. Nicholas Martin had had the farm, but then it had been taken by Frederick Allcorn, one of the three brothers to whom the Hall Farm at Rotherfield had belonged. Yes, I remember Sam Sands well. He lived in a cottage not far from the Mill at Huggett's Furnace and worked for the Allcorns nearly sixty years. His daughter is Mrs. Annesley, the washerwoman near Court Meadow, and you must have known his father and mother at Hadlow Down. They both lived to be many years over ninety.

'We had no eight-hour day then, when I went to service. Our regular work began at seven o'clock, but before that we were out and about, milking and seeing to the stock. We had seven cows to milk and feed, besides feeding the horses and teams of oxen. We began about half-past five, got all the animals comfortably tended, and then came to enjoy our good breakfast at half-past six o'clock. We could not have eaten comfortably before the animals had been tended.

'I dare say you remember the very long table in the farmhouse kitchen at Huggett's Furnace. We all sat down together at it, Master, Missus, maids, and men. We each had a large lump of fat boiled pork as big as my fist to eat with our bread, and washed it down with small beer which was made at home. Every farmer brewed, and made homemade cheese in those days, as well as baking bread, cakes, and pies. Oh! I have seen the whole of the oven floor covered with big loaves and then, when they were taken out, there were twenty cakes and pies ready to go in.

'After breakfast we went out to work. Master kept four teams of oxen and we used them to plough and harrow the fields and to prepare the hop-gardens and do the carting. I liked working with them better than with horses, and I will tell you for why. Maybe on level ground the horses are quicker, but if you have a bit of a hill oxen always keep up the same pace. They do not get out of breath like horses and have to stop now and then going up hill in order to breathe. I was trusted to drive a team of oxen to Lewes market. They were our young team five years old, and well broken. They fetched fifty-one pounds. They went up hill as fast as down.

'As I have said, we all sat down together to farmhouse dinner, and what good dinners they gave us. What a help pork was! When pigs were killed the hams and shoulders were cut off, and in process of time hung up in the chimney to be smoked and dried, while all the rest of the meat was left in the tub, ready to be taken out and boiled whenever it was wanted.

'Sometimes we had beef puddings, sometimes pork for our dinner, a good big bit of meat and with it plenty of homegrown vegetables; then fruit pie or some pudding to finish with. At six o'clock we came in again to supper, when everyone had a good basin of milk to drink and as much bread and cheese as he cared to eat. If the home-made cheese had got dry, then it was warmed in the oven, and we enjoyed it.

'There were two hirings a year for indoor men and lads. The six months from Lady-tide to Michaelmas wage was about five pounds, and Michaelmas to Lady-tide four pounds. So we got all our living and about nine pounds in wages for the twelve months. It works out at three shillings or four shillings a week in money. Our mothers used to wash and mend our clothes for us. No! there are no indoor farm servants nowadays, and I tell you for why – farmers wives are too "ladyfied" to look after the men."

'So you want to know how we got a light before present-day matches were made. I have got all the things ready to show you, so come along into the next room.'

He produced a tin box, containing scraps of cotton, probably part of an old handkerchief, and held over the box a broken flint and a file. He showed us some very thin pieces of wood about an inch wide and four inches long. The tips of the wood for three-quarters of an inch had been dipped in brimstone. Then, removing the lid of his tinder box, and, holding the flint above the tinder, he struck it sharply with the file, letting the sparks fall so as to ignite the tinder. He breathed gently to fan the sparks, put in his brimstone match and there was a flame sufficiently strong to light a candle.

Next he showed us a circular block of wood, in which was placed a split stick much like an inverted clothes-peg. Into the deft of the stick he put a rush which had had a narrow strip peeled off from end to end. This he lighted, and there was a rushlight.

Master Rogers told us that large rushes used to be peeled in the same way, then dipped into melted grease, enough times to make a candle of the requisite size – of course, letting each layer cool and harden before the next dipping – and that these home-made candles served for all ordinary lighting purposes. It seems that the brimstone matches were prepared and brought round for sale by travelling people who sold them from door to door, charging a penny for three bunches, each containing four or five matches.

N.B. August, 1927. – Master Rogers still lives, aged ninety-five.

A Sussex Farmhouse Servant in 1855

I WAS born in 1837 at Scooter's Bridge, two miles from Mayfield. My father would not let any of us girls go out to service while we were young. He said that the shilling a week which a child of twelve earned was more than swallowed up paying for her boots. So we went to all kinds of field work.

'Before I was married I went earing many a time. We lived about a mile from Mayfield, near Scooter's Bridge, and the mill was in the same neighbourhood. We did not take away the straw, but only the ears. We picked every ear up one by one off the ground, and as we went quite early in the morning the grass and wheat were often wringing wet with dew.

'When I had a nice bundle I laid it to dry on the bank in the sun, and so with every bunch till dinner-time. Then I cut off all the ears and carried them home in a bag. Next we thrashed and winnowed the grain and took it to the mill. Some people let the miller keep the offal (sharps and bran) from their wheat as payment for grinding the flour. But we used to pay him a trifle for his work, and have the offal returned for pig food. I have had five bushels of wheat to take to the mill for our season's gleaning. Once, the flour I had earned made bread enough to last all through hop-picking. But I got very tired of the round of work, and made up my mind I would leave home.

'I got up very early one morning, went to a neighbouring farmhouse, saw the missus, and got the place as general servant. I was then nineteen, and stayed there three years; my wages were three and ninepence a week.

'Three men were boarded in the farmhouse. There were ten cows for the men to milk. Milking did not come into my work, but they taught me there how to do it. Except a couple of hours during the afternoon, I worked from five in the morning till nearly ten at night. You see there were six people in the house: Master, Missus, three men, and myself. We baked, brewed, churned, made up fifty to seventy pounds of butter a week, besides doing all the washing, cooking, and cleaning that was needed. Then I had the little chicks and ducklings to mind, till they were big enough to sell to the higgler, and it was my place to catch them before he came, and take the money every week for those he bought.

'We had a very big oven; kneading all the bread was part of my work, and I can tell you the quantity of dough needed strength to work it. On baking mornings there was the oven to heat. We used very good wood in that farm, for we had hop-poles to chop up and burn in the oven, and that was much better than the ordinary brush faggot. I was very kindly treated in that place, and food was plenty. I always had an egg with my breakfast and half a pint of ale with my dinner. Whilst I was there the Master gave me a stuff dress, because I always cleaned his boots. Up to that time I had never worn any but a cotton frock.

'Now, I will tell you how I made the ale. On brewing mornings we began at four a.m., got the malt, scalded it and soaked it; then boiled it for an hour with a few hops; strained it through a strong cotton cloth, carried it down into the cellar, and put it into a big tub whilst it was still warm. We got thick yeast from the brewer's, put it into a basin, stirred it up well till it worked and foamed to the top of the basin, then put it into the tub of beer. After it had worked we poured it into a clean barrel, and let it work again over the bung hole for a day or two. Working made it fine, as thick scum would keep coming through the bung hole. As soon as it had stopped working we put paper over the top to keep out air. This we covered with skin, which had been dried, and on the skin wet ashes. Sometimes the ale was kept a year.

'About the meals, we did not sit down together. The Master and Missus were served at their table and cut off my dinner from the same as they ate. The three men had their dinner at the same time, but at their own table.

'My next place was a lighter one, for I went to the shopkeeper at Five Ashes, Mr. Thomsett, who had the house at the corner of the high road to Mayfield, and the lane leading to Hadlow. They kept three cows only. I had the milking and churning to do as well as keeping the dairy clean, and washing and scalding all the pans and the churn. But Mrs. Thomsett made up the butter and helped mind the shop. I did all the cooking and washing, ironing, and housework.

'On Sundays I had time off, and used to go to Chapel regularly. I remained there four-and-a-half years, and left to be married to the keeper at Isenhurst. Then he came to work under Mr. Taylor of Summer Hill, and we lived under him in the cottage with the spring of beautiful water, where you used to know me in 1875.

'I brought up five girls and four boys, who are mostly married round here. We used to fat chickens all the year round, so as to average the good and bad pay. We bought the chicks, giving one and eight pence to three and nine-pence each, according to the time of year. We used to go round with crates collecting, two or three evenings in the week. When we got them home we put them inside the barn in the cramming crates, which had slat bottoms, so that the droppings were cleared away twice a week. The crates were cleaned and whitewashed after every set of chicks. Sometimes we had quite a barn full of birds, and we kept the barn whitewashed also.

'Hand cramming needed doing very gently with careful stroking of the throat, so as to prevent hurting the bird. The crams were made of ground oats, mixed with milk for the first week, but during the second and third, fat was added. Each cram was two inches long and oval in shape. As a rule each bird had three for a meal. We gave one meal every morning and another at night every day except Sunday night. I used to sit, with my pellets beside me; one of the

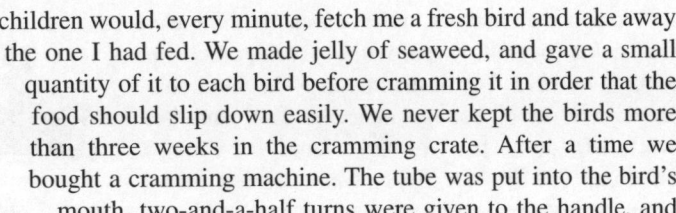

children would, every minute, fetch me a fresh bird and take away the one I had fed. We made jelly of seaweed, and gave a small quantity of it to each bird before cramming it in order that the food should slip down easily. We never kept the birds more than three weeks in the cramming crate. After a time we bought a cramming machine. The tube was put into the bird's mouth, two-and-a-half turns were given to the handle, and the meal went down easily, owing to being of a more liquid description, and then no jelly was required, nor did we need to stroke the throat, so I preferred the machine to hand cramming.

'After each bird was killed it had to be picked whilst it was still warm. Then a child took out all the stubs with a blunt knife, I put them in shape, and tied their legs, and then pressed the chicks under boards, with heavy stones or weights to "shape" them properly. At night, after they had become cold, they were packed into travelling crates or pegs, each of which held one dozen and despatched to London by the carrier. We always sent one and sometimes three crates to market three times a week, and mine sold quickly, because my birds had such good breasts. Price varied with the season. During summer three shillings per bird was all we got, but in early spring we had seven to ten shillings each.

'Then the feathers made splendid beds. We had no spring mattresses then. We dried the feathers in the top attic, turning them over constantly till they were dry. If we had not had a garret I should have put them into a bag in the sun to dry. Besides selling a quantity of feathers at seven pence a pound, I made six feather beds, each of which held forty pounds of feathers. I sold two beds at thirty shillings each before I came to Rotherfield to live with my daughter.

N.B., 1927. – Mrs. Wren has now gone to live at Tunbridge Wells with another daughter. She is ninety years old.

The Shepherd's Wife. March 6, 1922

'I LEFT home at Sevenoaks in 1865 to take a place as cook at the Hall, Rotherfield, then married Ernest Hurst, who was shepherd for Mr. Dodd, who placed us in a cottage near the Hall. My husband's wages were fifteen shillings a week, but we had to pay out of that sum half-a-crown for rent.

'You know the large orchard Scott had on the road to Rotherfield Station? That land, as well as some below Horsegrove, was in hops forty-five years ago, and I used to go there at hop-tying time. I have taken four acres of hops at twelve shillings and sixpence an acre. We tied the hops in May and twice later during season.

'This was where the new road to Station now exists. For hop-picking forty-five years ago we used to be in the gardens at seven a.m. As a rule we worked till half-past five or six p.m. We had a lead tally in return for the hops taken out of our bins by the tallyman. The number of bushels varied with the size of hops and abundance of yield; of ordinary hops we picked five; six or seven of very large ones. I have known eight bushels for tally worth one shilling each. Then sometimes the little colgates numbered only four.

'There was a great difference in the way the measurer filled the bushel measure. If he pressed your hops they went tightly down, but if he let you stir them up lightly and then flung them into the measure in an easy manner, then you got good return for your work. Jesse Hoath, of Coes Farm, was so kind in that way. He packed the hops as lightly as possible, saying he wished everyone to be happy and encouraged. I have, with my children's help, earned five pounds during a single hop-picking. That paid our firing for the year, and found a new pair of boots for everyone of the family.

'Women used to work in the harvest field. I have used the sickle myself. I particularly remember the autumn of 1875. My husband was a shepherd. We lived in a small cottage near the Hall and he worked for its owner. We had a family of young children. The harvest fields were divided into strips the whole length of the field and called "cants". Every man or woman was given a "cant" to cut with the sickle, and then bind the corn into sheaves. When you had finished your "cant" you passed all the workers who were busy on their portions, and took a further strip. These strips or "cants " were all measured and added together at the end of harvest, to see how much each person had earned. We were paid twelve shillings per acre and the ground was measured by Mr. Burgess, the schoolmaster.

'After an early breakfast I used to start with my children for one of the Hall fields, carrying our dinner with us, also sometimes a kettle in order to make some hot tea. Even the toddlers could help by twisting the straw into bands and also by helping me tie up my sheaves. The children enjoyed being out of doors. But cutting and binding our sheaves was not the end of our day's work. We still had to make the shocks. Many is the time that my husband came round to us when his own day's work was done, and we worked together setting up the shocks by moonlight. I was a proud woman when pay-time came, and I received four pounds, and was told by Mr. Dodd that it was the largest sum he had ever paid a woman for working with the sickle.

'At one place where we worked, a gallon of skim milk a day was supplied us free. And didn't the children thrive! In those days we could not buy quaker oats, but sometimes I used to get Scotch oatmeal, which with milk made a splendid breakfast. Then we had hasty puddings and plenty of rice boiled with milk.

'Our garden gave us lots of vegetables. We always tried to keep two pigs – one to sell for enough to buy the next pair of little ones, and pay the miller's bill. The other was cured for ourselves, so with plenty of vegetables and the refuse boiled up for the pigs we managed. I cannot tell you exactly how we spent our money, but I remember that if I had not enough to get something one week we waited for it till the next.

'I have often made mottled soap myself. When we had some fat I melted it down and boiled it in strong lye made from wood ashes, and very useful it was. In those days we burnt no coal.

'Though we had to be careful of every penny and had to work hard we were quite contented, and everyone was a good neighbour. I never had a misword with a neighbour in my life, and the children, though they had no shop playthings, were as happy as could be. They played about with what-ever they found and amused one another. I had five boys and three girls, of whom I lost only one.'

N.B., August, 1927. – Mrs. Hurst keeps house for her grandsons at the age of eighty-three.

A Sussex Septuagenarian, born 1845

HOW did we live seventy years ago? Very simply, we worked hard, but there was much love to one another in the family, and we were very happy. There was little schooling, but the elder children rocked cradles, played with the little ones, and helped father and mother do all sorts of easy light jobs. My mother died when I was seven, so my father was left with six small children to bring up. Two were older and three younger than me. We lived deep down in a wood, far away from other people, close to the farmstead and other cottages. Once a week my father would get up at three o'clock in the morning to bake our bread. He was a farm labourer, with wages of six shillings a week in money, besides six gallons of flour. Flour was dear in those days. It cost one and fourpence a gallon. So our home-made bread was very precious.

'Though grandfather at the farm was very poor, he used to spare us milk, and also give us rabbits which ran wild. We had a good garden, where father grew lots of vegetables, and our yearly pig which we cured made us always have a bit of meat in the house, though we could not afford to buy any at the butcher's shop.

'And now about our pig. When it was possible for father to do so, he bought two little pigs every spring – paying seven shillings or a little more for each. We fetched in ferns and leaves off the rough to make their beds, and fed warm vegetables to them which I used to boil and stir up with a little meal. We could not pay a big score to the miller, so father hired a quarter of an acre of land and sowed it with oats in order to get grain to ripen the pigs. The second pig we always sold, so the money over, after we had paid the miller, went to buy material for clothing us all. Then the manure made the garden stuff grow.

'When big enough to help him, father took us into the woods, where he cut the eleven-years-old saplings and larches for hop-poles, and made faggots of the limbs. We shaved the hop-poles, collected the branches, and helped him tie the faggots. Later on we went hay-making and earned one shilling a day each. We started work at eight o'clock in the morning, and often worked till quite late. At five  p.m. bread and cheese (home-made) and tea were brought us, and then if we worked late we were served with another lunch.

'In harvest time we took our sickles, cut the corn, tied the sheaves, and set up the shocks. In the spring we made the round of the hop-garden, and tied the hops about two feet from the ground. This was repeated twice during the season, the third time we carried a step-ladder, so as to reach the upper vines. And last of all, during six weeks of Autumn we went hop-picking, and the children did enjoy being out of doors all day, and seeing the big kettle over the sticks and the flames rising below it. They used to pick into trug baskets while the grown people stood at their bins. How useful our sunbonnets were for all these out-door jobs, and how many of them I have made.

'I first went to school when we moved out of the wood on to the high road and I was ten years old; later I went regularly for six months. No, I did not learn much needlework there. We had a good, kind neighbour who knew how to cut out and make all manner of things, and she taught me how to make father's shirts, and before I was twelve years old she had cut out and shown me how to make his cloth trousers, and I had the finishing of them. My sister. went out to service so I had to keep everything tidy. Many is the smock frock and pair of cord breeches, besides a coat for father, I have made. A cottage in those days cost one and sixpence a week, and had about a quarter of an acre of garden.

'I cannot tell you how much I earned by my outdoor work, because we helped father, and then it was all added together once a year. The rent and price of wood for firing were kept back, and then each of us had a strong pair of boots for winter, and our old ones mended up, and there was a nice little sum left.

'I married when I was just under twenty. Had eleven children and brought them all up except one who died of whooping cough. Five of my sons and twelve grandsons went to the Great War. We are a long-lived family. My grandfather lived to ninety-three, and grandmother to ninety. One of my uncles died lately aged eighty-eight.

'What I particularly remember is the way that we used to help one another. There were no village nurses in those days. When a woman was confined her neighbour came in and out to look after her and the children, and keep things straight and clean. Then in her turn she looked after the next one who needed help. I remember once, a woman was confined, and her husband laid up with a broken leg. Another neighbour and I nursed both till they were well again. Nowadays folk do not neighbour in that way, and I do not think they are as happy as we were. My age is seventy-seven, and I can get about the house and do my own cooking, though I cannot go to shop.'

N.B., March 8, 1927. – She is no longer a septuagenarian, being now eighty-two years old.

Horace Head of Five Ashes

HORACE HEAD, who left Five Ashes in 1879, gave me the following information 'When the end of harvest had come we decorated with rosettes all the horses that drew the loads.

'Humphrey Beal and his brother used to thatch all the stacks for miles around. The stacks were raised on metal "staddles" some three feet high, so that every stack appeared to be walking on legs. That kept rats from reaching the grain. The harvest home feast was laid in a large barn, and the long table had lots of flowers on it, while from the dark ceiling many flags hung down. The Master carved the roast beef, and sat with the Missus and their elder children at the top of the table. Then there was roast mutton and all sorts of vegetables in plenty. After the meat came plum pudding, and didn't we enjoy our big helpings?

'Then followed toasts, and the children went away. Afterwards we had songs. The Master and Missus stayed for two or three songs and then left us to amuse ourselves.

'The barrel of beer was always taken charge of by one of the principal men, who drew as was required. The guests were entirely men and boys who worked on the farm; I never saw women or children there.

'At harvest our employer always told the men who bound the sheaves to leave plenty of wheat for the poor to glean. I have known a family who gleaned enough to make six sacks of flour. They took the wheat to the miller after it had been thrashed out with a flail.

'The miller ground the wheat for every family. There was no money payment made him for his trouble, but he kept the offal, that is, sharps and bran, and gave back the flour. Very important was this contribution towards the winter food of the family. Every woman kneaded her own bread, then baked it in the large brick oven which belonged to every cottage and farmhouse. These ovens were heated by burning faggots inside until they became cavities of glowing heat. It was very interesting to look into one of these glowing, fiery caverns six feet deep, and broad and high in proportion, when the charred wood was being swept out and the oven being prepared to receive a batch of bread sufficient to feed eight to twelve people for a whole week. And when the bread was drawn out didn't it smell nice! I have seen in some farmhouses as many as twenty pies and cakes ready to replace the loaves which had just come out of the oven.

'Sometimes the cottager baked only once in a fortnight; but that was the exception. In the past every cottager kept his pig, and I have been told that the rule of a quarter-acre garden for every cottage held good throughout the Hadlow estate, whether the farm to which the cottages were attached were situated in Hadlow Down, Buxted, Framfield, Mayfield, or Rotherfield.

'People were happy and contented on plain food, and children earned a few pence by going out to work on Saturdays, threepence to sixpence a day at weeding. I have seen thirty boys pulling kelp and thistles at Isenhurst. We went out to regular work at ten to twelve years of age, but had earned considerable before then, doing odd jobs.

'I went to school at Hadlow Down. Mr. Edwards was our clergyman, and Cripple Wood, as we called our one-legged teacher, was the schoolmaster. He taught us very well, and then when we went to work there were night schools in both villages which were very well attended. In those days all we needed was to read, write, and figure well and we learned to do all those things.

'At Hadlow Down we paid one penny a week each for our schooling, and before winter every boy had a strong smock frock given him, and every girl a red cloak, besides stockings. And how we enjoyed the summer treat at Hadlow. After games we sat on the sloping lawn under the big oak tree and held our mugs (which we had brought with us) for tea as often as the jugs came round, and ate bread and butter and cake till we had had enough.

'I remember Mr. Ansell[1] very well. He had such a team of farmers and working men – Butcher Packham, the three brothers Hemsley, known as King, Butcher, and Rugged, were some of them. On Saturday afternoons, when Mr. Ansell returned from London, the men used to meet in the large meadow in front of the house and play cricket till dark. Sometimes there was a regular match. He used to bring down his friends from London to play against Hadlow Down and a very good showing the villagers made. Once the Earl of Sheffield brought his team over and then was there not a good running?

'Sometimes married men played the single ones. And we boys – how happy we were – looking on. Sometimes there were hundreds of people looking on. They came from all parts.

'No, there has been nothing doing there, not since. How the family was missed! After the matches people all went to the large room over the stables to have supper – I mean the players. Not those who had been looking on. For them, plenty of forms had been placed as seats around the place. One particular thing that I remember when I was young was the happiness all around us. We children were happy and so were the older folk. Certainly we had not much money. I used to think as much of a farthing or a halfpenny to spend at Mrs. Piper's as folk do now of a shilling, and we had no grand food in those days. Plenty of skim milk and vegetables, home-made bread and pork were our every-day food Of course, we had cheese, and sometimes butter. But the thing was the way in which neighbours were ready to help one another, not only with nursing during sickness but in all manner of friendly ways. Though wages were sometimes only eleven shillings per week, yet with our many privileges we were happier than folks are at the present time. A carter had a cottage free, besides two hundred faggots. Oh! what fires the old roots made which belonged to the man who went wood-cutting, and had the roots he grubbed out besides the brush which he cut away in preparing the hop-poles.'

[1]Ansell Day (1826-86)

A Waterloo Veteran

DURING the Great War, numbers of young men enlisted from villages of Hadlow Down and distinguished themselves. A portrait of one of these young fellows reminds me of his great-grand-father, Sergeant Martin, who served in the Battle of Waterloo under Colonel Le Blanc, a great-uncle of my own.

As a girl I met the veteran, who turned to my mother and said,' I well remember your uncle, Ma'am. I was wounded, and could hardly get along, so the Colonel he gets off his horse saying, "Martin, I am more fit to walk than you are, get up directly." I did as he bade me, and he walked all the way to Brussels by my side, whilst I rode his horse.'

It was only the other day that I saw the tombstone in our village church, inscribed 'William Martin, and Elizabeth his wife." On it was written, 'Thou hast covered my head in the day of battle.'

The old couple died in 1878, he was eighty-six and his wife eighty years. They spent their declining days with their daughter and son-in-law in a picturesque farmhouse, which stood back in a garden all aglow with flowers, especially many sorts of polyanthus of every possible colour, which their daughter was famed for raising.

There was a deep lane in front of the garden, and a splendid yew gave a grateful shadow to the passer-by on a hot summer day. I had an amusing experience there. Seated sketching in the lane I became aware of a man's figure near. Without moving, I said ' Good afternoon.' A voice replied, 'Good afternoon, Miss, you do not seem to remember me.'

Having been away from the neighbourhood for several years, I did not expect to recognize my sometime neighbours, so replied, 'No, ought I to remember your name?'

My visitor said,' I take it very hard that you do not know me. I am the Waterloo veteran's son, and when I was a young man and you was in long clothes you had a nursemaid named Caroline. Well, I was a-courting of Caroline, and we used to go walking together, when she was sent out with you; and if we took a long walk she used to get tired and hand the baby to me. I tell you, Miss, 'tis many a mile I have carried you, so I think it very hard that you do not remember me!'

'I Fed My Folk Properly'

BUT what were our villagers like years ago? Quiet, silent people. Unready with their tongues to promise, but with true, warm hearts ready to devote themselves entirely to the good of those whom they respected and loved. You had quietly to get to know these people and then you found in them unexpected depths of attachment.

The women were good home-makers. One of them said, speaking of her finely-built sons, 'I always fed my folk properly. Even when we could not afford much meat, I saw to it that I cooked plenty of vegetables. Then my men ate a good bit of cheese, and I never starved them on baker's bread. I always make my own bread, and it nourishes them. Sound bread and cheese make strong men.'

Our working people must have endured hard times fifty or sixty years ago, when flour was dear, weekly wages only ten shillings a week, and schooling for their numerous children had to be paid for.

Men who had the care of stock were provided with 200 faggots free, as well as their cottages and gardens. The gardens averaged a quarter of an acre in extent, and there were grown potatoes in quantity sufficient to store for winter use, roots of various kinds and green vegetables enough to serve for daily use.

During winter many men went wood-cutting, and their little lads went with them, and learned how to collect brush wood, tie faggots, and help generally.

The Wood Reeve and Other Characters

JOHN PARKES, who used to be the Wood Reeve at Hadlow, was so well acquainted with every tree under his care, that he could tell his questioner not only where any species was to be found but also any peculiarity of bark or growth in any special specimen. John left school at eight and went with his father for some weeks into the woods every year afterwards. He said that from the time he went to work regularly at ten he had kept a diary, and put down every day's work and his earnings.

He and his forbears worked for at least four generations of my ancestors. In bygone years the little boys were proud to 'help father' and later earn pennies for the family purse by picking stones in the meadows, scaring birds off the corn, or working under some gardener for sixpence a day on Saturday.

Then the delights of the hop garden! Perhaps father was pole-puller, an honoured and responsible task. Mother would tidy up the house after early breakfast, and with the infant in her arms, start for the hop garden. The elder children would carry rugs, a kettle, and the lunch and dinner for the family.

I understand that, with these various helps from wife and children, a working man's income in the middle of the nineteenth century averaged a pound a week, and then his wife, if she were a good manager, cleared an extra pound every season from each of her seven or eight hens. So with their productive gardens they lived comfortably, though frugally.

The women not only baked the bread and pies but took fruit enough to make one gallon of wine for Christmas, and saved plums, etc., by placing them in bottles which they stood inside the brick ovens after the bread had been drawn. They also made their own vinegar.

As late as the 'seventies some of the farmers employed hired men whom they boarded and lodged in the house. Alfred was an instance of what thrift can do for a young man. At twenty-seven he left his indoor place and married, being able to furnish a comfortable home with over sixty pounds which he had saved.

How the Labourers Became Farmers

THIS is what Henry Smith of West Hadlow Cottage, Hadlow Down, told me in July, 1922. 'I do not know why my father did not name my eldest brother after himself, but the fact remains that I, the youngest, answer to the same name he had. My father was a bricklayer and builder and brought up all his three sons as carpenters.

'He was a Hadlow Down man and the owner of two little properties there. One, named " Hyders," consisted of two houses situated in the village in the centre of very long gardens. Many years ago—1824—there was no church at Hadlow Down, and no religious service, except an occasional visit from a local preacher.

'My father was a Wesleyan. He decided to do what he could for the good of his own family and those of his neighbours. So, about ten years before I was born, he built a Wesleyan chapel himself. It still stands in the village, though for many years it has been used for a carpenter's workshop and is now out of repair.

'The year I was born the village church was built, the two principal subscribers being the Earl of Liverpool and the Squire of Hadlow, who each gave £100. The great mover in this work was Mr. Hall, who lived at Buxted Lodge in the village of Hadlow Down, and wrote to many people, including His Majesty the King, and the Duke of Wellington.

'I was a high-spirited boy and was always getting into scrapes, so one night my twin brother and I paid a visit to an orchard and helped ourselves to apples. Little did we imagine how severe our punishment was to be. Father called us to him and said how ashamed he felt of our conduct, and that in future, instead of going to school at Hadlow Down we should go to the Old Manor House, Rotherfield, where Mr. Fenner taught a private school. That meant walking five miles every morning before nine o'clock, in order to be in our places punctually, and another five miles home at night. I kept this up for about a year and a half. At that time the Manor House was let to more than one family of working people, and Mr.
Fenner hired one of the large rooms to use as his schoolroom. He lived at Town Row Green and came into Rotherfield every morning to teach his pupils, of whom there must have been about twenty.

'Mr. Fenner was dressed in the old-fash-ioned way. He wore a large black stock and high collar with points in front. We boys were amused by his collar being so stiff, that he could not turn his head to look round, unless he moved his whole body. He was very con-scientious, always keeping his word even in tri-fles.

'I remember his promising a Rotherfield woman that when he walked to Tunbridge Wells he would bring her back a parcel from there. Alas! he forgot it, until he reached Cowford Bridge on his way home. Then he thought of the parcel, retraced his steps several miles, fetched it, and delivered it to her.

'Mr. Fenner allowed himself one indulgence every year. On his birthday he went to the "George Inn," ate two pennyworth of bread and cheese, and drank one pint of ale.

'Our master, like myself, was very fond of bulls-eyes. So now and then, when I wanted a ride home, and the miller's cart was going through Hadlow Down, on its return to Buxted from Rotherfield, I used to buy a pennyworth of sweets and give him some of them, and in return he would let me off early enough to climb upon the miller's cart.

'Mr. Edwards was the clergyman at Hadlow Down, having come there when I was an infant. And Mr. Martin was the schoolmaster. What a contrast his pay was with what schoolmasters get nowadays. He had £40 a year on which to support himself and family. He got some pay for being Clerk at the Hadlow Down Church, and also a trifle from Buxted.

'Mr. Edwards took great interest in the school, often teaching there for two hours at a time. Then he conducted a night school for the elder boys who went to work. Sometimes he would take a class of day school children home with him, and teach them grammar in his study.

'After my year and a half at Rotherfield I attended Hadlow Down School, and had many a les-son from Mr. Edwards. He was a thoroughly kind, good-hearted man, but eccentric and quick tempered. Many a box on the ear has he given me, and I certainly deserved one the time I scooped out the middle of a turnip, put a lighted candle inside, and tied it to his gate post.

'One of his habits was to take long walks; I have known him start for Maresfield, five miles off, late at night, quite alone, and cover the whole distance in his peculiar manner, which was to walk six steps, and trot the next alternately.

Mr. Edwards took great pains in teaching us, and brought forward more than one clever lad.

'Mr. Bryant, the shopkeeper at Hadlow Down, had a son William. Mr. Edwards taught him a great deal, got some assistance from the Shinners' Company and helped him through College. He became a master at Tunbridge Grammar School, and eventually head of the commercial side.

'Three-quarters of a century ago there were no organs in churches or chapels in the country, the musical portion of service being led by a band containing a variety of instruments. At Hadlow Down Church, Jack Wren of Blackboys played the bass viol, his son the bassoon, and Walter Bean(who died in this cottage before I took it some forty-five years ago) the clarionet. The instrument which later on took their place was an organ on which the tunes were ground out.'

P.S., March, 1925.—Henry Smith of Hadlow Down has recently died at the age of ninety-one, loved and respected by all who knew him.

N.B., July. 1927.—His twin brother has just passed away.

Does anyone now remember the cry in 1886 of 'three acres and a cow' and the article written by my brother's friend, Dr. Jessop, in the *Nineteenth Century* entitled 'Little Ones in Norfolk', which did much to stop the agitation for cutting up large estates into three-acre lots?

Of course, the idea, 'three acres and a cow', penetrated into Sussex, and, among other people, our former gardener, Solomon, who had remained in charge of the Hadlow gardens under three successive owners, was bitten with the idea.

I met him one morning, so stopped as usual for a little chat. 'Won't it be nice, Miss, when everyone has his three acres and a cow?' 'I am not so sure of that, Solomon.' 'Why not? Think of having as much milk and butter for the family as they can eat, as well as plenty to sell.' 'No, Solomon, not as an *extra – instead* of your cottage and wages as Hadlow gardener.' 'But I do not want to give up my work and wages.' 'How are you to keep them? If all England is divided into three-acre plots, what becomes of the estates? They will be cut up and, then all you will have to live on will be what you can make off your three acres and a cow. Then, if every family keeps a cow where will you sell your milk and butter? What will you do for food and clothing if your wages stop?

Solomon thought for a moment or two, then said: 'I think I am best off as I am.'

This led to my remarking to my brother that I could find plenty of people close by who had, by hard work, frugality and integrity, raised themselves into the position of working farmers, though born in a labourer's cottage. So we agreed that I should see what I could discover of my neighbour's histories. I also enquired if a man were likely to do well on a small piece of ground without earning extra money. The first point I ascertained was, that during the period 1846 to 1886 much land had changed hands and many small pieces had been bought by thrifty individuals. I append my notes in full of some out of the twenty cases. One of the tradesmen of Hadlow Down said:

'I find no difficulty in showing you plenty of men, who in their own time – or that of their fathers' – have risen from the ranks.

'How have they done it? In no case by depending on the produce of a small piece of land. Everyone of them went to work for wages, or fattened fowls, or in some other manner earned extra money. As to myself, my father was the carrier between Hadlow Down and Lewes. He saved a little money and bought ten acres of land which he farmed, continuing his journey to Lewes. My eldest brother was apprenticed to a miller. I was learning my trade, that of a carpenter, when, twenty years ago, my father was killed by an accident. I came here and kept things together as well as I could for a year, by which time, my brother, being out of his time, came home, took to the farming, going out to work between times. I returned to my trade.

'By degrees we have bought small lots, till now we possess thirty acres of land, and have hired Toll Farm, about as much more. We have a fine herd of Sussex beasts, and now my eldest brother is taking a farm of 100 acres (Wilderness) and my youngest brother has gone into our own cottage. All the men round have done the same. They have saved money, then borrowed a sum to pay the in-going inventory – in some cases have been allowed to have the inventory and pay off by degrees.

'You ask for instances of men now who are getting on. Take John Blank, estate carpenter to Mr. Hum. Some years ago he moved into the cottage with one and three-quarters acres of land at the foot of Tinker's Lane. He has now moved into the opposite house and is doing well with his twenty acres. His near neighbour has gone on in the same way, only a little in advance of John. Then Herbert, who has bought four and a half acres down in the valley, is doing very well, making a large sum by his poultry, and selling a good deal of butter. Oh yes, he told me he received last year sixty pounds from the sale of butter and calves alone. He keeps Jersey and Alderney cows, and fills up time at his trade of boot-maker.

'Henry left school at eight years old, and helped his father at work, especially in wood-cutting and planting in Hadlow woods. He worked on as ordinary labourer on the estate, had a large family and became very poor. Times improved, the children went out to work, and service, and he took a gardener's and stockman's place for six or eight years. He was allowed the keep of a cow besides wages. His wife borrowed money to buy the cow, and about eight years ago they were enabled to take a cottage with twenty acres of land. They have now a fine flock of poultry, four or five good milking cows, supply the great house (Sir George's) with eggs, cream, milk and butter, and have brought up about half-a-dozen young beasts every year. Henry Parkes goes out to work in any capacity, and, when I last saw him, he and his youngest boy were painting at the lodge of Sir George's. George A. is an ordinary labourer, not very strong, but industrious and with a most capable, hard-working wife. All the family are turning out well. He went some five years ago to a farmer's in Waldron parish. He has brought up a couple of young beasts and now this Michaelmas has moved to a little farm, near Little London, Waldron, of about twenty acres.

'My next example is that of a strong, fine young workman at Hastingford, with a young family of five children. Two years ago he took a farm in Buxted, named Foxhole, of forty acres. Last year I was informed that the Foxhole butter was some of the best in the neighbourhood.

'The most recent cases I know are the following:

'William —— has worked during a good many years for Pursglove at Buxted. During some little time he has had, besides his work, two to three acres and a cow, This Michaelmas he has taken a nice compact little farm, Spoods, of some thirty or forty acres.

'Henry —— brought up as under-gardener at Buxted Park for about ten years, has had two cows on a little bit of ground, continuing all the time to go out to work, recently as bailiff at New House, Buxted. He has now taken a farm and enlarged his stock, and seems to be doing well.

There were three brothers, whose nicknames were, King (a very good cricketer), Rugged and Butcher. The two elder ones took three acres of wild land, sowed oats, and worked hard as labourers. In process of time King took a large farm, Inchreed, which he worked for many years, his brothers helping him at first. Then Rugged took Crowpits, about thirty acres. Now, for the last ten years or more, Rugged has had a good farm near Blackboys, and Butcher, the youngest brother, having married a daughter of Master John Daniel of The Hole, has Crowpits, which he and his sons work in conjunction with his father-in-law. John Daniel's father was keeper at Hadlow. John himself helped his father in the first place. When he was a big lad he worked under the estate carpenter, while much re-building of farmhouses and lodges was going on. He also worked under bricklayers on the estate. Married at one-and-twenty, he continued working with bricklayers, or at any kind of work. He took a small piece of five acres of grass land near the village, kept a cow, fatted fowls, went out pig-killing all round the country, and, in fact, did anything which came to hand. He never thought of depending on his five acres. Then he moved to Cross-in-Hand, where for eight years he worked sixteen acres in the same manner. For the last twenty-nine years he has had the Hole Farm of 100 acres. Notwithstanding having broken a leg, and reached the age of seventy-two, he is an active man ready to undertake an eight or ten miles' walk or do a day's work. His wife was a very capable woman, who never stopped her work a minute whatever visitors came in or allowed anyone to hinder her. For many years she made sixty pounds a year by her poultry and eggs. She used to start at four a.m. with a wheel-barrow filled with chicken food, and feed poultry in a meadow half a mile off.

'One of my neighbours was carter at Broad-reed till about 1868, when the new line was formed between Uckfield and Tunbridge Wells. He took his horse and worked on the line as a navvy. In process of time he became a clerk and engaged another man to go with the horses. Some eight years ago he hired Broomfields, which is a farm of about 150 acres, and, with a capable wife and six or eight sons, besides children of school age, has worked till now. A year and a half ago he rented an additional farm, Five Chimneys, of about fifty acres. His eldest son, James, has, till lately, been working for him as a labourer, but has now set up for himself, in a little lot of fourteen acres, continuing to go out to work between times. His second son, Richard, is in charge of Broomfields, whilst the father lives at Five Chimneys. I forgot to mention that between working on the line and taking Broomfield my neighbour had a small farm near Crowboro' Rocks, thirty acres.

'Mr. Jesse —— is an old man of about eighty, whom I sometimes see. He was an ordinary labourer at Huggett's Furnace. Then one of the Martins took a farm of some seventy to eighty acres named Covels in Rotherfield parish, near the border of Hadlow Down. He took Jesse on as foreman. This was thirty-five years ago. Then he changed his mind, and thought he did not care about farming, and offered Jesse to start him in the farm, by letting him enter with prom-ise of everything as it stood (Mr. Martin having paid the in-going valuation) and that Jesse might repay him the valuation by degrees, at his own time. Jesse accepted the proposition, and in a few years had paid off the entire sum. He has brought up four sons. The eldest son has a farm called Sandhills in Rotherfield, and one of his sons lives with the old man. Together they work Covels. Another son has a large farm, Street, in the parish of Framfield. Another son has a Hadlow Farm called Stockland. About three years ago the youngest son took Hastingford Farm and is reputed to have the finest team of cart-horses in this neighbourhood. Thus Jesse and his four sons, with the assistance of his grandson at Covel, have four large farms averaging at least 100 acres each, and some being over that in extent.

The Yeomen

LET no one infer from my notes that we had no well-to-do farmers, survivors of the old yeoman class, in Sussex.

One family is that of the Allcorns, or Allchorn as it used to be spelt, who had owned Rotherfield Hall for generations, then sold it to Mr. Dodd. Long afterwards it was bought by Sir Lindsay Hogg, who laid out gardens and in many ways restored its ancient beauties.

There were three brothers Allcorn, two of whom I knew. George, the Rotherfield Rate Collector, and Frederick, born at the Hall in 1819, who died at Crowborough during 1900 after he had retired from farming Huggett's Furnace where he went in 1853. In the seventeenth and eighteenth centuries Sussex had important iron works, but when the oak trees had been cut down which were used as fuel to smelt the local iron, the land returned to cultivation, and Huggett's Furnace no longer was a centre of iron works. It was there Sam Sands worked for sixty years. One day I called at the house about midday. The large kitchen had a long table in the centre, at which were seated, in old English fashion, all the members of the family, as well as the hired men. Game was not often served in our house, and I gave an exclamation of sur-prise, when I found that partridge pudding formed the staple dish. Mrs. Allcorn would not hear of my sitting down to the long table, but took me into the large, comfortable sitting-room, and served me with a portion of the partridge pudding; certainly the most delicious pudding it has ever been my lot to taste. Huggett's Furnace is the only house where I have tasted the ancient British beverage, mead, which Mrs. Allcorn possessed the recipe for making. She was famed for the lightness and delicacy of her "Flead cakes" which no one now goes to the trouble of making. I was struck to find how much leisure her servants enjoyed. Certainly, they began early, being about their duties by 5.30 a.m. The washing-up after the midday dinner completed, the maids had some hours every afternoon to devote to their own sewing, with the result that each one had a good store of well-made garments on leaving, as well as a fund of gratitude to, and affection for, their kind mistress.

When Mr. Frederick Allcorn retired in *1875,* giving up the tenancy of Huggett's Furnace to his only son Fred, the farm continued to be noted for its splendid herd of Sussex cattle.

The stackyard there in olden times was a sight worth seeing. High barns enclosed one side. Another was bounded by the narrow footpath which extended in front of the windows of the house. The whole yard was strongly fenced with rails; troughs held the food, and about twenty head of cattle busied themselves eating and otherwise enjoying life. Mr. and Mrs. Allcorn retired to a house near Hadlow Down known as Five Chimneys, owing to the fact that around the centre one four others are placed. There is another set of chimneys built in the same style at Cuckfield, and these two examples are considered unique in Sussex.

Another prominent figure at Hadlow Down was Mr. Frederick Allcorn's nephew, William Allcorn of Pigsfoot, of whom his grand-daughter writes as follows: 'William, son of James Allcorn, was born at The Hall, Rotherfield, in 1829, and died in 1919 at Oaklands, a house which the Marquess of Abergavenny had built for him in 1903. He lived the life of an ordinary energetic working farmer, but was always fond of sport. His father was for many years keeper at Eridge Park, and although William was never in the Marquess of Abergavenny's employ, yet he did much to preserve the game from foxes. When Lord Henry Nevill lived at Hadlow my grandfather managed the farm for him.'

Five Ashes

A WEALDEN village is so named from a clump of five ash trees which must have grown on their knoll for a couple of hundred years, before Mr. Hughes had them grubbed out (probably during the 'sixties), in order to build the shop and post office. They were such fine trees, and behind them was a yard, where bullocks were kept. There are some old poplar stumps in front of the inn, and I have known people point to them as if they were the original ashes! The War Memorial on the little green is opposite the bank on which the five ashes stood so many years ago.

One of our patriarchs was born in 1800, near Inchreed Farm and died at Five Ashes during 1882. His picture was painted by D. E. Robins as he sat by his little round table in the small cottage of his daughter, Mrs. Field, and shows the open hearth, with warming-pan and bellows hanging over the chimney piece. I remember once seeing festoons of home-made sausages hanging from the old oak beams of the ceiling.

Thomas Streeter was one of a large family who married in due course, and had seven children. One of his daughters, dying in 1919 at the age of eighty-seven, left three generations to survive her.

He and his wife were thrifty people and brought up their family on labourer's wages. I knew one of his sons, George, who had raised himself to the position of a well-to-do farmer, and when he retired from New Pinn had a large inventory(worth over £1,000) to receive. He had had no advantages of present-day education, but he and his wife were industrious, careful people, who wasted nothing.

It must have been about the year 1884, that, requiring an under-housemaid I engaged a niece who had been working for this honest couple for three or four years. Mary asked me to see the contents of her box when she came. I was astonished to be shown every sort of undergarment for day or night wear, and to find that Mary possessed eight of each description......all made of calico she had bought from her wages of eight pounds a year, made, trimmed, and feather-stitched by herself.

There had been a time in Thomas Streeter's life when he was badly off. His last piece of hard work, i.e., quarrying stone for a house which was being built, had been accomplished during 1856, since which time he had only been equal to doing odd jobs. It must have been about 1866 when he was laid up with asthma from which he never recovered sufficiently to go to work. His son-in-law offered him house-room if he could find his own food. The parish allowance was only two and sixpence per week; he could not exist on that. Naturally, he shrank from going into the workhouse, but for some time it appeared inevitable. His clergyman, the Rev. R. Kirby, spoke to one of the old family for which in happier days he had worked, saying that for another two shillings and sixpence a week he might be spared this indignity. So till the time of his death the sum he had was an extra half-crown weekly, and it sufficed.

It struck me as strange to find that he ate alone, instead of with the others, his little round table with a white cloth being placed near the fire, whilst his daughter and son-in-law used a square table beside the door. But later on I found that that is the way in the cottages, probably in some cases in order to let the old folks eat in peace, without being disturbed by children. He was comfortably. dressed in his grey linen smock, sometimes in winter supplemented by a cloth coat.

In July, 1921 there was a fete at Skipper's Hill to gather funds towards the erection of a church at Five Ashes, and I took Thomas Streeter's portrait over, and it was displayed as that of one of the patriarchs of the village, and aroused much interest among the visitors, as well as some of the old man's descendants.

The present owner of Skipper's Hill has kindly given me the following information:

The name (which is on the oldest map of Sussex in the British Museum) comes from this hill having been used as a beacon for the smuggling ships; lighted up was a signal that all was clear.

It is now nearly fifty years since the Rev. R. Kirby erected a school-house in this hamlet, and till five years ago services were intermittently held there on Sundays, to the great benefit of the people, who appreciated a simple service which the unlearned could follow. I have seen those old and middle-aged people who could not read, and probably had no one to read to them, sitting intently listening to the lessons for the day and to the sermons.

There was an old man of those parts who had lost his eyesight but came regularly to Hadlow Down Church, led by an octogenarian neighbour. Obadiah Cottingham leading blind Hezekiah Stapley, followed by George Fulleron his wooden leg, were rather a pathetic sight, as Sunday after Sunday they tramped along and then sat together in one of the front benches. They were none of them scholars, but Hezekiah said to me, 'I love to hear the clergyman's verses in the Psalms; they give me much to muse on during the week.'

People talk of attracting congregations by means of musical services. I wonder where they will find more earnest, attentive congregations than Hadlow Down possessed during the 'eighties.

With the exception of three or four families who had their own pews, the congregation was divided thus. The men had the north aisle, the women and married men the south aisle, and the boys and girls of the Sunday School filled the west benches. 'Tis but a small village, but Mr. Longland preached such interesting sermons that one seemed to see the individuals of whom he was preaching. Then Mrs. Longland devoted herself to training the choir of men and boys(and, if I mistake not) allowed other members of the congregation to attend the practices. There must have been eight benches on the north side of the church holding eight persons in each. Sunday after Sunday I have known all these benches nearly filled with men and youths. And how they used to sing! Canticles and hymns resounded, and then we read the Psalms and joined in the prayers. After Mr. Warner came, the congregations still filled the church, owing to his good voice and clear delivery.

It is interesting to think that our neighbouring village of Cross in Hand was the rallying point for our forefathers whence they started for the Crusades. Cannot we imagine those brawny men, with sword, shield and helmet, each holding on high the emblem of his salvation ere starting on that distant journey?

Village Clubs

IN a little cottage at the entrance to the Wilderness Lane lived old John Dean and his wife, all alone except for their pig and a few fowls. They used two fields, and so were included as rate payers, though really among the poorest of the population.

Old John had joined a Benefit Society in youth, and paid his subscription over fifty years. His old wife, being very infirm, found it beyond her strength to lift over the fence the pail of pig-wash she had carried from the cottage to the stye. The old man saw her difficulty, and helped her raise the pail. Someone had observed them, reported old John to the Society, and he was turned out, and so lost the small weekly allowance to which he had become entitled in virtue of age, infirmity, and the long period during which he had paid his subscription to the club.

These Village Clubs seem to have been managed on a very insecure basis. A number of young fellows would start a Benefit Club. Each member was to pay so much a month and in return was entitled to receive sick pay when unable to work, and often a small allowance in old age. This sounds satisfactory, and would have been so had the surplus funds of the Society been deposited year by year to form a sinking fund. Alas that was hardly ever done. These meetings of the club often took place at the public house, the innkeeper was probably an official, and the *benefit* consisted in the members enjoying a good dinner once a year at the inn.

This feast took all the money saved during the year. As time went on young men did not care to join. They said, 'If we join this club we shall have to support all the old members, so we will leave them to look after themselves and start one of our own.' I knew one case, where a man, having paid in for nearly sixty years, was left destitute in old age because his club had broken up.

Does one wonder at improvidence, when providence is so rewarded? The rule about doing no work whilst in receipt of club pay was most strictly enforced. I have heard of a man being turned out of his club because he put a couple of sticks on the fire, by which he was sitting.

But to return to my friends, Master and Missus Dean. When I knew them he had lost all claim to the club, and used to potter around his 'Missus' and do little jobs. They had four hens from which they got enough eggs to pay the miller for ground oats on which the hens were fed, and perhaps leave a trifle over towards their weekly flour.

Autumn was coming on, and Mrs. Dean said to me, 'I'm afeared, Miss, I must kill that hen you admire so much.' She was a large dark Sussex with pheasant-coloured feathers round her neck. 'Food is dear, she has left off laying, and I can nowise afford to keep her.' Not realizing the old woman's need, I said, 'Oh, Mrs. Dean, not my pet, I hope —— '

It was perhaps a fortnight later when I next called at the cottage. 'Please, Miss, I hope you will not be angry, but I had to kill your pet hen.'

'Why should I be angry, Mrs. Dean? She was yours, not mine.

'Well, I had a little flour so I divided the hen into four lots, and made four little puddings. My Master and I we had one pudding between us the first day. The next day what was left from that one – and so on; each pudding made two dinners for both of us. So I hope, Miss, you will not think I was very extravagant in killing and eating the old hen!'

How would any of us have contrived sixteen dinners from one old hen and a little flour?

Economical Bonnet Buying

HERE is another instance of the frugal life the cottagers used to live. A labourer's wife, when in bad health, said once to Mrs. Day, 'You see, Madam, perhaps you think me extravagant in having bought myself a bonnet, but you see mine was quite worn out, and so Polly – that is my eldest daughter, you know – Polly, she is always so considerate like; says she, 'Mother, buy a black one, and then you see, Mother, if you die, it will be ready for me to wear at your funeral.'

The bonnet, however, was not needed for Polly's use, as the mother lived many years afterwards.

A Book Bargain

MRS. APPLE consulted me as to an investment she had made. She was 'no scholar' but her old man was uncommon fond of reading', so when he had a paper or book he was contented and never grumbled.

'My neighbour up the lane left lately and I went to see her when she was packing. "What shall I do with this big Bible? "says she, "I have no room for it anywhere. Look ee, Mrs. Apple, will you buy it for half-a-crown?" I took it in my hand, saw what a lot of reading there was in it, and thought it would keep my husband busy for a long time. So I trotted home, fetched a half-crown that I had saved, bought the book and took it home, and put it on the little round table. When my husband had had his supper he said, looking at the book, "What have you there?" "That's for you to tell me," I said, "because you can read, which I can't." So he put on his specs, and now every evening he reads, and you cannot think how good-tempered he has been lately Now he reads to me regular. So, Miss, do you think I was very extravagant in spending my half-crown?'

Soup

IT must have been in 1852 or 1853 that times were bad for farmers. Many of the farms were thrown on hand. My mother could not afford to increase the weekly wages, so called some of the men for consultation.

'Can I help you in any way during this coming winter?' 'Well, Madam, we have been talking it over, and made up our minds to ask you if we can have nice soup, such as you have given us from time to time, provided twice a week. it would help.' So a second copper was put into the back kitchen. Eliza was a first-rate cook and agreed to make the soup twice a week. Some of the neighbours sent vegetables to supplement those grown at Hadlow. Flour, rice, oatmeal, etc., were bought by the hundredweight – Soyer's recipe proved invaluable – the butcher was liberal, and the result was, that, for an outlay of £25, soup was made and distributed at the rate of a quart each, twice a week, to every member of the labourers' families. I believe the bi-weekly quantity made was forty gallons. Children on their way home from school brought cans to be filled. If any remained after all the farm workers had been served, outsiders might buy it at one penny per quart. Distribution lasted over five months.

'Sophy's School'

BESIDES the national school at Hadlow Down there was a dame school in the village, kept by a tall, thin woman who lived in a small cottage. The room had a table in the centre, and there were benches for the children to sit on, one being quite low for the tiny tots. In this primitive schoolroom were gathered over twenty boys and girls, representing the families of the farmers and tradespeople.

Mothers used to say, ' I send my children to Sophy's School, because she allows no rough manners. Then see what good needle-work she teaches.'

For many years I kept as a specimen of stitching, hemming, and gathering, a pinafore made by a child of eight in Sophy's School.

Finding that the Family Bible, so treasured by every self-respecting cottager, was not available for use by the children, I offered to give a New Testament to every child who would learn perfectly the six verses which end the first chapter of St. Mark. The elder ones were promised a whole Bible for reciting the second of Kings, the fifth chapter, with its vivid account of Naaman's cure.

If I mistake not, every scholar earned a book, one of the Bibles going to a boy of ten, who subsequently won a scholarship in the Uckfield Grammar School.

The Wealden People

OUR genuine Sussex man or woman used to be hardworking, frugal, and contented. I have been reproved by more than one farmer for saying I wished the weather would change before haymaking-time. 'We mustn't complain,' he would say, 'God sends the weather, and He knows what is best.'

The men were always ready to give a helping hand if needed. One evening five or six men had come to my house for a reading. It was haytime and my few haymakers were working to save the crop. A farmer looked out of the window and, turning to the other men, said, 'An ounce of help is worth a pound of pity; instead of sitting here, let us all go out and work.' Out they went and worked till nine o'clock, saved my little crop, and charged me nothing, but said they were pleased to give any assistance in their power. The honesty and integrity of these men was striking. They never scamped their work, but would labour for extra hours when needful, never accepting overtime wage.

Their generation has nearly passed away, as I am writing principally of my experiences among them during the years from 1874 till 1892. They had good gardens in which they grew most of their simple fare. These people were not appreciated as they ought to have been, because their manners were not similar to those of townsfolk, and an ancient lingo still prevailed which was not understood. The townsman did not realize that 'I have no mislike to you, for none of your family ever did me any harm' means 'I am very much attached to you, and would go through fire and water to rescue you, or any of yours.'

Their particularity about truth was very striking. If a woman could not remember exactly what day of the week an event happened she would say, 'I do not wish to tell a falsehood, but I cannot tell if it took place last Wednesday or Thursday.' If townsfolk knew the Wealden dwellers' sterling worth and honest affection they would respect and look up to the countryman.

Of old it used to be said that these Sussex country people dreaded the very thought of a sea voyage, and that the boys rarely became soldiers and never sailors. Let me mention an incident of about the year 1853. The Squire had died, leaving a large family, the elder ones already at college or training for professions. The second son having a taste for mineralogy studied as a mining engineer and went to seek his fortune in the gold fields of Australia, where, like so many of our brightest and most adventurous young men, he met with disappointment and sickness.

News came to his mother that he was ill, and soon the tenants and labourers with whom he had been a favourite, from his love of outdoor occupations and sunny disposition, heard of it. Three men (each unaware of the others' intentions) came to the house, and asked to see the mother. Their request was the same in each case,' Let me go to Australia and fetch Mr. Edmund home.' 'I will work my way out', said one, 'in order to save you the expense of my fare'. Not one of the three men asked for any pay, though they were all poor men. The married man merely said, 'I know you will not let my wife and children starve whilst I am gone.' The estate carpenter, with whom Edmund had worked in anticipation of leaving home, was most emphatic in his desire to be of use. And now people say falsely that there was no link of affection between the families of squire and labourer. Does a man offer to undertake a voyage of several months, as it was in those days. during which time he would forgo all wages and personal comfort, unless he cares for and loves the person he hopes to serve? I trow not.

Wealden Characteristics

OUR village folk were too independent to make my visits an excuse for getting gifts. Our intercourse was entirely of a friendly nature in the hundred and twenty houses where I was welcomed. The only exception was that of a 'pattern house-keeper' whose furniture, polished to perfection, was decorated with antimacassars of her own making, and quite free from dust. She always implied that she should like a gift, and, in later years, when her husband became an invalid, she would get sympathy from all by talking of 'poor dear Joseph' till the clergyman would give coal, and the minister grocery tickets, whilst house-rent, brandy, and soup were supplied by the gentry.

When I first knew Mrs. Joseph her sunbonnets were my admiration, and she earned quite a nice sum every year by making them in readiness for the haymaking season, and also by making round frocks which she smocked most exquisitely.

During the 'eighties there was a large exhibition held in Brighton and I saw in the schedule prizes offered for Sussex smock frocks. Accordingly, wishing to uphold the honour of our village, I bought enough linen to make two frocks, and handed half of it to Mrs. Joseph, who at the close of the exhibition received the first prize, i.e., twelve shillings and sixpence. She must then have been under fifty. I took the second half of the linen to a widow aged seventy, who lived with her son in Poundsley Lane, on his wages as an agricultural labourer. When the awards were made, ten shillings was sent as second prize. Taking the money I started to walk to her cottage, but met her on the way. I told her she had earned a prize, and laid the money in her palm. For a minute she could not speak. Then she exclaimed, 'Gold for me! I never expected again to earn so much money, but I tell you I am thankful.'

A striking point about my neighbours was then thirst for Bible teaching and their desire to spread the good news. My gardener's son asked if he might bring some mates on a certain evening. 'Tramp, tramp', like soldiers marching they sounded. On opening the door seventeen young men entered, and for some years attended the Bible class.

Then the elder men came, one of them calling for his neighbours whose cottages he passed, and bringing his chum (aged seventy) with him.

In gratitude for the use of books, lights and firing, Kemp made a big missionary box, which, placed outside the door of the room produced two pounds in six months. The women made clothing and the girls knitted socks to send to Canada.

Mrs. Cott lived near the village, with her 'old mad' who could still keep the garden tidy, while she saw to her three or four hens with their chickens. She was too feeble to join the working party. 'Let me have a shirt to make at home', she said, and she made one a month for three years till, becoming a widow, she left to live with a daughter. I forgot to supply the sewing cotton, so the old couple went to bed quite early, and spent the money they had put aside for lamp-oil in buying the cotton. Besides their rent their united income was five shillings a week. Who of us exercises such self-denial as they did?

From 1872 I had been constantly at Hadlow Down, but it was in 1879 that I returned to settle in my old neighbourhood and exclaimed, 'How different are the people of the Weald to those who live in Brighton! Here the middle-aged are all over seventy and the old folks vary from eighty to ninety years of age. There were a dozen cottages within a radius of a quarter of a mile of my house. I ascertained that fifteen of the men and women living in them were over eighty. One woman was ninety-two and would start after breakfast for a farm one-and-a-half miles off and return by eleven o'clock carrying a dozen new-laid eggs up Tinkers Lane Hill.

In nineteen hundred and eight, while staying at the vicarage, Mr. Warner was good enough to let me make extracts from his registers. I took the names and ages of fifty men and women I had known in Hadlow Down. Of these, six attained the age of seventy years, eleven seventy-five years, twenty-five eighty years, and eight ninety years.

When I lived at Hadlow Down I was interested in observing how many of my neighbours had Bible names. I will quote a few: Aaron, Abraham, Amos, Boaz, David, Caleb, Ezra, Esli, Eunice, Esther, Ebenezer, Hezikiah, Jeremiah, Obadiah, Jesse, Joseph, Isaac, Jacob, Samuel, Solomon, Tamar, Ruth, Sarah, Naomi, Michael, Ephraim, Obed, Lois, Benjamin.

Then we had Augustus Caesar, Cicero, Virgil, Horace, Mark Antony, Venus Pandora, Luther.

I have seen the statement made that mothers of a former generation laid most of their infants to sleep in the churchyard. So I have been collecting information from my neighbours. In this locality, twenty families had two hundred and six children. Of these, two hundred lived to maturity, and were all brought up on mothers' milk.

When I came of age I undertook to complete the house in which I afterwards lived, and my brother said: 'These Hadlow Down men are absolutely trustworthy. Choose one of them to work for you, and he will look after your interests before his own.'

And so I found it, for I never had an unjust act done or a piece of work scamped by one of them. But then, I only knew them after they had had the benefit of Mr. Edwards's and Mr. Reginald Kirby's teaching.

A Personal Note

S OME of the years of my early girlhood were spent in Brighton, but I went to Hadlow Down constantly, thus keeping up an interest in the people whose families had worked for my ancestors for many generations.

One of these loyal men regretted that a house, begun by my eldest brother, should stand unfinished when the old family left the neighbourhood. Acting on John Daniel's favourite proverb, 'An ounce of help is worth a pound of pity', he got planks, with which he boarded up the window spaces. He also replaced any tiles which had moved, attended to the young trees which had been planted in the garden, and in every way looked after the forsaken building for years. And all this without fee or reward, entirely from love to the old family.

Little as the world appreciated them, the Sussex folk were a noble people who would scorn to tell a lie or defraud their employers of an hour's time. Surrounded by the beauty of the Weald, they grew up to love nature, and looked up from nature to nature's God, whom most of them served from day to day.

It is of these people I have jotted down a few memories. Mine was a lonely childhood. My father died when I was a few months old. Times were bad for agriculture; my mother was burdened with the responsibility of finding tenants for the numerous farms, which covered two thousand acres of land, in Mayfield, Hadlow Down, Rotherfield, and Framfield. Some farms she had to take in hand, and for all the forty cottages tried to keep up my father's rule: 'A good roof, a well, and quarter of an acre of ground for each.'

My grown-up brothers were preparing for their professions. By the time that I was two-and-a-half years old one had started for India, another for Australia, and only the youngest remained at home.

I went with my nurse maid to feed the nestlings in Deep Hadlow woods, or pick mulberry leaves for the thirty thousand silkworms which were kept in the large room above the stables.

Sometimes the carter would take me to see the animals in the yards, and what an interest I took in watching the sheep being washed in the pond preparatory to shearing time; and in admiring the decorations being put up before the harvest home supper.

The school treats were held on our lawn. When four years old I trotted round with the cake. 'Take some more', said I to a boy. 'Please, Miss, I can't, I have eaten seven pieces, and my pockets are full!'

Our original family name was Daye, but as early as 1750 it was spelt Day, as we know from the records of Mayfield parish, for in that year the first school was established, and Ansell Day, Gent., subscriber and trustee, is mentioned.

William Day, who died in 1807, was no mean artist. He made one of the earliest private collections of minerals. His son took up geology ardently, and their specimens are now in the Central Library, Finchley Road, and are used by teachers constantly.

Ansell Day, born in 1826, became a solicitor. He gave much attention to the improvement of labourers' cottages, and by his articles in the *Herald* obtained assistance for the starving peasants of Kerry during the 'little famine'. He was also author of' Russian Government in Poland'.

Henry George Day, Fellow of St. John's, Cambridge, took holy orders. He was a keen geologist, and assisted the late Professor Sedgewick in arranging specimens in the Cambridge Museum. His daughter is a Doctor of Literature.

Francis was a born naturalist. In India he became Inspector-General of Fisheries, and subsequently Commissioner for the Indian Department at the Fisheries Exhibition in 1883. His rank was that of Surgeon-General. He was one of the first men to receive the Order of Companion of the Indian Empire, and his books on ichthyology are not forgotten.

INDEX OF PEOPLE'S NAMES IN
Glimpses of Rural Life in Sussex

Introduction

"Nowadays folk do not neighbour in that way."

What of the approaching twenty first century? Crystal Balls were never reliable and are best avoided. Today in spite of the many pressures, Hadlow Down is a pleasant rural parish and thought by most to be a good place to settle in. Long may it continue to be so.

As we look back over the years we can see how much the nature and structure of the village has changed. We are no longer a community of largely servile tenants frequently remaining in the village from cradle to the grave but have exchanged our status for that of the owner occupier. The value of our properties exert different pressures on our lives, whether for good is a matter of conjecture. It was noticeably common for our forebears to move surprisingly large distances when unencumbered by property, all that was required was to give up one tenancy and take on another. Cecil Godley remembers how "keeping your ear to the ground" was of paramount importance in order to know about properties that might be coming vacant, indeed the tenants frequently knew what was happening before the landlords. With tied cottages so commonplace, jobs and homes could be changed and travelling to work did not present a problem. Today many people choose to stay living where they are happy and settled with a mortgage even though it is 'the devil you know', and at the same time accepting commuting to work, over frequently enormous distances.

Hand-in-hand with the housing revolution we have seen huge increases in property values partly caused by better off families migrating from the towns to enjoy the good life in the country and undoubtedly in Hadlow Down fuelled by the strength of the south-east's economy. The result now is that young people often experience difficulty getting on the housing ladder, possibly forcing them to leave the village. The building of St Mark's Field [fondly known to many as Brookside Close] as starter homes for locals is a practical step toward overcoming this problem and easing the pressure of change. At the same time older people find the need to move because of the lack of facilities, such as shops and public transport.

The smallholders, so important in the early days of the century, have long gone and the family farm along with agriculture in general is fighting a rearguard action for survival. No longer is this country's economy founded on agriculture with a huge manufacturing base; the silicon chip and the 'computer age' has changed all that, allowing, even forcing, different work patterns. The trend for people to work from home but still be linked to their head office has been possible for some time; now there is growing evidence of firms beginning to actively encourage the practice. Possibly working from home will, in the future, change the dormitory village we are in danger of becoming, and encourage the return of some retail services in the village. The retail trade has also suffered change. As the local towns grew after the Second World War so customers were lured away from the village shops. In turn hypermarkets and out-of-town shopping malls are helping to inflict similar ignominy on many town high streets.

The availability of mass transport in the shape of the motor car has allowed greater freedom for the individual although frequently at the expense of the environment and his neighbour. The constant stream of ever increasing vehicles passing through our village brings problems in the shape of noise and pollution for residents, as well as danger for both motorist and pedestrian. Residents understandably retreat behind high hedges and close-boarded fences, whilst campaigns are waged to reduce the speed of the through traffic. When the main road was first 'upgraded' from the B2102 to the A272 our local Parish Council adopted a policy of resisting any improvements to the road or pavements in the hope that one day the classification might be put back to a B road. For many years that has seemed an unlikely possibility, but now as the century draws to its close, a wind of change can be seen blowing through the shires. Mr John Prescott, [Minister of Transport] has declared a moratorium on road building, at the same time making it quite clear that the British people's love affair with the motor car must change and alternative methods of transport must be found. Interestingly when thirty years ago the railway line from Uckfield to Lewes [midst a storm of protest] was closed, it seemed to most folks that there was no chance of it ever reopening. Today however for the first time and to the credit of the campaigners who have kept the pressure on, there are signs from our elected masters, that the line might be reinstated. This of course may all turn out to be so much political hot air blown away by the commercial interests of the automobile industry. Even supposing there is another transport revolution, how much effect, if any, it might have on our community here in Hadlow Down, remains to be seen.

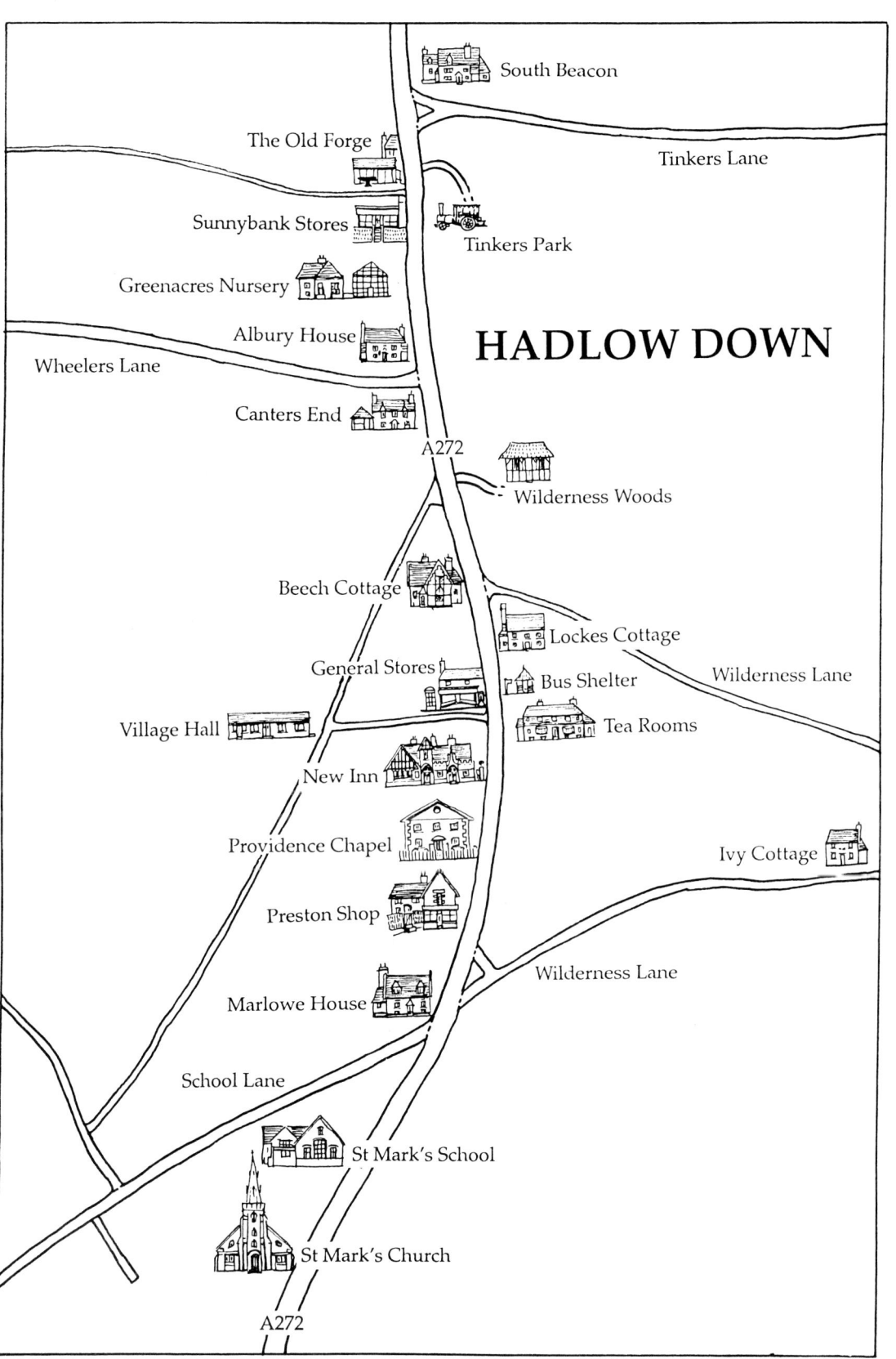

Hadlow Down

What's in a name?

Originally it is felt there would have been a clearing in the forest here-abouts with a settlement, probably governed by a Saxon with the name Headda. Headda's leah, or clearing, in time developed to Haddelegh. In the early 1300s the Down was added to denote the hill sloping to the valley. It took another 200 years for us to become Hadleydown and then another 250 years, when in the late 1700s the name Hadley Down emerged. Today's Hadlow Down is only a mere step away from that. Perhaps with a more literate population and better communications, the evolution of our name will cease.

Many would argue that the heart and life of the village springs from its school. During the 1950s and 60s there seemed to be a national mania to close as many village schools as possible and bus the children to the nearest town. Although attendance at our school went through several lows and there must have been many good economic arguments for closure, we were spared the axe. Today's national policy appears to have eased the pressure on rural schools, the local authority are committed to investing in our buildings and the school is flourishing, with lively staff, active governors and pupil numbers at a healthy level.

Perhaps the national decline in religious influence stands out more clearly than any other change. The two chapels in the village have both closed and the Church which in 1913 required enlarging is today generally under-used. This position is reflected nationally although it can be argued is often accentuated in a community like ours when the policy of the United Benefice is adopted. Perhaps it is to be expected that if one incumbent is asked to do the work that three did before him, then a decline will follow. During the last ten years or so the Church of England has undergone an economic revolution devolving much more financial responsibility on to individual churches and their congregations.

For the first half of the century home entertainment for the majority was minimal to say the least, so any form of public fun and games was to be welcomed. Today we tend to think our lives are busier than ever, although there is plenty of evidence that our grandparents lived lives equally full as ours, even if their work and the pressures were quite different [when George Bracher took over The Forge in the 1890s the employee walked to work from somewhere near Tunbridge Wells!]. Due to the development of the cinema and subsequently the television and computer we are now used to a very sophisticated level of home entertainment along with well-equipped leisure facilities within easy reach. This may help to explain why sometimes village events are poorly attended.

Evaluating the changes of the last 100 years or so and their effects on us is no easy task. Certainly we have seen great alterations to every aspect of life but so have most, if not all, generations before us. Change there has always been and we must assume always will be. Maybe the speed of change sets us apart; certainly in the second half of this century the speed has been cyclonic. It is to be hoped that reading this book will provide an insight into times that today are gone for ever, and provide the reader with an opportunity to evaluate the changes. No attempt has been made to produce a complete work; it should be viewed more as a compilation of facts gleaned from those who know the village best.

Chapter One

THE MAIN ROAD

by Peter Gillies

"We knew nothing about the fancy biscuits, tinned salmon and other delicacies which the grocers offer now to rich and poor"

The centre of the village has always been spread along, what is now the A272; formerly the B2102 and prior to that just called Main Road or even High Street. Not very imaginative perhaps but certainly accurate even in earlier times, it was not only the major arterial road through the parish but also the centre and heart of the village. The only name that might have been more appropriate is Commercial Road, because unlike today there was a hive of business activity, all along the street which sustained and in turn was supported by the life of the village.

Starting at the junction of School Lane and Main Road opposite Fir Tree Cottage stands what is now called **Marlowe House** [Residential Home for the Elderly] formerly Four Ways but originally built by Charles Lang Huggins as Holiday Cottage. Although it was probably not intended to be a commercial venture, more of a service for friends and staff from London, it must have offered a contribution to the local economy with holiday makers staying in the centre of the village. There can be no doubt the building served the local community in a more sociable way. (See Chapter 5.)

Holiday Cottage – renamed Fourways, now Marlowe House.

The *Sussex Express*, November 1912

READING ROOM RE-OPENED

"The room at the holiday cottage which every winter is kindly placed at the disposal of the villagers by Mr Charles Lang Huggins has again been opened, and on Wednesday last, the first evening of the season, there was a good attendance of members who participated in billiards, cards and other games."

Preston House and shop accommodated the Bakery, Sweetshop, Corn Merchant, Coalman and General Stores. The shop and outbuildings were built around 1900 by Mr A. E. Smith and his wife Elizabeth [Grandparents to Dawn and Gerald Standen]. Dawn can remember how the window would be full of sweets and other foodstuffs [largely unwrapped] and a big fluffy cat asleep in the corner, that nobody seemed to mind. Many people remember the cakes, which used to lure the children in on their

Bill Ruff
Baker at Preston House

Preston House and shop, circa 1907
from the left, Marjorie Ann Smith (born 1897), Elizabeth Kate Smith (born 1901), Dorothy Smith (born 1895)

way to and from school. Bill Ruff was employed as baker until the Smith's sunset years. Mrs Smith died in 1942 so her husband A. E. Smith carried on with the help of his youngest daughter, Kate, and Kittie Mitchell [née Godley]. When eventually the shop was sold Bill was able to take on the tennancy in his own right. His son-in-law [Fred Dennett] carried on the business when Bill retired in 1949. The shop finally closed as a General Stores in 1954 after over 50 years of continuous service.

Marjorie Jarvis remembers…

"I can recall the Bakery which was situated at the back of the shop where all the bread was baked by Bill Ruff always on faggots. His speciality for little boys were the bread rolls, these cost a half penny and would be collected by the children in the morning on route to school. The bakery also served as a venue for the cooking of all the Christmas Turkeys and the villagers used to arrive with their turkey and Bill would cook them and afterwards the people would return to collect their birds and then carried them down the road back home for their Christmas dinners. In fact the person who actually cooked the birds was a Mrs Smith and she used Bill Ruff's facilities".

Since the closing of the shop it has had a chequered career. For a while a green

Fred Dennett in the doorway

grocer's shop flourished. Since then spending much of its time selling antiques, briefly a craft shop but never again managing to become an integral part of village life.

When The **Providence Chapel** opened in July 1849 it is impossible to imagine that financial gain entered anybody's mind, apart of course from the gigantic effort that must have gone on before hand to raise the money required for building. The foundations were however laid, for many years of service to the local community. It is clear from the accounts that The Chapel was never allowed to run in deficit but just managed to pay its way, always contributing to the local economy in a gentle manner. Whilst many people made their own way to Providence on a Sunday, there were those who required a taxi and those who on arrival required somebody to look after their horses whilst they attended to their devotions. The boiler didn't light itself, the graveyard had to be tended

Providence Chapel in its heyday

New Inn, Petrol Station and Garage

and local craftsmen, all of whom were paid, attended to maintenance. So for 138 years Providence Chapel contributed to the spiritual and practical welfare of Hadlow Down.

Next of course comes **The New Inn**, dealt with in some detail elsewhere. For as long as anyone can remember it has run in conjunction with the garage which supplied taxis, carried out repairs, sales of fuel, spare parts and even the occasional new vehicle whilst the Hotel brought visitors to the Village. As is so often the way with self-employed people, George Standen never really managed to retire, it was more a case of 'gradually phasing out' during the late 60s, so there was a steady but relentless change in the emphasis of the garage business as repairs dwindled and sales of spares from the scrap yard increased with lorry haulage becoming more significant. Gerald describes himself "as the most reluctant publican of all time". There was nothing he liked better than to be able to jump into his lorry and metaphorically head off into the sunset in order to escape the pub trade, which he had disliked from an early age. Dawn's husband Johnny Johnson was also a self-employed owner lorry driver, so all through

Gerald with his Foden lorry, circa 1962

the 1950s and 60s these two men stimulated each other with the maintenance and operation of their lorries, using the scrapyard and pub as a base.

The date the **Post Office** started is unclear but the O.S. map of 1899 indicates the P.O. on the site where it remained for over 90 years. In the early years of this century the same building housed the Telephone Exchange which was situated in the front room of the Postmasters house. Described by Cecil Godleys father as like "a huge piano" each call was answered in person and then the necessary connection made manually by pushing the plug into the correct socket.

Marjorie Jarvis…

"When the family moved to Hadlow Down, the only available public telephone was inside the post office and this also had to be used for the purpose of receiving telegrams which were subsequently written out by hand and then delivered on a bicycle by the post master. In due course, a small telephone exchange was installed in the downstairs lounge and this had to be operated 12 hours a day, a task that fell mainly to the two daughters. The first subscribers were Hadlow Down 1 which, was reserved for the Post Office. Hadlow Down 2 was Brigadier General Godfrey Faussett who had previously been in command of Maresfield army camp and now lived at Annes in Wilderness Lane. Telephone 3 was for

Gatehouse where Miss Hughes lived and telephone No. 4 was Verpilleux [a French family living in. Wilderness Lane]. No. 5 was Midford living at Nurney Cottage. No. 6 Holt at Gill Hope. No. 7 was the Lawrencens at Nurney House. No. 8 the Yearsley family and No. 9 The New Inn. The exchange was powered by a huge bank of batteries which were installed in a special shed erected at the rear of the premises and housed in a steel rack".

Although the original exchange was updated whilst it was in use, it was finally declared obsolete and in 1939 a modern automatic mechanical exchange was built at the top of Wheelers Lane. This continued to be used until the Uckfield Exchange was converted to a digital exchange in 1992 and all the Hadlow Down telephone numbers had the prefix 830 added.

"My father used to sell a certain amount of tinware, buckets and watering cans etc. and these were always hung up in the ceiling, very cleverly positioned to catch the drips of rain which came in from the leaking roof!!"

From the left Frank Powell [brother of Min Powell school teacher], Spencer Sands [lived with his mother in Rose Cottage], H.T. Richards [Windy Dick], Minnie Richards and their daughter Marjorie Evelyn, John Simmonds known as "Ferret" a casual worker who did all the dirty jobs and lived in a shed on Waghorns Common circa 1913

Mr and Mrs Richards continued in the P.O. right up until the closing months of the Second World War when they decided to retire. With tenure of some 36 years behind them an era came to a close as they sold up and moved on.

Glenis in the New Inn P.O.

The shop and P.O. continued to be a successful enterprise for many years until in December 1991 the shop lost the Post Office franchise. For a while the village hardly noticed, the facility remained unchanged, only the stewardship had passed from Jim Dixon to Glenis Pitson. Sadly, once the two businesses were separated it appeared to sound the death knell for the last remaining village shop. When at the end of November 1993 the P.O. was given notice to quit in the shop, it looked as though the village would have to do without, until Dawn and Gerald offered a space in the front entrance of The New Inn. From December 1993 until November 1997, Glenis Pitson, Post Mistress squeezed herself into the tiny space available [approx. 7ft x 12ft] and provided the service. The shop died during the summer of 1997 with a burial in September 1997, when Jim and Maggie Dixon sold up and moved away.

As the fortunes of the New Inn changed so the manager, Martin Clarke needed the entrance hall and front room, occupied by the P.O., to be restored to its former glory.

Bob Lake and Martin Clark restoring the front room, May 1998

The last Rites

Celebrating the opening of the new shop/P.O.
back row: Elizabeth Herbert and her son Lance, Betty Hawkins and sub-postmistress Glenis Pitson
seated: Nell Terry, Gladys Milham and Rosamund Thomas

13

Beech Cottage

Again the village was faced with loosing its P.O. After a period of some two months a new era began on what appears to be the final act of the P.O. saga. Led by a group of concerned villagers The Village Shop Support Group was formed. Without delay they obtained a splendid temporary building and situated it in the entrance to Wilderness Wood. During February 1998 the new shop and P.O. combined opened with Glenis again at the helm. Following a year of dismal trading the curtain finally fell in April 1999 with closure. Will there be an Epilogue?

Immediately adjacent and east of the P.O. stood **a large wooden workshop**. Little is remembered except that it was a two-storey building and from the upstairs it was possible to see sailing ships in the channel, as indeed it was from the Cecil Godley's field behind Rosebank. The workshop belonged to Mr J.Preston Smith, J.P., local builder and was finally demolished around the 1920s. Clearly marked on the 1910 O.S. map is a saw pit indicating at least that it was a commercial site for the production of timber at the time.

Further down the road used to be **Beech Cottage** originally built by the Abergavenny Estate as two cottages, one for a farmworker, the other to house the Estate Carpenter with a workshop behind for his use.

George Henton and his shop at Packhams Farm

In later years it was occupied by Fred and Kathleen Harrison. The workshop use continued for Fred. As a local builder he could use the asset in conjunction with his outside work, so providing him with employment and the local populace with a much needed service. The property was demolished in 1991 with four dwellings being erected in place of the one.

In the early years of this century, **Packhams Farm** stood on the corner of Wheelers Lane and George Henton's butchers shop is the view that would have greeted Hadlow Downers.

The buildings to the rear were used for the abattoir so the business was not only self sufficient but almost certainly local with George buying from nearby farmers or if necessary at Heathfield Market. When George retired his son Stanley took over and continued until 1954. Today the shop is closed and the property renamed Canters End.

Canters End is one of the few bright spots left on the commercial horizon today, run for many years by Molly Thompson and since her death the riding school is in the capable hands of her longtime assistant Vannesa Malthouse.

Albury House is how we know it today, but that certainly wasn't its original

Lot 6 (Coloured Green on Plan).

A similar Freehold Detached Cottage

(Adjoining Lot 5), containing 3 Bedrooms, Sitting Room, Kitchen, Scullery, Larder and W.C.; with rain-water Tank, deep well and good Garden.

This lot is sold subject to the right of the owners and occupiers of Lot 5 to draw water from the well on this lot.

It is let to the Chief Constable of Lewes on a quarterly tenancy at a rental of **£11** per annum.

name. Around the turn of the century, in response to a desire in the village for a local policeman, Mr C.L. Huggins of The Grange built Bermuda Cottage as a police house. The first incumbent was Mr Bert Alce who was a true community bobby, liked by all in the village and especially the authorities, because at that time, gypsies were a perennial problem and Bert was adept at managing to move them on when everybody else had failed. In 1919 after 15 years of service Bert wanted to retire, and there was

Station: Buxted, S.R.

Phone: Hadlow Down 27.

HADLOW DOWN, UCKFIELD,

Sussex .... *March* 193 7

M *The Exors of Mrs Emily, Maria, Leeves,*

Dr. to - - - -

A. W. DABSON,

Builder, Contractor, Decorator & Undertaker.

	£	s	d
Interred at St Marks, Churchyard, Hadlow Down Jany 20th 1937 Supplying polished elm coffin, with brassed furniture, and best swansdown drapery complete with Personal attendance.			
	6	18	6
Supplying Hearse, & 1 Mourning Car	2	5	0
Churchyard fees. Vicar, Sexton, Grave, Supplying 4 Bearers	2	2	0
£	11	5	6

nowhere for him to go, so the powers that be decided he could stay in the house, which again meant the village was without a policeman. Bert's retirement lasted for 35 years until his death in 1954. The chief constable of Lewes, as head of the Sussex Police Force, rented the house from Mr Huggins, a fact that is clearly shown in the sale particulars for The Grange sale, dated 1919.

Greenacres was for many years the home of Arthur Dabson and his family; Builder Decorator and Undertaker. Sadly one son, Cyril, was killed over Germany and his brothers had already made careers elsewhere so when Arthur passed on the business ceased, until a few years later when Greenacres Nursery opened providing a source of fresh local-grown salad crops. Unfortunately the green houses standing on the exposed backbone of the parish couldn't withstand the Hurricane of 1987 and the resulting devastation forced the venture to close.

Sunnybank is another property owned by C. L. Huggins, he bought it in 1895 for the princely sum of £60. Mr Charles Locke, who was the village shoemaker living and working in Lockes Cottage, still so-named today, moved and took the tenancy. When the workshop was built and why he moved is not clear. In 1919 the dispersal of The Grange estate began and for the Lockes as sitting tenants it was clearly an opportunity not to be missed. Miss Amelia Locke paid £300 to secure their future.

Eventually the bootmakers business closed and Sunnybank became a Newsagents/ general stores; probably spending more time vacant trying to attract its numerous tenants, than actually trading. When the highway was the B2102 it no doubt provided quite a service for the eastern end of the village but with the upgrading of the road causing increased traffic, as well as the lack of pavements, parking and general decline in village shops at the time, the inevitable was finally faced in 1985 when the shop closed.

Lot 5 (Coloured Blue on Plan).

A Picturesque Freehold Cottage

occupying a delightful situation adjoining the road leading from Hadlow Down to Five Ashes, and containing 3 Bedrooms, Sitting Room, Kitchen, Scullery, Larder, W.C., etc., with Boot Maker's Shop adjoining, and a good Garden.

There is a large Rain-water Tank on this lot, and the Purchaser will also have the right to take water from the deep well on Lot 6.

This lot is let, with other property not forming part of the present sale, to a tenant of old standing, Mr. CHARLES LOCKE, on a yearly tenancy, at £16 per annum for the whole (the tenant paying rates), and the rent apportioned in respect of this lot for the purpose of the sale is £14.

Sunnybank Stores as a newsagents Circa 1984

The following from The *Sussex Express* 7th November 1913 may be relevant.

"BOOT CLUB – It is several winters since Mr T Long the headmaster of the schools, prompted by the sad condition of the footwear of some of his scholars, formed this club, and a great boon it has proved. The rules laid down require that every member shall be a regular attendant at school and no member of the family to which he or she belongs may participate in the generous bonus which is added to their contributions of 1d or 2d per week. The patrons are Mrs C. Lang Huggins and Mr T. J.G. Duncanson. So fully are the benefits appreciated that the sum of over £20 is this year being expended on boots for the members who number nearly 70, but of course, this outlay would not be possible but for the handsome contributions of the Patrons. The boots are all purchased from tradesman in the village."

The last property on the Northern side of Main Road is **The Forge** run for many years by George Bracher as a tenant of The Grange estate; he started before 1900 although the date is unclear. In 1919 when The Grange held their first sale, son John had already taken over the tenancy so the family seized the opportunity and bought

Lot 4 (Coloured Green on Plan).

A VERY DESIRABLE

FREEHOLD PROPERTY

Having a frontage to the road leading from Hadlow Down to Five Ashes, comprising

A capital Brick-built Blacksmith's Forge and Workshop,
And a Brick, Cemented and Slated Cottage,

Containing 3 Bedrooms, Sitting Room, Kitchen, Scullery, etc.; with Garden, etc.; let to Mr. JOHN BRACHER on a yearly tenancy at **£19** per annum.

---

both the Forge and house. When retirement became due, George left the forge and house for his son John [Jack] and moved into the house opposite, Bracherlands. Jack continued as village blacksmith until around 1950, only enjoying two years of retirement before his death in 1952. He had no sons and trade was dwindling with horses in decline; furthermore, a new introduction 'The Farm Workshop' was becoming fashionable. Jack always hoped someone would take over The Forge even wondering if petrol pumps might be added, but it was not to be. Another inevitable closure as the broom of change swept on.

If we cross the road and commence our journey back from the top of Tinkers Lane we start with **South Beacon**. Originally built by the Day family but in the early part of this century it was purchased by a Dr Phillip Harmer and used for many years as a private asylum. Miss Wheeler who was a trained Matron lived in the Wren's Nest, now called Thimble Cottage and Little Hadlow also formed part of the complex. The inference is that Dr Harmer's treatment of his patients was rather ahead of his time. They were evidently allowed great freedom in the village and surrounding area.

Cecil Godley remembers...

"...several patients, one who used to walk every day to Buxted just to see a train pull in to the Station and then walk back again. And Jimmy Matthews, he was liked by all, he used to attend the dances in the Red Triangle Hut, taking his music and a persuasive line of chat to persuade the M.C. and pianist to allow him to sing. He always managed it and the two songs were always the same 'Daisy Daisy' and 'You are My Hearts Delight'. Other patients formed a regular, if odd sight around the lanes. There was apparently no objection from the villagers, with many positively in favour, until it came to 'passing Harmers at night' and then with patients leaning out of the windows and shouting at you on both sides of the road, many were less sure as it was a question of running the gauntlet. That wasn't the only problem as Phillip Harmer's son Willy kept a huge [thousands?] flock of White Leghorn chickens in the field opposite South Beacon. The birds would roost up some tall trees on the roadside so "the cackling came from all quarters". There were two fatalities at least, in the asylum with the inquests held within the property where the deaths occured, as was the custom then."

Dr Harmer also believed in recreation for his charges. The field behind South Beacon, now The Brooms Vineyard was really part of Broomfields Farm but the good doctor managed to hire it from The Eridge Estate and used it as a golf course and cricket ground. Cecil remembers how Frank Barden used to work for Dr Harmer and one day was told to go into bat first so that when he was out, there would still be time to return to work. Frank preferred cricket to work and managed not to be "out"! How the asylum brought a lot of work and prosperity to the village. The doctor, like other estate owners, was sensitive to trade fluctuations always sharing out the orders amongst all the tradesmen. Sometime between

South Beacon

the wars Dr Harmer and his patients left Hadlow Down moving to West Sussex and selling South Beacon to a Mr Green from Cross-in-Hand who redeveloped the property into several dwellings as it is today.

Tinkers Park with its annual Traction Engine Rally has been a regular feature in the village since 1966. It was started by Claude Jessett, mainly for interest and as an extension of his hobby, plus the added advantage of trying to raise money for the charity of his choice namely Cancer Research. With the huge influx of visitors the event brings each year, some benefits for locals are inevitable ranging from selling refreshment in the New Inn and visitors to the Vineyard or taking a stall at the Auto Jumble in order to sell unwanted goods; if all else fails it's just plain good old fashioned entertainment.

Wilderness Wood was taken over by Chris and Anne Yarrow in 1980 and run as a working wood and woodland trail ever since. It has been home to the temporary P.O. and shop whilst the barn and yard are frequently used for village functions. The woodland business continues to help keep the spotlight on Hadlow Down.

On the corner of Wilderness Lane, inside Wilderness Wood it appears there used to be **a general shop**. Cecil Godley can remember his father, Luther telling him of its existence selling buckets and ironmongery etc.

On the eastern side of Wilderness Lane stands **Lockes Cottage** one time home of the Godley family. Then it was usually necessary for a family to take on anything that came along in order to make ends meet. Luther Godley was a dab hand at bicycle repairs and so the house collected the reputation of being the Bicycle Shop. Mrs

Presentation of a certificate from Cancer Research to Claude Jessett on his retirement from the Rally in 1983. From the left on the engine: Owen Mitchell, Ken Langley, George Epps. Standing: Chris Rodgers, Peter Haining, Bertha Mitchell, John De Havilland, Joyce Jessett, Stephen Epps, Claude Jessett, Graham Arding, Geoff Tait, Cecily Hunt, Reg Hunt, Jim Blades, Kevin Page

Godley also did her bit by taking in lodgers. So when Bert Alce stayed on in the Police House his replacement [P.C. Armstrong] went to lodge in Lockes Cottage and the blue light proudly proclaiming County Police, for a time, graced the front of the house. Eventually an official Police House was built in Five Ashes so Hadlow Down lost its village bobby for good.

Outside Lawtons stood the **bus stop and shelter.** The Maidstone and District Bus Company served the village for over 40 years, providing the only and much needed public service. With the proliferation of the motor car so the service became less profitable and gradually diminished from its peak when the village enjoyed an hourly service to today's timetable of two buses per day on three days a week. The Shelter was built in the 1950s by Fred Harrison and Owen Mitchell for the Parish Council, so had done sterling service. Faced with increased maintainence for a redundant building that was now becoming used by the youth of the village for dubious extra curricular pursuits, the council decided in 1998 to offer the shelter to the parish. It was sold to Anne Zenka, for £50 as a garden summer house. The site is retained in case there is ever again the need for a bus service.

We return to the centre of the village where **The General Stores** stood oppo-

The hub of the village. Stores, Post Office and Pub looking west

site the P.O. a large shop supplying a wide range of goods perhaps more hardware than the others but still providing much needed competition. Towards the end the business had several owners who wanted to try their luck, at one time three in one year! Eventually realization dawned that it couldn't be kept going and closed as a stores in 1969. A limited amount of hardware was stocked for a while and a tearoom opened up in the west end. In 1978 it became a tearooms only and they finally closed in 1981.

Trade of course did not have to be static. The **onion johnny** came over from Brittany each year and used to visit us periodically, pushing his bycycle with the handlebars loaded with strings of French onions. Rain or shine every week Mr Green arrived selling fancy cakes made by Weekes Bakery of Uckfield. Being rather disabled he hobbled badly so it was a source of wonderment to most how he got up Buxted Hill when the box on the front of his trade tricycle was loaded. Probably looked forward to with greater enthusiasm was the 'Eldorado Stop me and Buy One' tricycle selling ice creams which made once- or even twice-weekly visits. They all stopped because of the Second World War, with only Mr Green trying again after the conflict.

Although not situated on the Main Road it is impossible to ignore **Ashdown's Bakery** representing as it did an essential element of Hadlow Down's commercial life. Around 1880, Ivy Cottage in Wilderness Lane was the home of Henry Ashdown [bricklayer], known to all as Orpy, and his parents. Orpy suffered a gun accident

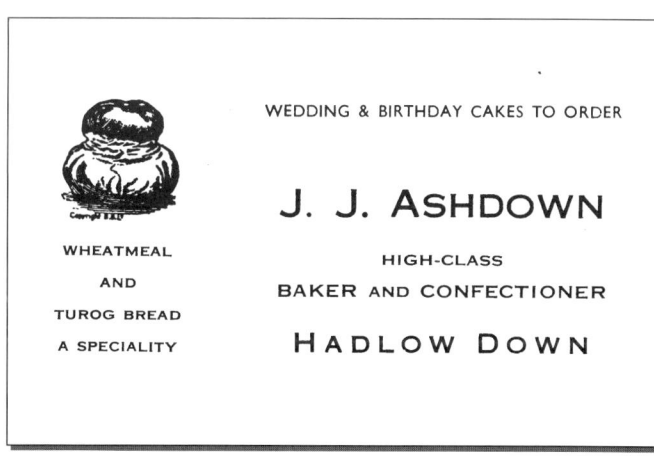

WEDDING & BIRTHDAY CAKES TO ORDER

J. J. ASHDOWN

WHEATMEAL
AND
TUROG BREAD
A SPECIALITY

HIGH-CLASS
BAKER AND CONFECTIONER

HADLOW DOWN

loosing his left hand, thereby having a hook fitted to compensate. Faced with the burden of looking after a disabled son, Mrs Ashdown, clearly a resourceful lady, rose to the occasion. Already baking for the family, and still using her domestic oven, she increased production, sending Orpy out around the village to sell the fare. Output increased rapidly and an extra oven was built in an outhouse with a purpose built bake-house following after only five years. In 1893 the domestic ovens were soon replaced by a commercial steam oven, initially fired by faggots, then converted to coke. When it was finally removed to make way for an oil-fired replacement it was reputed to be the oldest of its type still working. In the fullness of time Orpy's nephew, James, took over the business, followed by his son Ernie. The enterprise continued until 1964 when Ernie's failing health forced closure. The Bakery like all the ventures in Hadlow Down took its place in the web of commercial activity, served the community faithfully and for over 60 years

Orpy Ashdown

nurtured three generations of the same family. Today re-named 'Cobwebs', the bakery is still the home of the Ashdown family.

Today the Main Road can continue to be used as a mirror for the commercial life of the parish although on a much smaller scale. We have two late twentieth century businesses running, namely Canters End and Wilderness Wood both of which are open to local people, although they obviously attract customers from a far wider area. The third is Synergy Training Design Studios, very much a product of the modern information technology revolution and ready for the twenty-first century; capable of

Ashdown's delivery van

operating successfully anywhere in the world using the Internet, e-mail facsimile machines and in desperation, Snail Mail. Undoubtedly other concerns across the parish are equally diverse and have been just as successful at adapting themselves to fit the modern world.

The new oil-fired oven

Lines on the laying the first stone
of St Mark's Chapel, Hadlow Down
21st April 1835

The Stone is laid – The building soon appears
   and soon the Church it's head erected bears!
While all assembled at the glorious shrine
   the songs of numbers hail the Power Divine.
In Heaven, his dwelling place, Jehovah hears
   enthron'd on high, he yet regards our prayers.
Daughter of Liverpool! thy fairy hand
   hath touch'd the corner-stone with magic wand.

Quick at the touch the solid walls arise
   and mounting upwards, shoot into the skies.
Oh! may this Church, uprising from to-day
   recall the sinner from his evil way.
Teach him to tremble at the Lord of Heaven
   by whom eternal punishment is given.
And may it aid and comfort the distress'd
   and point the place of everlasting rest.

Wordsworth! thy name exalted praise demands!
   a monument of thee this Temple stands.
At Cambridge honour'd with the noble care
   of talents rising and unfolding there.
Yet, urg'd by duty, we behold thee come
   for Israel's God to build an earthly dome.
Proud of our nobles, we may well relate
   the gifts of Delawarr, the good and great.

Camden! thy name too on the list is found
   fond to distribute Light and Truth around.
This act, immortal, more adorns thy braws
   than all the wreaths increasing fame bestows.
Happy that land, whose Lords are foremost seen
   the welfare seeking of their fellow men!
Thrice happy day! may others such succeed
   and sinning nations to their God be led!

May Heav'n propitious, grant us peace and love
   and life eternal in the world above.

Rev John Kirby   *Vicar of Mayfield*

Chapter Two

ST MARK'S CHURCH

by Sarah Welbourn

"If you expect a good crop of peas and potatoes you must plant them on Good Friday."

The collection of letters that now live in Lewes Record Office tell us the story in 1835/36 of funding and building the first Anglican Chapel in Hadlow Down; but they tell us so much more. Through them like a voyeur from a train window, we share for a fleeting moment the lives of their authors.

The Rector of Buxted at that time was Dr Wordsworth [related to the Poet, William.]. Well connected at Cambridge a man of influence, held in high regard, whose advice and approval were constantly sought.

His clerical neighbour was the vicar of Mayfield Mr John Kirby. Because the village of Hadlow Down lay across the borders of Mayfield and Buxted parishes he was a joint holder of the living with Dr Wordsworth and sadly became embroiled in personal controversy before very long.

Our own Dr William Edwards, the first minister in Hadlow Down, found his new flock hard to shepherd and his intervention, however divine he thought it, was not always appreciated.

Mr Benjamin Hall of Buxted Lodge [today called The Grange] was a man of moral excellence and extraordinary energy whose idea the Chapel was. In his first letter to the Archbishop of Canterbury he explained the Chapel was needed "for the use of the parishioners prevented by distance from attending their respective churches of

Buxted and Mayfield". He also said, "there are very many poor children wandering about the lanes in ignorance of almost every duty, moral or religious." In his reply the Archbishop promised "to do all in my power to forward its success", but he went on to warn that raising funds would be hard and that aid from the Society for Building Churches and Chapels rarely exceeded a fourth of the total cost.

The Church of England had entered the nineteenth century unreformed, but in 1834 a new Ecclesiastical Duties and Revenues Commission began a process of reform which led directly to the building of two thousand new churches. Hadlow Down would be one of them. Undaunted by the Archbishop's warning Mr Benjamin Hall employed Johnson's builders and an architect, Mr William Moseley, who submitted plans based on a Chapel he had recently built in Forest Row [He was also the Architect of Uckfield Holy Cross Church]. The letter accompanying the plan, which is missing, describes provision for eighty two persons in "pew accommodation". These pews were privately paid for on an annual basis together with two hundred and sixty "free sittings", and a gallery in the west end providing for eighty free children.

Circa 1900

The commandments would be written and an altar table provided. Heating was installed, surprisingly "by hot air" and Lord De la Warr donated rough stone for the walls, valued at £200. Buttresses, tower and spire being of sawn faced stone "neatly scrappled and tooled edge". In brackets Mr Moseley adds here "that this form of construction would save upwards of £130". A dubious saving as we now know that the weight of the stone spire proved too great and ultimately provided a serious structural problem.

Showing capped off stone spire in bad structural condition. Viewed from the school playground

Our collection of letters reveal some strong emotions, emotions that are of course, the same today, but it is the language used to describe them that is quite different. Many words are used where few would do, but 'the many' seem rather beautiful. The following letter dated 18th October 1834 was sent to Benjamin Hall, as news of the intended Chapel had travelled to Kennington in London and Mr William Edwards was applying for the appointment of Minister.

"May I be permitted to ask you a more than ordinary favour" he writes "would you have any objection to use your powerful interest with Dr Wordsworth, or whoever the Patron may be, to procure me if possible this little appointment – I do not I assure you covet for want of any other engagement, or from mercenary motives", [in future letters he constantly refers to the pitiful income he derived from the Chapel] "but because it is precisely that sphere of action for which I have long sighed I am persuaded that a country parish is that post where a clergyman if so disposed, may make his influence most felt, and therefore be most useful. As I have a little income independent of my profession I should be able to devote myself exclusively to my duties as clergyman I should desire nothing so much as to spend and be spent amidst my little flock. If a small school, either daily or on Sundays can be established you would always find me most happy to lend myself to it. A residence in the country would be rendered the more agreeable to me as my good and admirable wife does nothing less than dote upon it and I believe will never rest till she becomes my helpmate in the moral and religious improvements of some rural spot like yours".

We hear very little more about Mrs Edwards, but in December 1836 her husband did write that she had fifty poor women to clothe, so we just hope that her predicted dedication held fast!

Benjamin Hall now threw his inexhaustible energy into the appeal, this was the hardest task, the majority of the inhabitants of Hadlow Down were the poor and their poverty was acute. Even work on the land was being squeezed by the introduction of agricultural machinery, this had caused serious rioting only two years earlier in what became known as the Swing Riots. There had been no improvement in provision for the poor since the reign of Elizabeth 1. In 1834 these riots led to the Poor Law Amendment Act to which Mr Edwards once alluded.

> "There is an outcry amongst the poor men of Hadlow Down and a complaint that the farmers, though reliant on their rates, do not employ more hands than before the alteration of the poor laws".

Funds for the new Chapel therefore would come from a very small percentage of the local inhabitants. Cleverly a list of subscribers itemizing names alongside their donations was printed and published for all to see. It was social blackmail and seems to have worked. If people saw that you had made no donation you would be shamed into rectifying the matter, or on seeing your neighbour had given a greater sum, you might indignantly, up your own.

Team work is essential when a group joins together on a project of any kind, but it is often the case that two members seem quite unable to get along with each other. Although it is apparent that Benjamin Hall used his influence to procure the post of Minister for Mr Edwards the two had a strained relationship from an early

SAINT MARK'S CHAPEL,

HADLOW DOWN, SUSSEX.

HADLOW DOWN is a hamlet, lying partly in the parish of Mayfield, and partly in that of Buxted, in the county of Sussex. Its population of late years has increased very considerably, and appears likely to continue to do so. The central point of the hamlet is about equally distant from the Parish Churches of Mayfield and Buxted, namely, not less than three miles and a half; and is at a still greater distance from any other Church or Chapel of the Church of England. Within the distance of a little more than a mile from the same central point, the population of the two parishes (on the increase, as it has been said) amounts, at present, to between six and seven hundred; whose attendance for Public Worship, at their respective Parish Churches, is, on account of distance and other causes, in a very great degree inconvenient and impracticable. It is considered, therefore, to be highly desirable that a small Chapel, possessing a joint Burial-ground, &c. should be erected, as near as may be to the centre of the district; and that a resident Clergyman should be fixed there, with an Ecclesiastical District, assigned out of the two parishes, for his special charge and pastoral superintendence.

In the earnest desire to accomplish these objects, the present appeal is made to the piety and charity of the Land-owners and others of the two parishes; and to other benevolent Individuals who may be disposed to promote the good work. The Inhabitants within the district, it may be proper to add, consist principally of cottagers, and of farmers of small occupations. It is estimated that for the erection and the completion of the Building for Divine Service, a sum of not less than Eighteen Hundred Pounds will be wanted.

The Endowment, to secure the important benefits contemplated, ought not, it is considered, to be less than One Hundred Pounds per Annum, certain income. Towards this amount the Incumbents of Mayfield and of Buxted have (in addition to their Subscriptions in the List below) declared their readiness to charge themselves and their Successors to the extent of Fifty Pounds per Annum, provided an equal sum per Annum can be obtained, in permanent income, from other quarters. For this latter purpose a gross amount of nearly One Thousand Pounds will probably be requisite.

A Residence House for the Minister, is further, in the highest degree, desirable: but it is considered that the immediate objects of the present Appeal ought to be, in the first place, the Building and the Endowment.

Benefactions in aid of the design will be received by the EARL of LIVERPOOL, *Buxted Park*; the Rev. Dr. WORDSWORTH, *Rector of Buxted*; the Rev. JOHN KIRBY, *Vicar of Mayfield*; WILLIAM DAY, Esq., *Maresfield*; BENJAMIN HALL, Esq., *Buxted Lodge, Hadlow Down*; and at the Banking-Houses of Messrs. HURLY & Co., *Lewes*; and of their Correspondents, Sir JAMES ESDAILE & Co. 21, *Lombard Street, London.*

SUBSCRIPTIONS.

N.B.—In the following List the letter (*b*), or (*e*), severally, denotes that the sum to which it is prefixed is given for the sole use of the Building, or of the Endowment, respectively. Of the rest, much the greatest portion has been allowed by the Benefactors to be appropriated in equal shares, to each of the two objects; and it is presumed, it will be most satisfactory that the *same* rule of distribution be followed, in those comparatively few cases where no special direction has been received.

	£.	s.	d.		£.	s.	d.
HIS GRACE THE ARCHBISHOP OF CANTERBURY ..	100	0	0	Rev. Dr. Wordsworth, *Rector of Buxted*	100	0	0
The Earl of Liverpool, *Buxted Park* ....(*b*)	20	0	0	Rev. John Kirby, *Vicar of Mayfield*	50	0	0
The Ladies Jenkinson, *Ditto* ....(*b*)	20	0	0	Wm. Day, Esq., *Maresfield*	100	0	0

[*Subscriptions continued.*

2

	£.	s.	d.
Benjamin Hall, Esq., *Hadlow Down*	15	0	0
Do., a field of four acres towards the endowment.			
Mrs. Hall, *Hadlow Down*	5	0	0
Mrs. Goring, *Wiston Park*	100	0	0
John Woodward, Esq., *Uckfield* ....(b)	100	0	0
Rev. Wm. Woodward, *West Grinsted*...........	10	0	0
Rev. Alfred C. Lawrence, *Sandhurst, Kent*......	20	0	0
Mrs. Lawrence, *Ditto*	5	0	0
Captain Hurdis, R. N. *Uckfield*	5	0	0
T. F. Marson, Esq., *Regent's Park*	20	0	0
Rev. Thos. Wilkinson, *Curate of Buxted*	10	0	0
Miss Wordsworth, *Rydal Mount, Westmorland*	5	0	0
Mr. John Wordsworth, *Buxted Parsonage*	5	0	0
Rev. Charles Wordsworth, *Ditto*...............	5	0	0
Rev. Christopher Wordsworth, *Ditto*	5	0	0
Mrs. Davis, *Uckfield*	5	0	0
Mr. J. Holland, *Buxted*	1	0	0
Mr. J. Catt, *Ditto*...........................	1	0	0
D. Hay, Esq., *Kennington, Surrey*	5	0	0
J. Davidge, Esq., *Clapham*	2	0	0
Mr. G. Davidge, *Kennington*	2	0	0
Mrs. Pugh, *Newington, Surrey*.................	2	0	0
Rev. Thos. Brown, *Ephraim Place, Tunbridge Wells*	20	0	0
James Davidson, Esq., *Combe Banks, Uckfield*	5	0	0
Earl De La Warr, *Buckhurst Park*..............	25	0	0
Do. the site for the chapel and burial ground.			
Countess De La Warr	10	0	0
Mr. Wm. Russell, *Mayfield*	1	0	0
Mr. Elias Bryant, *Ditto*	1	0	0
Rev. James Aldridge, *Curate of Maresfield*.......	5	0	0
Joshua Watson, Esq., *Park Street, Westminster* (e)	25	0	0
Miss Watson, *Ditto*........................(e)	15	0	0
Miss Hoare, *Hampstead Heath* ··············	20	0	0
Mr. Serjeant D'Oyly........................	5	0	0
Rev. Henry Hoare, *Vicar of Framfield*	10	10	0
The Lord Bishop of Chichester	20	0	0
Mrs. Law, *Horsted Place*.....................	10	0	0
Rev. P. G. Crofts, *Malling House, Lewes*	10	0	0
Rev. Dr. D'Oyly, *Rectory House, Lambeth*	25	0	0
Mrs. D'Oyly, *Ditto*	5	0	0
Robert Holford, Esq., *Lincoln's Inn*..............	20	0	0
Mrs. Thomas Woodward, *Uckfield*	5	0	0
John Fry, Esq., *Mayfield*.....................	10	0	0
Mr. Nicholas Martin, *Ditto*	5	0	0
Mr. Wm. Brissenden, *Ditto*	4	0	0
Mr. Thos. Norman, *Framfield*	2	0	0
Mr. Thos. Herriott, *Buxted*..................	1	0	0
Mr. Edward Willett, *Ditto*	0	10	0
Mr. Thomas Ware, *Ditto*	0	5	0
Rev. Wm. Edwards, *Curate of St. Mark's, Kennington*	10	0	0
Rev. J. G. Weddell, *Battersea*.................	5	5	0

	£.	s.	d.
Rev. C. Lane, *St. Mark's, Kennington*	2	2	0
Rev. H. S. Plumptre, *Lambeth*	1	0	0
Rev. G. Vale, *Feltham Vicarage*................	1	0	0
Randall Jackson, Esq., *Brixton, Surrey*	2	2	0
E. N. Thornton, Esq., *Streatham, Surrey*	2	0	0
Mr. Thomas Luck, *Buxted*	1	0	0
Mr. James Garson, *Mayfield*	0	5	0
Mr. William Ashby, *Buxted*	0	5	0
Mr. William Tooth, *Mayfield*	1	0	0
Mr. William Mann, *Ditto*....................	1	0	0
Mr. T. P. Durrant, *Ditto*	1	0	0
Mr. William Baldock, *Buxted*	5	0	0
Mr. John Jarratt, *Ditto*	2	0	0
Mr. John Newnham, *Uckfield*	5	0	0
Rev. Edward Langdale, *East Hoathly*............	1	0	0
W. H. Lidbetter, Esq., *Uckfield*	2	0	0
Mr. Wickens, *Buxted*	10	0	0
Rev. —— Pemberton and Friends.............	11	14	0
Mrs. Kirby, *Vicarage, Mayfield*	5	0	0
Mr. J. Kirby, *Ditto*	2	0	0
Mr. Michael Baker, *Ditto*	0	10	0
Mr. George Daniel, *Ditto*....................	0	5	0
Mr. Richard Garson, *Ditto*	0	5	0
Rev. Dr. Walton, *Birdbrook Rectory, Essex*	5	0	0
Rev. Watson J. Thornton, *Llanware Rectory, Ross* .	5	0	0
Henry Sykes Thornton, Esq., *Clapham*	10	0	0
Rev. Dr. Dealtry, *Chancellor of Winchester*	5	0	0
Hon. M. General Trevor, *Glynde, Lewes*	50	0	0
Rev. Archdeacon Watson, *Hackney Rectory*	5	5	0
Rev. Henry John Rose, *Fellow of St. John's Coll. Cam.*	5	0	0
Sir Thomas Maryon Wilson, Bart. *Searles, Fletching*	20	0	0
Rev. John Brown, *Vice-Master of Trinity Coll. Cam.*	5	0	0
Rev. George Peacock, *Fellow of Trinity Coll. Camb.*	5	0	0
Rev. Thomas Thorp, *Ditto*	5	0	0
Rev. Francis Martin, *Ditto*..................(e)	3	3	0
John M. Heath, Esq., *Ditto*..	1	0	0
Rev. J. W. Blakesley, *Ditto*	1	0	0
Rev. Charles Perry, *Ditto*	5	0	0
Rev. Professor Musgrave, *Ditto*	5	0	0
Rev. William Whewell, *Ditto*	3	0	0
Rev. William Carus, *Ditto*	5	0	0
Rev. William Law, *Ditto*....................	2	0	0
Rev. R. W. Evans, *Ditto*....................	2	2	0
Rev. J. A. Jeremie, *Ditto*....................	5	0	0
Rev. Marmaduke Prickett, *Trinity College, Cambridge*	1	1	0
Rev. J. F. Isaacson, *Fellow of St. John's Coll. Cam.* (e)	3	0	0
Rev. William Selwyn, *Prebendary of Ely*	2	2	0
Mr. Charles Jarratt, *Buxted*	1	0	0
Mr. William Gorringe, *Ditto*	2	0	0
Mr. John Rose, *Mayfield*.....................	1	0	0
Mr. John Kenward, *Uckfield*	1	0	0

stage. Unfortunately for the Rector of Buxted Dr Wordsworth, this developed into something rather more than that during the building of the school between August 1837 and April 1838 and he became piggy in the middle. In a letter from Benjamin Hall in which various expenses are first discussed he suddenly writes.

> "From Mr E I have scarcely experienced the attention of a stranger, much less any kindness or respect, but the day may arrive when he may see the error of treating me thus".

Six weeks on and another letter from Benjamin indicates a further deterioration.

> "After all our exertions, trouble, anxiety and expense for which we have repeatedly received your very kind acknowledgments neither Mrs Hall or myself expected to experience the ingratitude we have done from Mr and Mrs Edwards. To perplex and annoy and to treat with scorn and contempt the opinions and advice of others was plainly manifest to be a leading feature in their conduct, and you will excuse my stating to you, my fixed determination no longer to submit to such treatment".

Although he writes 'I thought you ought to know', we can interpret this as meaning 'you definitely don't want to hear it' and it is very probable these were Dr Wordsworth feelings when yet another letter complaining about Benjamin Hall went on to say

> "there is another very important aspect in which I am anxious to open my mind to you.But I am informed of good authority indeed it is current about two months ago there was a meeting called amongst the common tradespeople of Mayfield to consider what steps were to be taken in regard to Mr Kirby's debts. It was stated at this meeting that his debts amount to £3,000 in the town of Mayfield alone and he owes one tradesman as much as £800; instead of paying his outstanding bills he gives notes of land".

This seems an extraordinary sum for 1834 and we wonder what is meant by 'notes of land', indeed whose land? Sadly no further mention is made of the matter.

If Dr Wordsworth ever made a daily list of duties to be done he must surely have added "thank God" to the one he made for April 24th 1838 when a letter from Mr Edwards ended with "Mr Hall called on me and we are at present on a very comfortable footing, thanks to your decision and authority".

A number of ecclesiastical grants were available and applied for, but one appears again and again 'Queen Anne's Bounty'. Queen Anne herself was a staunch high Church Protestant. Her creation of the grant, restored to the Church, a fund to increase the incomes of the poorer clergy, which Henry VIII had taken for his own use. Mr Edwards wrote "I have received the glad tidings that they will meet us with another £200."

Whether Mr Edwards ever asked for advice on the running of his new Church is unknown. However we do know he got it, he replied to Dr Wordsworth "I shall pay particular attention to what you suggest respecting the separation of the sexes in the Chapel, and observe for a few Sundays whether any inconvenience arises from the congregation sitting promiscuously together in the free seats. I have no doubt you have some very good reason for your suggestion and I shall closely observe the general behaviour of the congregation." Sadly we never hear the results of this close observation.

Viewed from the Main Road before remodelling

Early in 1836 the Chapel was near completion. The Archbishop of Canterbury found the first Friday in May would suit his convenience for the consecration service and Dr Wordsworth was asked by his Grace to preach the sermon. Mr William Edwards was soon to have his Chapel but not a residence to accompany the living. Still residing in Kennington, he now became very anxious that the grand occasion should be used to raise funds for his house and asked Dr Wordsworth to press his cause publicly from the pulpit. This was desirable he explained because

> "without the authority of the pulpit they would probably give little or nothing".

An elite 500 attended the Chapel on Consecration day. Dr Wordsworth's discourse was pronounced excellent, and Exodus provided a fitting text: 'Put off thy shoes from off thy feet, for the place whereon thou standest is holy ground'.

Quite rightly Mr Benjamin Hall was highly praised as "an excellent individual who has so unceasingly exerted himself in this good work". As promised from the pulpit Dr Wordsworth pleaded firmly the vital cause of the collection.

> "For a residence for the Minister that he may be always in the midst of the flock committed to his charge".

An amazing £50-60 resulted; this left only £400 outstanding.

THE VICARAGE, HADLOW DOWN.

The Village must have felt rather quiet after the great day passed, but not for long, in November a violent storm hit it. Mr Hall's house was unroofed and they were up all night. There was not a house in the neighbourhood, which was not damaged and innumerable trees of full size blown down. It occurred between ten and one o'clock in the day. There is however no mention of St Mark's being damaged, but the new Chapel had other problems, fifteen months after its consecration clear symptoms of dry rot appeared. Mr Hall urged "something should now be done on that account". Whatever that something was, it could not solve the problem. Seventy seven years later in 1913 the Chapel was described as being in bad structural condition as well as being old-fashioned, and was entirely reconstructed enlarged and rebuilt by Mr Benjamin Hall's great nephew Mr Charles Lang Huggins Esq. J.P. of Hadlow Grange who generously undertook to do so at his own expense. The architect was a Mr Fellowes Prynne and the stone for the rebuilding was quarried from behind the part of The Grange which is now called Little Manor. Mr Mitchell from School Lane Cottage was the clerk of the works for the builders (Miller and Selmes from Eastbourne) who won the contract. David Barden helped with the work and when it was finished he erected the weather-vane, deliberately putting it upside-down for a joke. Sadly, his humour was not appreciated and instant dismissal followed.

The new Lady Chapel

Hanging in the Lady Chapel is an oil painting of the Magnificat which was painted by Mr E.A. Fellowes Prynne, brother of the architect. The original sketch for the picture was exhibited in the Royal Academy in 1897 and the finished work shown there two years later. Mr Huggins purchased the picture to hang in his own private chapel in The Grange but decided to make it available to a wider audience and presented it to the church.

1913

Hadlow Down Churchyard.

Ours is one of the most beautiful and well-kept village churches in Sussex, but the churchyard which surrounds it gives the appearance of sad neglect, especially in the summer when it is overgrown with grass.

At a recent meeting of the Parochial Church Council, it was decided to take steps to make the churchyard more pleasing to look at and more worthy of its sacred purpose.

The present condition is chiefly the result of relatives failing to keep their family graves in good order. Some have left the neighbourhood and so are unable to fulfil their duty to the departed, while others tend to become less and less careful, so that in course of time the graves are neglected entirely.

The chief difficulty is caused by the mounds, kerbstones, trees and shrubs, which prevent the free use of a mowing machine or scythe. The cutting has to be done by hand, which is a slow, expensive way. If the graves were flat the churchyard as a whole could be easily and frequently mown like a lawn. Framfield and other churchyards are dealt with in this way and, the result is most satisfactory. We are hopeful that some day, not far distant, our own will be a place of beauty too.

It is proposed to begin by levelling the mounds, over the graves of those whose names are unknown

—and there are many such— and then to deal in a similar way with others, unless objections are sent in by the relatives to the vicar *before Christmas*. Such objections will be respected on the understanding that the relatives themselves undertake the responsibility of keeping the graves in order.

Those graves that have no headstone will be marked by a simple cross, bearing the name if known.

In future all *new* graves will be level, with headstone or cross only.

We fully recognise that to make alterations in a churchyard involves the risk of distressing those whose departed ones are buried there, and we are most anxious not to wound the feelings of any. But to improve the appearance of their resting-place is surely to honour the dead. If friends would but see our purpose in this light, few, if any, objections will be raised.

The work can only be done gradually as funds permit, and the cost will be very considerable. So we appeal to all who have an interest in our church and its churchyard not only to approve of our plan but also to contribute to its cost as liberally as they can.

G. H. WARLOW, vicar.
(For the P.C.C. Sub-Committee.)

October 31*st.* 1931.

The remodeled St Mark's had electric lighting and was consecrated in October 1913. The Bishop of Chichester, attired in Cope and Mitre was preceded by his chaplain bearing the Pastoral staff. The Hymns 'Come Holy Ghost our hearts inspire' and 'All people that on earth do dwell' were sung with great fervour. The proceedings ended with the Hymn; 'The Church's one foundation'. This time St Mark's foundation was a stronger one. Whether it is today is quite another story.

It is interesting that in 1931 the P.C.C. clearly felt the churchyard was letting down the side in the appearance stakes and something needed to be done. An appeal was launched and as is clearly stated "the cost will be very considerable" to level mounds, remove kerbstones, trees and shrubs to enable cheaper and faster mechanical mowing of the grass.

Today, judging by the number of levelled mounds and removed kerbstones the scheme must have been something of a failure. Ironically an appeal now would almost certainly be received with hostility at the destruction of the wild orchids and natural habitat which is so widely acclaimed. Indeed Framfield which was held up as a paragon of virtue has in recent years been subject to a request to let part of their churchyard revert to a wildlife sanctuary like Hadlow Down. Today our little piece of paradise is overseen by 'The Living Churchyard', a Church and Conservation Project based in Stoneleigh Warwickshire.

Wild Orchids 1998

Sussex. AT THE GENERAL SESSION OF THE PEACE of our Lady the Queen, holden at Lewes in and for the County of Sussex on Monday the fifteenth day of November the Thirtieth year of the Reign of our Sovereign Lady Victoria, by the Grace of God of the United Kingdom of Great Britain and Ireland Queen, Defender of the Faith, and in the Year of our Lord one thousand eight hundred and sixty nine, Before The Right Honourable Henry Thomas Earl of Chichester, Robert Willis Blencowe, Esquire, The Right Honourable William Earl Waldegrave,

and others their Fellows Justices of our said Lady the Queen, assigned to keep the Peace in the said County, and also to hear and determine divers Felonies, Trespasses, and other ill Deeds done and committed in the County aforesaid.

These are to Certify that James Hallett

of Arlington in the County of Sussex, Yeoman, on behalf of himself and his Co-Trustees, hath at this present Session produced his Certificate, that a certain Building called "Providence Chapel" Situate at Haslow Down, in the Parish of Mayfield, in the County aforesaid was intended forthwith to be used as a Place for Religious Worship by an Assembly or Congregation of Protestants pursuant to an Act of Parliament made and passed in the Fifty-second Year of the Reign of His Majesty King George the Third, intituled "An Act to repeal "certain Acts and amend other Acts relating to Religious Worship "and Assemblies, and Persons teaching or preaching therein". And I do further Certify that the same was Registered and Recorded at this Session, pursuant to the said Act.

Langridge

Cl of the Peace for the County of Sussex

Chapter Three

THE NON-CONFORMISTS

by Peter Gillies

"What a number of dissenters this neighbourhood has."

PROVIDENCE CHAPEL

For nearly 25 years the congregation of Hadlow Downs Calvinistic Baptists had used numbers three and four Grange Cottages as their weekly meeting place. Mr James Hallet who had guided them for so long was now leading his supporters into the future; at last they were to open their new purpose built Chapel. If a Crystal Ball had been available it is doubtful if any one then would have believed a prediction, as they left the old building which was to be converted into houses, that the same fate would befall Providence Chapel nearly 150 years later.

From the *Sussex Express* Saturday July 7th 1849

"This village in the parish of Mayfield, presented a lively appearance on Thursday last, that day being fixed for the opening of a new chapel for the ministration of Mr Hallet.

The building is very commodious and will contain about 500, but on this occasion there could not have been less than 1,000 persons present, every nook being crowded and those who could not gain admittance surrounded the windows outside, which were thrown open to enable them to hear the discourse. The roadside was crowded with vehicles, which brought parties from Petworth, Brighton, Hailsham, Henfield, Cowfold, Hurst, Lewes, Hastings, Wadhurst, Tunbridge Wells, Berwick, Newick and many other places.

There was also a number of dissenting ministers present, and the singers from West Street Chapel, Brighton, Five Ash Down and other places assisted on this interesting occasion.

The services of the day were commenced by Mr Warburton of Trowbridge, Wiltshire who read I Kings Chapter 8 being the dedication of Solomon's Temple, and afterwards offered up a solemn prayer.

The Reverend Gentleman then preached a most admirable sermon from the text 'Salvation belongeth unto the Lord.' In the afternoon so large was the concourse of persons, that the services were performed in the open air, a wagon being placed near the chapel for that purpose.

Mr Grace of Brighton officiated and preached from Matthew, Chapter 16 verse 18 'Upon this rock I will build my Church, and the gates of hell shall not prevail against it'

[He obviously was not allowing for The Hurricane of 1987 which did prevail].

George Budd and passer-by survey the damage the morning after.

The Reverend Gentleman delivered a very powerful sermon, illustrating the text with his accustomed eloquence. Mr Warburton concluded the proceedings of the day by conducting the evening service, preaching an admirable discourse from the words, 'Thy blessing is upon thy people.'

The day was beautiful, and the happy countenances of the assembled multitude proved how good and how pleasant a thing it is for brethren to dwell together in unity, whilst it is cause for Christian thankfulness that we, by the blessing of divine providence, are enabled to worship in freedom and peace, under the protection of a mild and tolerant constitution".

Even though we know by its longevity of use that the Providence Chapel was a popular meeting place, it is still astonishing to hear how far the congregation came to wish the fledgling Chapel well. In spite of the list of far flung places, it is indeed fortunate, that the reporter bothered to add 'Wiltshire' when mentioning Mr Warburton's home in Trowbridge, for we would surely have wondered if there was a town of this name closer home.

The life of The Chapel quickly became an established routine of stability. The first Trustees, [7 including Mr Hallet as Chairman] were appointed three weeks after the dedication and stayed intact for the next 21 years. The second 'Memorandum of the choice and appointments of new trustees' takes place on the 16th March 1870 and even then 4 of the original members continued to serve. Mr Hallett was clearly a major player in the construction and opening of the building, he remained as chairman for the next 43 years. With such devotion it would be reasonable to expect him to move into Hadlow Down, he never did, living in Arlington, Mayfield and Brighton. On the 15th April 1892 for the first time a Hadlow Downer, Mr C J Locke [Village shoemaker] appears on the list but only as a witness to the now 12 Trustees supporting the new Chairman Mr C.J. Farncourt from Croydon.

Today the Trustees continue to attend their responsibilities by tending the graveyard and stewarding the accounts.

The early accounts for the Chapel are sadly missing. The first available is dated 1861 and shows the quarterly collections to be relatively constant giving an annual total of £15. 6s. 2d. Clearly this state of affairs was unsatisfactory, an attached note explains:

> "It was proposed by James Hallet and carried unanimously that the collections be discontinued and a weekly subscription instituted".

Evidently this had the desired effect because in 1862, the weekly subscriptions more than doubled to an annual total of £42.18s.11d. After suffering a small dip from this exalted height, they remained remarkably constant for many years. The absence of inflation and general stability must have been very reassuring to the trustees. The accounts for 1893 show for the first time a Fire Insurance Premium of 7/6d was paid. That figure was to remain the same for the next 57 years until 1951 when it appears as 11/9d. The Chapel never had a resident preacher always relying on 'supplies'.

Restored, converted with the downstairs windows fitted at last.

As the treasurers change, so do the presentation of the accounts, making comparisons difficult but most years the tea account was in surplus, with no doubt, the treasurer encouraging thirsty hymn singing.

Contrary to local belief the front lower windows have not been 'bricked up'. The original design allowed for a gallery above and a staircase either side of the front door. Had that ever been built the windows would have been installed.

Attendance at the Chapel had been in decline for some years and services were only conducted once on a Sunday instead of three times as in it's heyday. The Great Hurricane hit this corner of England on 15/16th October 1987 and sadly most of the roof was torn off.

The remaining faithful decided to "call it a day" and the Harvest Thanksgiving Service due to be held the following day was conducted in Mayfield Chapel. When negotiations with the insurance company were finally settled, the Providence Chapel was sold to Mr Geoffrey Sheard from High Hurstwood, who converted it into a dwelling. Today the graveyard is still owned and maintained by the faithful band of Trustees whilst the building after an agonizingly long wait has a new owner to carry it forward into a new chapter.

Footnote... The organ/harmonium was removed after the hurricane to prevent any damage from moisture etc. Efforts were made to find it a good home within the congregation but sadly nobody could find room for the elegant piece of furniture. Eventually and reluctantly it was sent to Heathfield Market and sold for £6.00.

GATE HOUSE BAPTIST CHAPEL

The two chapels have long been set apart by their nicknames, applied by the irreverent children of the parish. Providence Chapel as 'The Chanting House' and Gatehouse Chapel as 'The Tin Heaven'. Certainly the latter sounds more fun and with the corrugated iron structure, complete with bell on top appears to be less pretentious.

The founder of the Chapel was a Mr Henry Donkin who moved into Gate House on the corner of Stocklands Lane and School Lane around 1885. He had been associated with The Baptist movement all his life and clearly although ready for retirement from commercial life had plenty of enthusiasm left for his religious convictions.

The *Sussex Express* April 1915   Death of Mr H Donkin of Hadlow Down

> "... there being no Evangelical Free Church in the vicinity, Mr Donkin erected a building in his own grounds, and threw the doors open to all. This was the commencement of a prosperous village cause, of which he was the life and soul... Some eight years since, finding the burden of increasing years prevented him from carrying on the work as he would like it done, Mr Donkin removed the Church building to a site nearer the village and handed over the title deeds, including a plot on which to build a ministers house to the Baptists Union of Great Britain and Ireland. It has since been worked by the Kent and Sussex Baptists Association as a Home Mission centre and they have a Pastor in charge who resides in the district."

From Mr Donkin's obituary we can deduce that The Tin Heaven was built around 1885/90 and subsequently moved to its present site around 1907. Mr Donkin still wasn't satisfied.

"Mr Donkin's last act on behalf of the church was to hand a cheque for £250

Summer Fete at the Tin Heaven. Circa 1920

to the Superintendent of the Mission Rev J.P.Morris of Lewes for the purpose
of erecting a Manse for the use of the Pastor."

Clearly the Manse was never built and how different things might have been for
the Chapel if it had come to fruition. In October 1916 a report from the Headquarters
in Lewes states that the Manse fund stood at £300 in War Bonds plus a further £86 on
deposit "but it would obviously be unwise to proceed with the scheme at the present
time". A service was conducted in The Tin Heaven for Mr Donkin and then he made
his final journey to Uckfield to join his wife who had been buried there around 1908.
After many years of sterling service as a Home Mission in 1920 the work was 'upgraded'
to 'a Church with 20 members' and in 1922 a Rev E.J. Halford took the helm until he
retired in 1939 whereupon the work collapsed and closed down in 1940. Eventually the
premises were sold with half the proceeds being used to build the Moulscombe Church.

Apart from its use as a school canteen during the war years the building fell into
disrepair until being rescued as a chicken house in the early '50s. The building plot so
kindly donated by Mr Donkin was eventually exploited about 1964 and used initially
as a farm cottage. The whole property was sold to Mr and Mrs Parkes in 1975, when
the Car Valeting business we know today was established.

Sad and dreary days, circa 1975.

Circa 1997

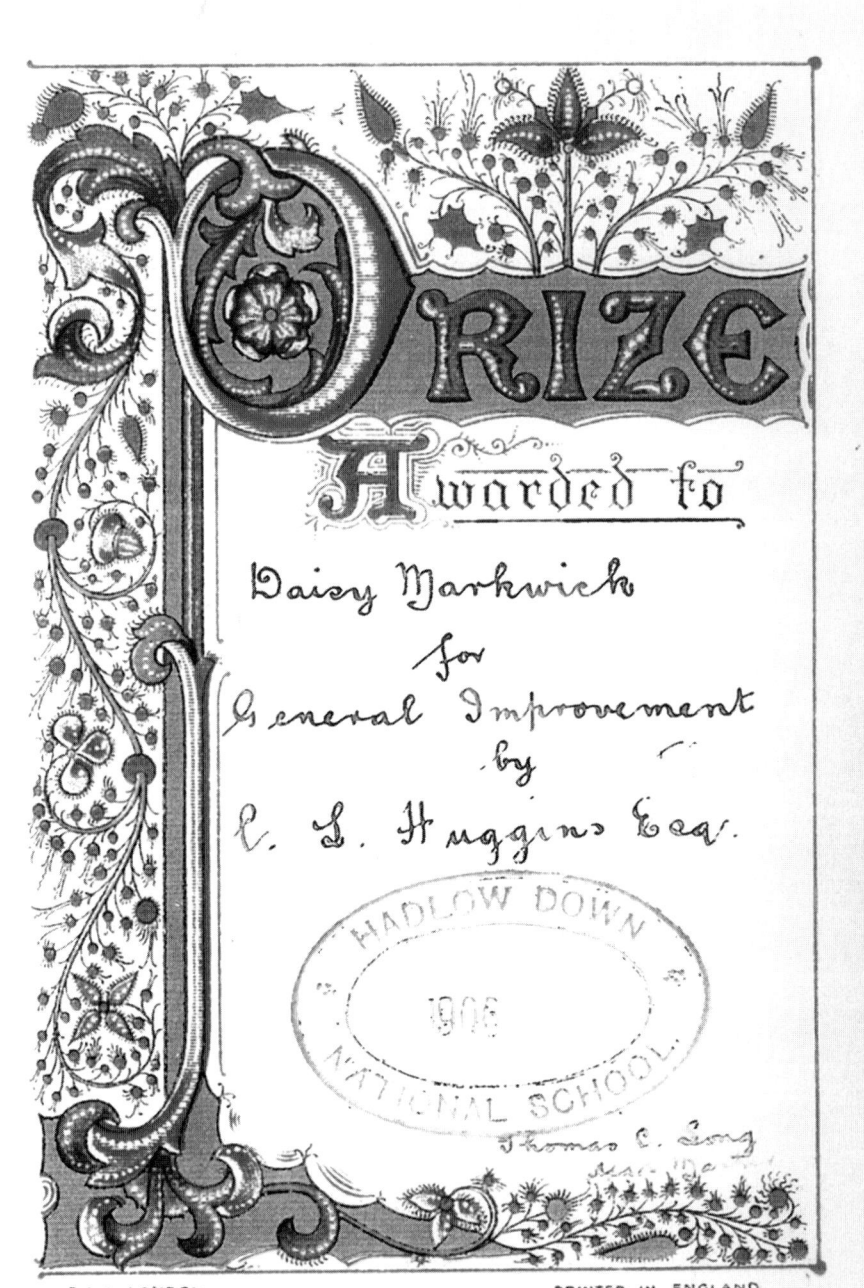

PRIZE

Awarded to

Daisy Markwick

for

General Improvement

by

E. S. Huggins Esq.

HADLOW DOWN
1906
NATIONAL SCHOOL

Thomas E. Ing

E S A LONDON.   PRINTED IN ENGLAND

Chapter Four

OUR VILLAGE SCHOOL

---

by Mavis Farrar

"…we paid one penny a week for our schooling."

This is not a scholarly history of St. Mark's, but a journey through the school's log books, accounts of the day to day running of the school. Unfortunately the records do not begin until June 1886. Previous accounts have been lost, but those studied for the present book describe characters and events which have helped make the school what it is today.

The first available book is a treasure house of stories. The head teacher is not named, but whoever it was had a wonderfully vivid narrative style, and manages to invest even commonplace events with a sense of drama. Here is her account, (the feminine touch is unmistakable) of her sister's illness.

> "On June 22nd my sister was taken very ill, her throat becoming so bad that she had great difficulty in drawing her breath. The Doctor tells her that her vocal organs are injured by excessive strain on her voice".

Later she records

> "My sister owing to an unusually severe bilious attack was unable to attend school",

and in December the most dramatic entry of all.

> "Owing to a frightful accident which happened to my mother, by which she was nearly burnt to death, my sister was unable to attend school this week".

Add to this the fact that the writer notes she herself had recently been "felled to the ground by a stone thrown by some passing tramps", readers may be forgiven for concluding this was a somewhat accident-prone family.

A sad entry on June 25th 1886 reads

> "Ellen Muddle, aged 12 died from inflammation of the heart' (a doctor believes this may have been rheumatic fever)"

and on Wednesday June 28th

> "many children having expressed a strong desire to follow their late, lamented little school-fellow to the grave, I gave them a half holiday to enable them to do so".

Is it cynical to wonder whether some of the company welcomed the opportu-

nity for extra time off and, perhaps, made only a fleeting appearance at the funeral?

School attendance, or the lack of it, was a prime concern . Almost every entry begins with a comment on the numbers present. The school attendance officer made frequent visits but, in spite of this, absenteeism was rife. Summer holidays began in late August, and lasted until about October 4th, which covered periods of harvest and hop-picking, but children still stayed away for every imaginable reason. St. Mark's had a wide catchment area, covering a number of outlying farms, so weather played an important part in the figures. Heavy rain or snowfall meant children who had to walk to school simply stayed away, but there were other less valid reasons. For instance Miss Day's tennis party required ball boys. Or Ernest Coles, reported to be sick on Monday, on Thursday was discovered to have been at work all week with his father in the hop fields. Among the records of absenteeism for the year, these figures make impressive reading. "John Winter 172 times. Harry Noakes 122 times". The long list finishes with "Elizabeth Martin 70 times".

Inspectors paid frequent visits. A report for 1887 notes (capital letters are his not the author's) "I was sorry to find that, in the Infants no action songs have been taught and that the Boys do not learn Hemming and Knitting".

No sexism nonsense here! During this year and 1889 there was serious over-crowding with 80 infants crammed into one room. How everyone was accommodated, never mind taught, is hard to imagine.

A pathetic entry in 1888 tells of Mary Ann Collins who complained that her arm hurt. A teacher examined her, and found her back was cut and bruised from a severe beating. Her adopted parents were reported to the police but, before action could be taken, the family disappeared. What happened to poor Mary Ann remains a mystery.

Another entry in the same year is more amusing. Harriet Jarret appears to have been a thorn in the flesh of the poor head teacher. First she

Tommy Long, Headmaster, and his staff.
One of the ladies is thought to be his daughter.
He retired in 1928.

refused to show her needlework to the Inspectors when requested to do so, then, at a later date, deliberately spoilt it. In an endeavour to strike terror into the heart of the sinner she was sent to the vicarage for a scolding. Alas! the vicar seems to have failed in his duty for she "returned triumphant". The slightly sinister comment follows: "Next time I shall deal with the matter myself". Harriet continued to cause trouble throughout her school career and although the names of pupils completing the course are seldom recorded, there is a final mention, perhaps reflecting the head's relief, "Today Harriet Jarret left the school".

In 1889 the Dame School, of which there is little on record, collapsed, and the village school inherited several children. A note of satisfaction can be detected in the entry about these children who "seem very backward and do not even know their alphabet".

December 1891 inspired an entry that reveals "George Peckham was punished for setting fire to the pinafore of Emily Winter during the dinner hour". This may have

Circa 1905

been because there seems to have been little supervision of those who stayed on the premises all day. The theory is strengthened by a paragraph which reads, "On Monday the fifth of November, during the dinner hour two tramps, a big lad and a younger one entered the school and chased the children who were staying there to dinner round their desks trying to catch them in order to thrash them. When I got back I discovered that one little girl had fainted while others were crying and dreadfully excited".

The following year Henry Lodge was appointed headmaster. He seems to have been a man who had a fondness for children. Rather touchingly he admits, "I have often been struck with the kindness and gentleness they display towards each other". On a more practical level he complains, on April 10th, ' Despite every care being taken the boys' offices have been very unpleasant the whole time I have been in charge of the school, and the hot weather of late has greatly intensified the evil... the need of a good water supply for the school both for cleansing and drinking water is urgently felt".

It is amusing to reflect that in 1999, when Phase 1 of the new building scheme is due to start, the first priority is... the lavatories!

In 1893 he decrees that, "if children arrive wet, they must be sent home" and "if not more than a third of the children are present the registers are not to be taken and the children who remain may amuse themselves with library books or games under the supervision of a teacher". By November the new stove had been installed, a positive move counter-balanced by the fact that the Infant classroom was infested with rats who ate the geography books and used dusters to make their nests.

Like most school teachers of the time Mr. Lodge had occasionally to resort to the use of the cane. He writes "This afternoon a boy in Mrs. Sand's class misbehaved and was made to stand on the bench. He laughed so I gave him 3 strokes on the hands with a few minutes between each. As he laughed again I gave another which brought him to a better frame of mind".

Well, in the circumstances, it would wouldn't it !

An interesting entry in the same year, particularly bearing in mind the modern habit of rushing to litigation, confirms that Mr. Lodge firmly refused to administer corporal punishment except in the presence of one of the Managers. "I do this for my own protection". So strongly did he feel that he threatened to resign if his request was not granted.

The Managers, it should be noted, were forerunners of the present Governors and, like them, were responsible for the running of the school. Prominent among them at this time, and certainly the most active, was Mr. Huggins from The Grange.

Hardly a week passed without a note recording his visit to the school in a helpful capacity. This connection continued through the years, and is one of constant support.

In June 1897 Henry Lodge did indeed resign, although it is not clear whether the question of corporal punishment was responsible. His place was taken by Mr. Charles England and the poor man seems to have been beset by troubles from the outset. In October Mrs. Sands resigned through ill health, but no replacement was forthcoming. Use was made of monitors, senior pupils who helped with the teaching, but if one looks at the short periods in which they were in office... William Packham February 2nd – March 25th... one wonders how effective they were. By November 19th, a brief, rather desperate entry reads, "End of a very bad week".

On April 18th, the following year, there is an incident which demonstrates the concern of the Managers. The vicar, Mr. Warner, visited the school and found there were no fires in the classrooms so, rather than delegate the job to somebody else, he set about trying to light the stove himself. He soon discovered that the only wood available was green and stubbornly refused to burn. The admirable Mr. Warner would not be defeated. He went out, bought a load of old wood, ordered some coke and lit the fires. He then registered a complaint. "It is not right to require teachers and children to submit to such inconvenience".

In the early years of the 20th century the records are chiefly noteworthy for the amount of illness which afflicted the school. In October 1901 the school was closed for a fortnight due to an outbreak of scarlet fever. In 1902 the sanitary authorities closed it from February 3rd–17th as one of the teachers suffered from diphtheria. In 1903 there were outbreaks of chicken-pox, measles, whooping-cough, mumps, scarlet fever, diphtheria, impetigo and scabies! Other afflictions of a more doubtful nature were as follows. "Three girls fainted in school today. I cannot account for this , nor can the vicar, who has been present when other boys and girls have been taken ill. Illness generally occurs during the scripture lessons" ... Why?

On June 2nd 1902 the news reached Hadlow Down that peace was proclaimed with the Boers. "To celebrate this the children marched round the playground and sang, Rule Britannia and God save the King and after giving three hearty cheers for His Majesty were dismissed".

The school was closed for a week to celebrate the coronation of Edward VII and the children were each given a commemorative mug by Mrs. Huggins. There are still some of these around in the village.

By 1903 the numbers in the school were beginning to fall, no specific reason is given for this but the following figures show the decline:- 1903 122 children, by 1922 this had fallen to 60, and by 1929 to 39.

In 1914 Mr. Huggins visited the school and addressing the children imparted the news that war had been declared by our country against Germany. Apart from noting that it was difficult to get coke for the boilers there is no reference to the shattering events going on in the world until the signing of the Armistice in 1918 and the unveiling of the War Memorial tablet in the church in 1921.

There is a similar lack of recorded information about World War II, but Chapter 14 is devoted to Meg Rostron's vivid first-hand account. Of recent years the log books become more factual and therefore, from the point of view of interest to the reader less entertaining. Even if this did not apply, access to recent log books is not permitted, so we can pause here and look backwards for a moment. From the human point of view there are questions to which answers would be welcome. Did Harriet Jarret, like many rebellious children, learn to channel her energies to a constructive end? Did John Winter ever regret his 172 absences and wish he had made more of his educational chances and what became of poor little Mary Ann Collins?

Imagination creates an unbroken line of children stretching from 1838–1999 who have influenced and been influenced by our school and, in the final words of the song the children sang in a recent play,

"St. Mark's goes on, and on and on... confidently into the new millennium."

Dawn Johnson

Kit Crossland
(Auntie Kit)

Gerald Standen

Chapter Five

THE NEW INN

by Peter Gillies

"On his birthday he went to the "George Inn",
ate two pennyworth of bread and cheese, and drank one pint of
ale"

The New Inn is as inextricably linked with the village as the Standen family is with the New Inn. Thomas Standen was the first of the dynasty when he took over the licence in April 1912 following Mr John Markwick's demise. Thomas had previously been the Landlord of the New Inn at Ridgewood in Uckfield, so was no newcomer to the trade.In the fullness of time his son George took over, he in turn handed over the reins to his children Gerald and Dawn, who remain in control today, totalling three generations of Standens at the New inn. Worthy of mention at this stage is George's sister in law 'Auntie Kit' an institution to the customers and a tower of strength to Gerald and Dawn, for many years.

The origins of the New Inn are obscure. Gerald Standen writes...

> "There was a previous pub built on the site also "The New Inn" which burnt down in December 1890. It was believed to be arson as the Bailiffs were in. My late Grandfather then aged 23 remembered drinking up the removed stock in the back land while the pub burned. The Bailiff was alleged to have said it was the first time he had been burnt out of a place, his previous experiences having been chased out by dogs, geese, a bull and a swarm of bees".

East Sussex Record Office Document (SAS HC 674)

Messuage or Tenement formerly a cot or dwelling but now used as an Inn and called the New Inn with barn, stables, outbuildings and four pieces of land

The original New Inn

adjoining and belonging and formerly Common or waste land of four acres in Hadlow Down in Mayfield formerly in tenure of Thomas Baldock now of Wil Russell abuting to highway from Rotherfield to Lewes on E and to Hadlow Down Common on N S and W.

The first publican that we come upon in Kelly's Directory of 1899 lists "Markwick John Tailor & New Inn". No other reference to his being a tailor has been found. He appears to have played an active role in village affairs, judging by the friendly societies and Victuallers meetings held there, he also ran a pack of hunting Beagles. Gerald can remember the remains of the kennels which were still in existence in 1934/5, as well as some large iron spikes and chains in the big oak tree down Hut Lane, used for hanging the dogs meat on.

Sussex Express December 1909

"NEW INN SLATE CLUB, – on Wednesday last the members of this club had their annual supper and share out in the commodious club room which was seasonally decorated for the purpose. About 50 sat down to a well varied menu of substantial fare provided by Host Markwick. Mr J.P. Smith occupied the chair and after the table had been cleared, submitted the loyal toast which was patriotically honoured. Mr. Long submitted the balance sheet and in so doing alluded to the large amount of illness prevalant in the village during the year and pointed out the advantages of the club especially to the working man. The financial statement was as follows: Receipts £63 5s. 11d; expenditure £23 9s 1d of which £16 10s. was for sick pay and £4 12s. for suppers. The balance of £39 16s. 11d allowed a share per member of 17s 3d.

To the able accompaniment of Mr E. Shoosmith a varied and jolly musical programme was carried out. Mr Thomas well sustained the comic element his amusing items being heartily received. Mr J.P. Smith moved a hearty vote of thanks to Mr Markwick and his family for the nice supper they had prepared. The evening which was one of the most successful and enjoyable that has ever taken place here was regretfully concluded at the call of time."

LICENSED VICTUALLERS AT THE "NEW INN," HADLOW DOWN, 1906 (PROPRIETOR, J MARKWICK).

Independent Oddfellows Society

The New Inn

Sussex Express
December 1917 –
a similar article but the journalist concludes with the following words:

"The evening passed quietly and pleasantly till "Act of Parliament" was enforced and the company then dispersed anticipating another happy gathering next year."

When Thomas moved to Hadlow Down the pub was owned by Southdown and East Grinstead Breweries, who continued until around 1918 when they sold out to Tamplins of Brighton. After 43 years, in 1953/4

HADLOW DOWN. (EAST.)

The Eridge Hunt on a tidy forecourt with hand powered petrol pump.

they were taken over by Watneys who were only in control for ten years finally deciding that the cost of repairs to the fabric didn't warrant staying on. In 1963 the pub was offered for sale allowing a consortium of the Standen family to take control of their destiny. The New Inn was finally a Free House. Ironically since then, Harveys of Lewes has been the preferred beverage, although our hostelry has never been owned by the brewery.

In 1912, when Thomas took over, the outbuildings were stables, so the concept of pub and garage together was well established. There were no mechanical repairs undertaken in those days but the business did sport a horse and fly as a hackney carriage with some livery especially on Sundays when people came, frequently for the whole day, to the Providence Chapel. The front garage as we know it today was originally the Coach House until it burnt down in 1926. Perhaps it was Thomas who helped trigger the Standen mechanical streak by buying his first car, a 1903 Clement Talbot, in 1913.

Son George [born in 1897], was fortunate indeed to receive professional driving lessons which undoubtedly stood him in good stead, during his spell in the Army

A few years later

Service Corps during the First World War and made reviving the lapsed taxi business, after the conflict, all the easier. Vehicle repairs were soon introduced and the first hand cranked petrol pump installed in 1925. A single pump was sufficient until 1949, when in anticipation of impending legislation a second, electric pump, appeared.

Ironically in 1966 new regulations deemed the modern electric pump as, out of date for use with petrol, by which time one pump was again sufficient and the original "winder" reigned supreme. In 1972 profit margins had been eroded to such an extent that retail sales were discontinued so then the only fuel at the garage was diesel oil for Johnny Johnson [Dawn's husband] and Gerald's own lorries. George's mother Emily sadly passed away in the flu epidemic of 1918 and father Tom died, leaving his son in command, in October 1933. By this time George's son, Gerald, was showing a healthy interest in all things mechanical. The liquor licence remained in George's name until his death on April 25th 1974, when the yoke passed with great reluctance to Gerald. "I like the people but hate the trade" he was heard to mutter. As the proliferation of the motor car continued, so it became increasingly difficult to warrant the purchase of a new vehicle for the occasional taxi job while the demand for public transport and taxis declined. The garage continued for several years under Gerald's stewardship relying on car repairs only, until finally Gerald's love of the scrap yard and old cars won through and the garage ceased trading.

The distinctive architecture of our present pub has led to many speculative stories about its design mainly the notion that it was built as a railway station ready for the track to be laid from Buxted at a later date. Gerald leaves us in no doubt about the authenticity of this statement.

> "The New Inn was not or was never intended to be a railway station. At the time it was built there were no plans to link the village to a railway system or even locomotives capable of dealing with the gradients involved. In old deeds of a property in what later became Hadlow Down there was mention of a proposed railway around 1840. As many historians will know, at that period there was a railway mania, with many schemes being dreamed up which never did or never could have reached fruition."

In June 1979 an unlikely event took place in the New Inn which might almost have confirmed the railway station rumour. The confectionery firm of Lyons Cakes approached Gerald requesting permission to film a commercial on the premises. It transpired they had spent some time looking for a building, which would most closely resemble an old railway station, and now declared our pub to be perfect. Ted Griffiths from Blackboys earned £180 for a day's work painting the front room. The plot was for a small boy to be 'lost' in order for the Station Master and his wife to take him in, sit him down and give him a delicious "you know whose cake". The whole place was taken over by studio lights, generators, cables and technicians. Nobody could go about their normal business. The film crew had no idea of the contract that had been agreed beforehand, so tried to make free with whatever they fancied. Gerald's patience wore very thin at one time suggesting it might be better if they 'bleeped off'. The only advantage was the canteen, which appeared to be open to all, and the huge pile of cakes that they couldn't be bothered to take with them when they eventually left.

The film cannot so far be traced in the Lyons archives and nobody has owned up to having seen it shown locally, although there is a rumour that it was shown in the Midlands.

Around the same time Auntie Kit appeared in a documentary, which was filmed in the same front room of the Pub. She co-starred with Sister Thomas from Mayfield, telling the story of a Rural District Nurse. History doesn't relate who played which part or what happened to the film.

The present pub was designed by an architect named Denman of Brighton who designed several churches and it is believed the railway station at West Croydon. His son the late Horace Denman who lived in this village into his nineties would often say, "I can't think what the old man was thinking about when he designed this place".

In the early 70s, the late John Booth, then of School Lane Cottage decided to write a book listing and describing his choice of the best pubs in the area. After considerable research and sampling of the available watering holes, his selection was made and The Drinking Mans Guide to Sussex and Kent Pubs was published in 1974. John's choice for the finest example was The New Inn at Hadlow Down. He said:

> "Let us have no polite hesitations about this statement, no careful conditional reservations, let the claim be made loud and boldly - The New Inn at Hadlow Down in Sussex is the best pub in the county and probably the best pub in England".

The forecourt in 1997

Clearly the book produced considerable interest and brought people to the village expecting to see what they IMAGINED to be the best pub in Sussex. Needless to say many were very disappointed but John defended his position explaining he hadn't said it had the thickest carpet, trendiest wallpaper or was the warmest only that it was the best drinking man's pub and many would agree. Even Southern television made a pilgrimage to interview The Landlord, who was very busy at the time in the garage and not at all impressed by the ballyhoo. The resulting film carried more than its fair share of bleep outs and left the hostelry's good name intact!

In 1988 John published a sequel called The Real Pub Guide. This time the description is a little more graphic no doubt intended to counter any flak before it hit the fan.

"Even the most devoted admirers of the New Inn would have to concede it looks a bit well, tatty… . The interior matches the exterior. To say it is unpretentious would be a wild overstatement. It's plain bare and rather gloomy… . Next door to the pub is a large sprawling scrap yard, a graveyard for ancient lorries and cars, which drives those who wish to enter Hadlow Down in the Best Kept Village competition to apoplexy… . It is a pub which is not a business in the way other pubs are businesses. It belongs to a different order of things and is a place where the pub is basically the home of the resident family and the operation of the pub is of secondary importance."

In those days it still sported Harveys barrels on the bar and had the reputation "for excellent beer at reasonable prices, but don't worry about the decor". Because of the proximity of Gerald's scrap yard, the saying used to be "pull up a gearbox and sit down"

Gerald by his own admission was always a reluctant publican [every excuse to jump into his lorry and head off was seized with alacrity]. Although he helped doing his fair share of the heavy work it was Dawn and Auntie Kit who welcomed the customers and kept the ship afloat. Auntie Kit, born Elizabeth Kate Smith 24/11/01 was and is a legend. Raised in the village she met, and married, Arthur Crossland who was working as a butler at Dewbrook, now called Moons Mill in Tinkers Lane, after the first war. All her married life was spent away from the parish. She returned to the village in 1940 owing to the invasion scare in Brighton and lived with her parents at Preston House. Eventually she moved into the pub where she worked unstintingly, only retiring a few years before her death, which was one week short of her 89th birthday on the 17th November 1990. Kit was certainly Aunt to Dawn and Gerald, being their mother's sister, but to the rest of Sussex it was pure and simple affection.

By 1985 the task of running a pub had taken its toll and the decision was made to quit. The New Inn and the field at the back were put up for sale. Braxtons of Uckfield as Estate Agents, recommended asking for tenders. Given the state of the property market, which was travelling like a sky scraper lift out of control, it may well have been a reasonable commercial decision, although the final outcome makes it doubtful. In the event several prospective purchasers were attracted and a company called Dexta Estates took a two year option on the property whilst they explored the planning potential. Eventually in June 1989 the bombshell dropped, the plan was to demolish the pub and post office in order to develop the whole site with 56 houses which would have more than doubled the number of houses in the centre of the village. With the village in turmoil, Tom Bridges, chairman of the Parish Council, declared the scheme to be "The Rape of the Village" which was a little premature, but he could have been right. Unofficially, Dexta Estates were warned that their plans had

Locals' fury at 'rape' plan

A MULTI-million pound housing scheme involving the demolition of Hadlow Down's pub and post office has shocked the village.

Dorking-based Dexta Estates has submitted an outline application to demolish the pub and stores to make way for new homes and shops in the centre of the village.

The company, which already owns nearby land with permission for homes, wants to build bungalows and cottages for the elderly, 12 starter units and 22 three, four and five-bedroom houses on 4.29 acres.

Owners of the New Inn, Gerald Standen and his sister, Dawn Johnson, and owners of the store, Jim and Margaret Dixon, have agreed a year's option on the sale of their properties to Dexta.

Mr Dixon put a £7 million price tag on the scheme but did not want to comment on the development because he is a member of the village parish council.

He is displaying the plans in his shop window and told the Express he hoped one of the planned shops would be a post office and store.

RUN-DOWN PUB

Mr Standen and Mrs Johnson said they could not afford extensive repairs to the run-down pub and were looking forward to retiring.

Parish councillor Tom Bridges has attacked the scheme as the planned "rape" of the village.

"Feelings about the plan are pretty high. It would tear the heart out of the village and nearly double the number of houses in the centre. I believe it's overdevelopment. The destruction of the pub and post office would reduce facilities with no guarantee they will be replaced," he said.

Cllr Bridges urged residents to attend the start of Tuesday's parish council meeting when questions about the scheme could be raised. And he is considering calling a special public meeting to discuss the proposed development.

● A separate application for the demolition of Beech Cottage, also on the main road at Hadlow Down, and its replacement by a bungalow, two chalet bungalows, a terrace of nine houses and two detached houses, has also been submitted to Wealden.

ignored all the social consequences for the existing village and certainly with hindsight little sound judgement appears to have been used. One of the reasons given for refusal was "the development being outside the village envelope". Didn't they know that at the outset? Or was it a case of massive over confidence clouding their judgment? Subsequently, with the help of a village liaison committee a revised plan was submitted, for only 26 houses, but by this time the scheme had a history and the property gravy train was running out of steam. With the second application also refused, the option expired, Dexta Estates retired and the village sighed as peace and security returned. At the time it proved difficult for the average villager to understand what was going on. At least three property companies sprang up locally, all trying to join the bandwagon, all hoping for a slice of the birthday cake. (Several of the parish councillors were also involved which caused some consternation.)

Every pub has its tales of practical jokes and worse. One concerned two regular drinkers back in the 70s. Auntie Kit was in the habit of putting fresh sandwiches in a plastic cabinet on the bar at weekends. There was also a fruit machine, now long gone, which had the standard red spherical arbanite knob on the chrome handle. With the first couple of pints downed and quicker than it takes to tell, the plastic knob and a tomato from Auntie Kit's dispenser changed places. The joke worked well, with the victim winning nothing except a shirtfront, full of juice and pips. As expected he was not best pleased, and complained bitterly to those concerned whose response was "Anyone who can't tell the difference between a plastic ball and a tomato shouldn't be let out on his own" Faced with such devastating logic he retired, only to be vindicated when Auntie Kit emerged from the back and gave the trouble makers the drubbing of their lives for unhygienically messing about with her display.

In 1972 this country was blessed with decimalization and George found the transition as trying as everybody else. The New Inn till at this time still sported a facility for ringing up guineas. It was suggested that a mechanical calculator with a paper print out would help and such a machine was duly obtained. George soon declared it to be absolutely useless, whereupon you might expect it to be removed; but no, in true Hadlow Down style it remained on the bar as a paper dispenser for customers betting slips etc.

In recent years the fabric of the building has deteriorated but the welcome for local people and devotees has remained constant. One night in particular is remembered when a group with a lively rhythm was playing in the back room. As the enthusiasm increased and the whole place throbbed to the beat, the ceiling gave up the unequal struggle of defying gravity and enveloped the entire company in a white choking dust. Gerald is adamant; "The loose plaster was prodded".On another occasion, a window fell out and as a temporary measure a piece of hardboard had to be nailed into position. Many were heard to comment on the improvements taking place.

In December 1993 Jim Dixon from the village stores lost the licence for the Post Office and for a time we were in danger of adding to the national list of villages without even a Post Office. Much to their credit the Standens came to the rescue and allowed Glenis Pitson, The Post Mistress, to occupy a corner of the front room in the pub.

Today the New Inn; "you either love it or hate it",continues to rumble on providing us with one enduring link with the past. Dawn and Gerald still want to

Note the Post Office sign on the door

retire and hopefully will be able to find a way to do so and leave the pub as a working and active legacy for the benefit of the village. In the meantime it was with considerable relief that the reins were finally handed over to Martin Clarke, the present manager in 1992.

A final quote from John Booth's, Real Pub Guide.

"There has always been a healthy lawlessness here which generations of policemen have fought to prevent especially in the matter of what are permitted licensing hours but Hadlow Down has long regarded itself as having gained independence from the rest of the United Kingdom. To all those who are uncertain about what a real pub is, we urge them to make a visit to the New Inn but to do so quickly or it may be too late".

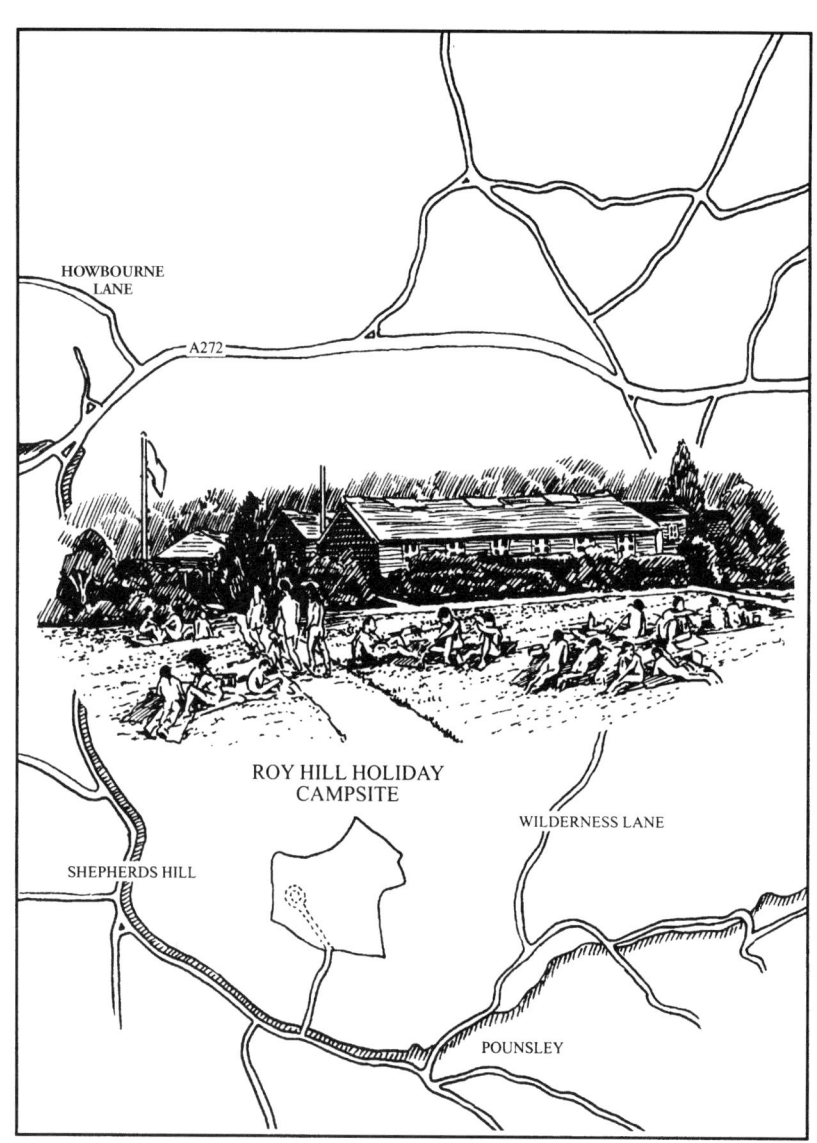

HOWBOURNE
LANE

A272

ROY HILL HOLIDAY
CAMPSITE

WILDERNESS LANE

SHEPHERDS HILL

POUNSLEY

Chapter Six

ROY HILL

by Peter Gillies

*"We mustn't complain, God sends the weather,
and he knows best."*

P ossibly this is Hadlow Down's best kept secret, although there is no evidence that it was ever intended to be a mystery. The reason for lack of knowledge or memory locally can now only be conjecture; possibly because the people involved in the scheme all came from outside the area and once here existed as a largely self contained community, without integrating themselves into village life, which meant that few villagers ever learned much about 'the visitors on the hill'.

The site was owned and run as Roy Hill Country Health and Pleasure Club by Dr McGregor Reid and his wife. Dr Reid had a practice in London, possibly providing a source of visitors. There was also a Mr Peacock, a non-conformist minister from London who was very involved, bringing several parties for holidays. The clientele may have been attracted from a wider area as well, possibly through advertisements but none has been found to date.

One story that gave rise to speculation occurred when Dr Reid wrote to Brigadier Godfrey Faussett who lived at 'Annes' in Wilderness Lane, saying that a line of fir trees growing on the boundary of his land caused the rising sun on midsummer's day to be obscured from the Doctor's view on Roy Hill and would it be possible to fell the offending trees. The Brigadier's thoughts are unknown but his reply was concise and the trees remained standing. Armed with this news, the holidaymakers became Druids, Solstice worshippers and no doubt worse.

The entrance road and camp

The only consistent answer to be given when enquiring about the site is "Oh you mean the nudist camp". On further examination few people can actually verify exactly what did happen, and whether nudism really was part of the regime. However one gentleman, who was a child at the time and lived locally, is adamant and told us that he and his friends ran wild using the woods as their playground, regularly going to watch through the wire fence as the holidaymakers "rolled naked in the grass in the mornings" as he described it "Dew Bathing". Most likely Dr Reid ran an alternative medicine practice with a slant on natural and herbal medicines. Certainly Mrs Pamela Greenwood, [nee Funnell] as a small girl living next door in Oakleys farm, remembers being asked to collect certain plants and herbs whenever possible, which were then used to make medicinal potions. Clearly some element of nudism did take place and undoubtedly would have fitted in well with the doctor's fairly advanced thinking on health care. Naturopathy [a system of treating diseases largely employing natural agencies, such as air, sunshine etc., and rejecting the use of drugs and medicines], is the description remembered locally. It should be stated that so far no trace can be found of Dr McGregor Reid in London listings of conventional doctors.

George Standen sometimes taxied travellers to and from Buxted Station, although clients could also be seen carrying their suitcases and walking along the lanes from the station, approximately three miles. A few local people worked there, presumably the groceries were bought locally, probably from Uckfield but generally it seems to have been a case of 'never the twain did meet'. The only other certain memories are of 'the large white flagpole and the tall water tower'.

Everything ground to a halt during the war allowing the authorities to use it as a base for an East Lancashire Regiment of the Royal Army Service Corps, during the summer of 1941.

Another rumour suggested the camp was used to house refugee children from the Spanish civil war. Considering the Blackboys Youth Hostel was used for this purpose [and geographically, is very close] it is felt this was probably a misunderstanding at the time.

After the war it opened again briefly as a holiday camp this time under new management. The owner, now described as 'a very upper crust lady', tried to run it for 'The Elite', presumably without success because it soon lay abandoned and was finally demolished in 1956/57.

Outside Dr McGregor Reid's private chalet.
From the left are: Under the umbrella unknown, Mr and Mrs Peacock, their son Ray. Seated at the table Mrs Alice McGregor Reid. The last two are unknown.

Chapter Seven

VILLAGE CHARACTERS

by Meg Rostron

"But what were our villagers like years ago?"

The 'Church Militant' was well represented by Miss Marjorie Banks, who lived with her mother Dr Banks at Fourways. Church Organist and Sunday school teacher, she did her best to discipline her somewhat unruly charges. Her voice as powerful as her personality could be clearly heard, whether leading the choir in 'Onward Christian Soldiers' on a Sunday, or 'Ten Green Bottles' in the charabanc on the way back from the Sunday school outing. She was a splendid organizer and we "flipped many a kipper" and played countless games of musical chairs during the church socials which she helped with.   Three cheers for Miss Banks.

The group of dwellings known as Grange Cottages housed the Kingsland family, The Sands and Mr and Mrs Simonds.

Mr Sands, disrespectfully known as "old Sammy", was a short fierce man, who tended the Churchyard and School grounds, cutting the grass with a swop hook. He also rang the Church bell on Sunday and every day at noon for the Angelus.

His son Alf had been terribly wounded in the Great War and spent most of his time sitting in their tiny front garden where he could keep an eye on the poppies "planted" on the triangle opposite, which was the custom on Armistice Day. Sometimes he would walk painfully down to the Church, creaking like an old leather shoe. There was no trace of bitterness on the face of this kindly man, who greeted every passer-by in his blurred voice. The human dynamo behind these two men was Lil, daughter and sister. Small, busy, with a no-nonsense manner and a caustic tongue, she nursed Alf, was an excellent dressmaker and did a lot for the Church, besides being Sunday school teacher to the infant class. She was also in the Red Cross and in due course received an invitation to a Buckingham Palace Tea Party for services rendered.

Mr Ruff the baker, with his brown walrus moustache, looked very much like "Old Bill" from the famous first World War cartoon; perhaps that is why the children tormented him so. They would run behind the horse and cart he used to deliver the bread, yelling "Old Bill Ruff!" He would scowl fiercely and flick his whip at them, as if they were so many flies. His wife, Rosie was a sweet little lady, very spry until well into her eighties. Bill was renowned for his delicious, spicy scones.

Meg's brother Chris Greenwood remembers George Pullen telling him the following.

> "Last night Rosie Ruff came to the cottage to see me. I was down the garden, she saw me and said 'give us a ride in your barrow George', so I said 'get your-self in then'. And she did, she set her little arse in my barrow and I pushed her round the garden."

Rosie was in her eighties at the time!

There was an advertisement for Reckits blue, [the pre-detergent clothes whitener] outside Mrs Smith's sweet shop, and the white haired lady depicted on it was the image of Mrs Smith herself. Forthright and outspoken, Mrs Smith liked to know everything that went on in the village, a new dress was sure to be commented on! She had a window full of sticky confections, such as liquorice bootlaces, sherbert fountains and gooey marshmallow cones as well as jars of bullseyes, acid drops and toffees on the counter. The more adventurous could perfume their breath with violet scented cachous. The twins Kitty and Bertha Godley sometimes helped out in the shop, which also stocked general groceries.

Sometimes the local copper, P.C. Glazier, [known to us kids as "Old Glass-eye"] would cycle through the village. Crime was rife in the country at that time... though it usually was nothing more serious than a dog without a collar, or worse still with no licence. Nevertheless a policeman who knew his patch was a great asset to the law-abiding majority.

On any afternoon you would be sure to see George Standen working in his garage. A large amiable, grey haired man, he loved his vintage motors, which he some-times hired out, as well as running a taxi service. Often the peace was shattered with a diabolical tyre pump he had, shaped like a Michelin Man on a motor bike, it could be heard at least half a mile away. George would put an accumulator on charge, which was a necessity if you owned a wireless set and wanted to hear "In Town Tonight" or "Bandwagon" on Saturday night.

Jo White, who owned the Village Stores was a quiet, burley man, and his assistant, Miss Storey talked nineteen to the dozen. Whether serving you with a pair of lisle stockings, a yard of elastic, or a tin of beans, she would chatter away about current events in the village, never gossip of course! She had the amazing ability of spotting Lady Hamilton, or someone of that ilk approaching the shop and adjusting her accent to 'posh' in mid-stream.

Mr and Mrs Richards at the Post Office led very busy lives. Apart from selling Postal Orders and Stamps, they also sold groceries and hardware. Mr Richards delivered paraffin etc. in his van or motor bike and side car. On top of all this they manned the telephone exchange, which was situated behind the counter. There were very few people lucky enough to have a phone in the early thirties, but with all that responsibility it was no wonder the Richardses were a bit grumpy with us kids, chorusing "shut the door!" in summer or winter. Mrs Richards was a very short lady, she hardly seemed able to see across the counter, Mr Richards was tall and thin with a moustache and never seen without his flat cap.

Mr Richards was known affectionately throughout the village as Windy or Windy Dick. There appear to be at least three versions for the nickname.

Meg Rostron...... Mr Richards was a very good card player and enjoyed a game with his friends. All was well until the stakes were raised a little higher than usual causing considerable consternation, hence Windy/prudence.

Marjorie Jarvis...... remembers her father working late in the shop on a Saturday evening, often until 10.00pm, as it was the busiest time of the week. Whilst Mum was shopping the children would wait and play outside frequently sitting on the wide window sills. As the evening progressed it all became too much for poor Mr Richards who would dash out of the shop and shoo the boys away from his window in case they broke it. Eventually a girl broke the window! Windy/fear or Windy/glass.

Gerald Standen...... Transport for any family was a slow progression in those days. Windy started with a pushbike, later a motor bike and sidecar, then a van and finally a Hillman car. His advancing years made him a very cautious driver, almost as if the new technology were more than he could handle Windy/caution.

Stan Henton was the village butcher, stout and jolly. He cut up the meat and served the sausages, helped by an assistant, while Mrs Henton, a pleasant woman with glasses and frizzy hair, acted as cashier in a little cubbyhole. Stan Henton did a lot of work for the village, especially helping with the sports at the annual Flower Show.

It was impossible to pass Mr Muddle's garden, at Bull Cottage without casting an admiring glance over the neatly trimmed hedge. His perfectly straight rows of carrots, peas and potatoes were a delight to the eye and made one realize that vegetables can be every bit as beautiful to look at as flowers

Mr and Mrs Steele ran the little general store at the top end of the village. It was a hard climb up the steep brick steps to Sunnybank Stores, and a hard place to make a go of. Rosy cheeked Sally Steele worked in the shop and looked after their small son, while Charlie Steele did the deliveries on his bike.

Jack Bracher at the forge was a huge man, who with his curled-back lower lip and enormous stomach was everyone's idea of a black-smith. What a fascinating place the forge was! As Jack hammered on a red-hot piece of iron it miraculously took shape and was dunked in a tank of water giving off a great hiss and a cloud of steam. The clattering bellows and glowing coals were a great attraction especially on a chilly winter's morning. Apart from shoeing horses, Jack Bracher could make a child's hoop, solder a milk bucket as well as many other useful things. In his spare time he swept chimneys.

Jack Bracher

Everyone seemed to have some special talent that made them useful to the community. Bert Smith, a sufferer from cerebal palsy was an expert mole catcher. The Smith family lived at Loudwell Farm in Tinkers Lane, and Mr Smith, a dairy farmer also helped out with his horses and farm implements at hay and harvest time, assisted by his sons.

The Mitchell family had a hop garden at Broomfield Farm [now Little England] which provided much needed cash to the local women at picking time. It was a far cry from the Kentish hop fields, just a kind of pleasant holiday, particularly for us kids who were allowed time off from school for the first fortnight in September.

Jack Fenner and his sister Emily who lived at the top of Wilderness Lane seemed to be true remnants of an earlier age. Bow legged, and wearing the traditional cloth cap, Jack's invariable greeting was "Marnin nice day." He still used the old style of address. According to his status a man would be Mas' or Mus', [Master or Mister] while touching his cap with a crooked finger. Jack did hedging and felling trees,

Hop pickers at Broomfield Farm
Note the inverted umbrella on the left of the picture for the children to pick hops into.
Back row, 5th from left: Nellie Civers, Mrs Ruff and Mrs Godley.
Front row, 3rd from left: Kitty Godley, Bertha Godley and Clara May Ruff

occasionally setting a bit of woodland alight with one of his bonfires, which caused quite a panic on one occasion during the war. He went everywhere on his old 'sit up and beg' bicycle with a sack....... the country-man's substitute for a hooded mackintosh, and his bottle of cold tea and a hunk of bread and cheese in a basket at the front. Reputedly born in a now vanished cottage deep in woodland on Scocus Farm, Jack and his sister had

Luther Mitchell cultivating the hop garden, Broomfields, 1940. A Fordson Model F, circa 1919, converted at a later date to a vineyard tractor.

both suffered the effects of rickets, the forgotten scourge of the olden days which affected bone development, and was caused by a lack of vitamins in childhood. Emily did a little housework for people in the village, but they were very poor. Jack was in his seventies when he dropped dead off his beloved bike, and poor Emily ended her days in an old people's home.

You were likely to see the two roadmen, Mr Balcombe and Bert French in Wilderness Lane. With their trusty swop hooks and shovels they kept the banks tidy and the ditches running sweet and clear...... the shovels were useful to lean on as well!

A stranger might have blinked in astonishment thinking he had seen a Frenchman driving cows up [or down] the lane, but it was only Alf Long, looking positively Gallic in his black beret carrying a hazel wand in one hand and a cigarette in the other, his whippets running at his heels.

Our oldest inhabitant lived at the intersection of the two Wilderness lanes. Bendy Cook was, as the rather insensitive nickname suggests, bent double. He was also totally bald. He bore these vicissitudes with the usual stoicism of the countryman, and managed to be quite cheerful.

Gerald Standen remembers Bendy Cook as a rather grumpy, self appointed guardian of Waste Wood who apparently took great delight in chasing Gerald and any

Woodgate Cottage, home of Bendy Cook,
where the two Wilderness Lanes join

other children out of the wood with his blunderbuss.

Peter Gillies remembers…… I met Lily, Bert and Charlie Leeves from Spoods Farm for the first time in 1966. Their parents, Edward and Emily had taken the tenancy in 1901 and moved in with three children Lily, Wallis and Frank. Brother Ted made his debut a few months later. Bert and Charlie completed the family but waited until 1903 and 05 respectively. A hard working and thrifty family they prospered and earned the respect of all that knew them. Frank and Wallis were both killed in the 14/18 conflict and Ted's unexpected demise in 1947 knocked the stuffing out of the survivors. Quiet unassuming steady and thoroughly reliable, the family had been raised with the ethos "Them as don't work, don't eat". Charlie was the optimist with a twinkle in his eye and ready for a joke. Bert the pessimist, described by his brother as "The Merchant of Doom" was dour and more difficult to get to know and Lily carried the burden of command heavily on her frail shoulders, each day, finding her less able to keep control of the situation. None of the three had married so no new influences had been introduced to them since their parents had died in the thirties.

Hay making was my first experience of their farming practices, the occasion being the merest puff away from 'Constable's Haywain'. The farm relied on:

Small scale enterprises.

Little or no cash investment.

Plenty of gruelling hard labour.

Make sure whatever you have for sale is good so it makes top money in the market.

The recipe worked and reflected itself in their frugal living.

Go to bed when it gets dark, that saves electricity.

Get up early gives a long day.

Eat whatever can be grown in the garden and stored.

Do all the cooking with firewood, (that means on the open fire in the sitting room and don't worry when a gob of soot lands in the custard.)

Don't have days out or luxuries, we didn't need them yesterday so why do we need them today?

Mod. – cons. such as telephones, televisions, refrigerators and washing machines just didn't even get a thought and who needs a car when you've got a perfectly good push bike and if neccessary a tractor. When on one occasion there was a strike and the newspapers failed to appear for a few days the decision was made, "If they can't send us a paper we won't bother to buy it again" and they never did, it was the ultimate in consumer resistance.

Lily died in 1967 so Bert had to take up the business reins, making all the decisions with Charlie remaining "the boy" running the errands. Many a trip to Lewes or Haywards Heath Market we made with Charlie sometimes to sell a beast more usually to buy a calf for rearing, but always with strict instructions. The regime worked. As the years rolled by so Bert developed a yen for a Jersey cow. Until then only beef breeds had found favour with more latterly Friesian crosses filling the gap. For the first time Charlie rebelled, defiantly refusing to go to Market with instructions, because "I'm sure to buy the wrong un and get the blame". Eventually it was agreed that Bert should go and negotiate his own deal. Haywards Heath was the choice, presumably some prior information told us there were to be some animals of the right type on offer. We

Bert and Charlie Leeves, 1970.

84

set off through Buxted and reached Coopers Green, whereupon Bert announced "Coo I haven't been down here for a long time". "How long" I asked idly, concentrating on the road. Sucking through his teeth in the customary manner was no longer possible for Bert and dentures would have been considered a luxury, but after quite a pause he said "Ooooh about 25 years"!

The animals were inspected and I assume a decision made although I don't remember being privy to it. The sale commenced with several lots going under the hammer before we were interested, allowing us to relax and watch the proceedings. Only when the bidding was under way for our first lot and Bert started asking me where the price lay, did I remember how deaf he was. Sam Knight the auctioneer was a brusque and busy sort of chap with a clubfoot, huge gabardine raincoat and a brown trilby hat. He seemed to have set the pace of his life to beat his gammy leg and he certainly didn't hang about on the rostrum. By the time he had a bid and I had shouted it in Bert's ear, (no finesse or secret bidding in our corner) Sam had moved on so we were out of date. There was every danger of the animal being sold to someone else with our business brains three bids behind. With no thinking time, I shouted and panicked, Bert nodded sagely and Sam just grabbed the bids. Fortunately the early hopefuls looking for a bargain dropped out as we settled down to slogging it out with just one or two others. Sam, bless his heart, saw my predicament and deliberately gave us time, setting the pace of the bidding to my old friend's infirmity. Whether Sam had a compassionate streak after all or he was just shrewd enough to recognize a determined punter I shall never know, but we emerged triumphant and as usual Tom Appleby, Carrier, from Piltdown was duly engaged to bring the prize home.

Album.

Chapter Eight

FROM THE FAMILY ALBUM

*'Little as the world appreciated them,
the Sussex folk were a noble people."*

Circa 1910

Corner Cottage was moved to this location after 1905

Wilderness Lane West. Ivy cottage, now Cobwebs, is on the left and Fir Tree farm on the right.

Tullys farm, which became Millers Farm, and is now Tullys in Five Chimneys lane

Gatehouse, the thatch on the right is a summerhouse and the little girl clearly likes being photographed

Remembrance Day Parade with the Mayfield Silver Band during the 50s

Tom Standen to the left of the pub sign

The Eridge Hunt. Left of centre is Charlie Bishop in the white shirt on the soldier's right, Charlie Muddle in front of him and Jimmy Edwards of television and film fame on the white horse.

Granny Sivers outside Curtains Hill Farm cottage, today named Civers. She was widowed early in life and found it necessary to take in washing to make ends meet. Although there was a spring on the property, it used to dry up in the summer time and so all the water was drawn and carried from Curtains Hill well. She cared, particularly for the Church Vestments and Altar Cloths.

91

January 14th 1933 Ruth Sivers, seated, married Albert Packham, on her right. Mum, "Granny Sivers" is on the brides left. Outside Sivers cottage.

The Rev John Alan Warner, vicar of this parish from 1888 until 1916, in the Vicarage doorway. At the time of rebuilding the church in 1913, part of the school playground was taken to enlarge the churchyard. The Rev Warner's grave was dug spanning the original boundary, so he lies in the new and the old. The reference to the Aeroplane is unclear. No mention has been found of an aeroplane landing in the village so it is most likely to be referring to one of the rare sightings of a flying aircraft.

Sussex Express

November 1913

> Much interest was caused in the neighbour-
> hood on Monday afternoon when about 1.30
> pm an aeroplane, flying fairly high was
> sighted. It approached from the direction of
> Brighton and proceeded northwards over
> Crowborough at a rapid speed. The machine
> appeared to be of a new type.

If all aircraft over the parish today were to be recorded by the local paper, it would require a major publication each week!!

Flower Show Committee Circa 1937
Standing from the left: Sid Smith from Loudwell, Cyril Muddle, Dud Simmonds, of The Grange Cottages, Albert Wood, then, everybody says it should be Cecil Godley but Cecil is adamant it's not him! Peter Chewter.Seated: Charlie Muddle from Bull Cottage, Steven Divall gardener at the Toll, Mr Jakeman gardener at Hadlow House, Frank Barden and Harold Kingsland gardener at The Grange.

Parked in Dawn Johnson's field, between the New Inn and Providence Chapel July 27th 1922

Each summer this mission caravan, denomination unknown, came to the village and provided fun and instruction for the children. Joyce Jessett remembers being told about a similar mission that visited a site on Broomfields Farm and baptised people in the river.

Fancy Dress Parade Circa 1945
Back Row John Muddle, Muriel Knight, Hazel Packham, Adult unknown, June Toop, Adult unknown, Richard Knight, Jean Kingsland, Hubert Knight, Chris Greenwood [as the political slogan, "Houses for all"] Front Row John Archer Evacuee, dressed in rabbit skins and newspapers, depicting "No blooming coupons", Phyliss Packham, Sally Taff, Jennifer Hazleden, Elizabeth Rickets [Union flag], Margaret Cottingham, Wendy Hartfield, Chris Rickets, Victor Toop.

The iron industry in the Weald dates back to the Romans and beyond. However, it was during the 16th century that this area became famed for its production of ordnance. Testing was obviously necessary and one site in the parish was Gun Bank Farm. The guns were situated on the south side of the river in Blackboys and fired over the water and adjoining meadow safely into the earth bank of the wood. The guns could be cooled using the stream and inevitably some balls were lost. The present owner, Steve Biggs, has found two, believed to be from deck cannon; they weigh 1.6 and 1.8 kilograms each. Although there must have been other sites in the parish none have come to our attention. One rather smaller ball was found some years ago on Scocus Farm.

Poultry represented a very large part of the farming economy, with both laying and fattening flocks. Cramming was an enormous and very widespread industry which had been carried on in this area for at least 150 years. With the trade requiring farmers, butchers, millers, crate makers, higglers, transport, feather buyers, auctioneers and consumers most people in Hadlow Down would have been drawn into the net somewhere along the line. Cottagers would keep just a few fowls, smallholders perhaps a few hundred and larger farmers kept flocks of thousands. Chicks were reared locally but frequently imported, often from Kent and on occasion from Southern Ireland. Generally those who hatched and grew the chicks, often free range, passed them on, frequently via the higgler, to specialist

Wallis Leeves at Spoods farm, cramming chicken
December 1915 Six months later he died in the trenches
in France

crammers who preferred not to be involved in rearing the birds. The fatteners usually kept them for five weeks. For the first three, they were housed and fed intensively, followed by two weeks of twice daily cramming. Which meant filling the crop with a gruel, consisting of ground oats, butchers fat and skimmed milk. The trade suffered a serious decline during the second world war and died out soon afterwards.

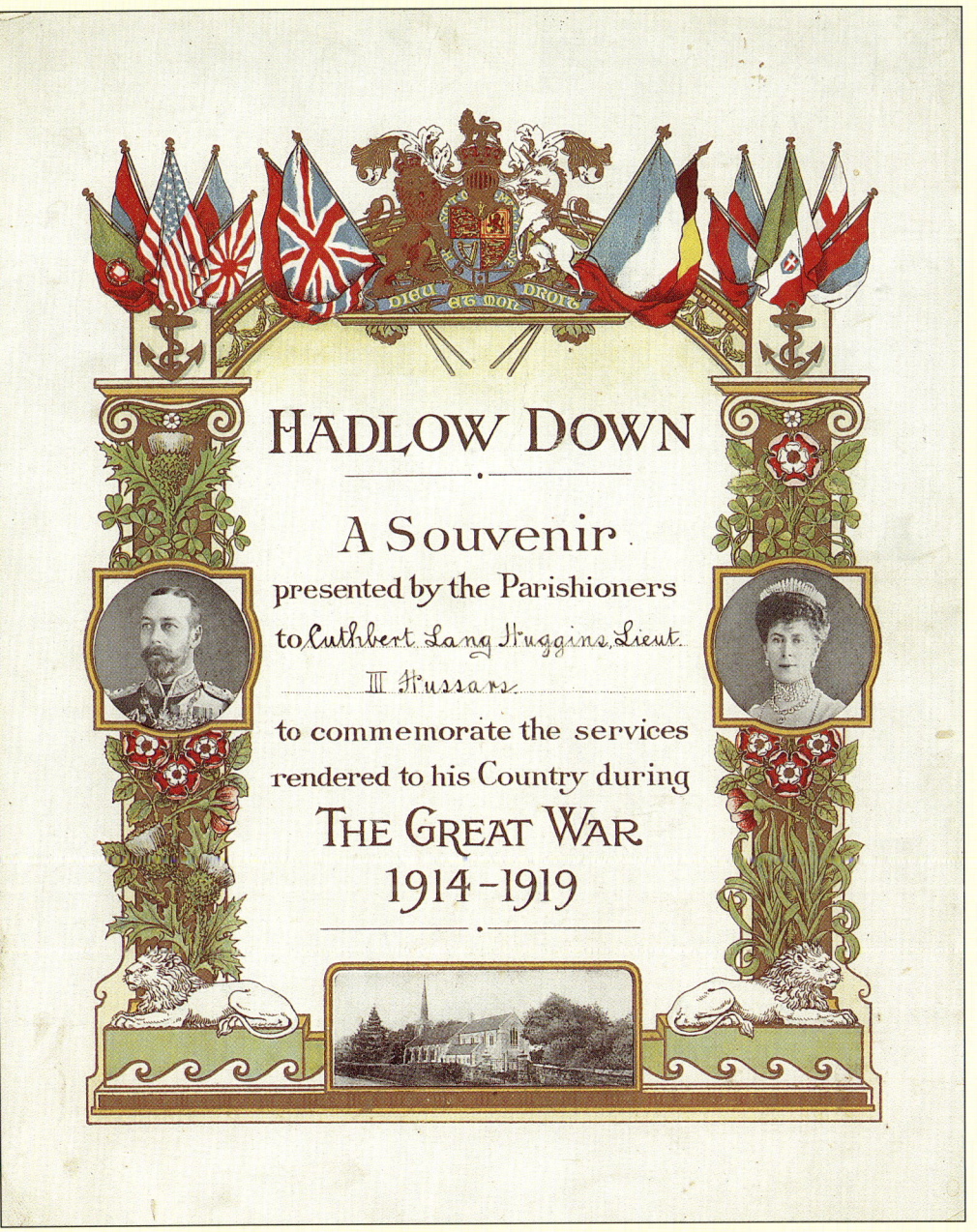

HADLOW DOWN

· A Souvenir ·

presented by the Parishioners

to Cuthbert Lang Huggins, Lieut.

III Hussars

to commemorate the services

rendered to his Country during

THE GREAT WAR

1914 – 1919

DIEU ET MON DROIT

Awarded by the Parish Council to all men
who returned from the Great War

Before rebuilding

After rebuilding

Hadlow Down crested china

John Loader Maffey married Dorothy Gladys Huggins

Presented to exhibitors at the early rallies

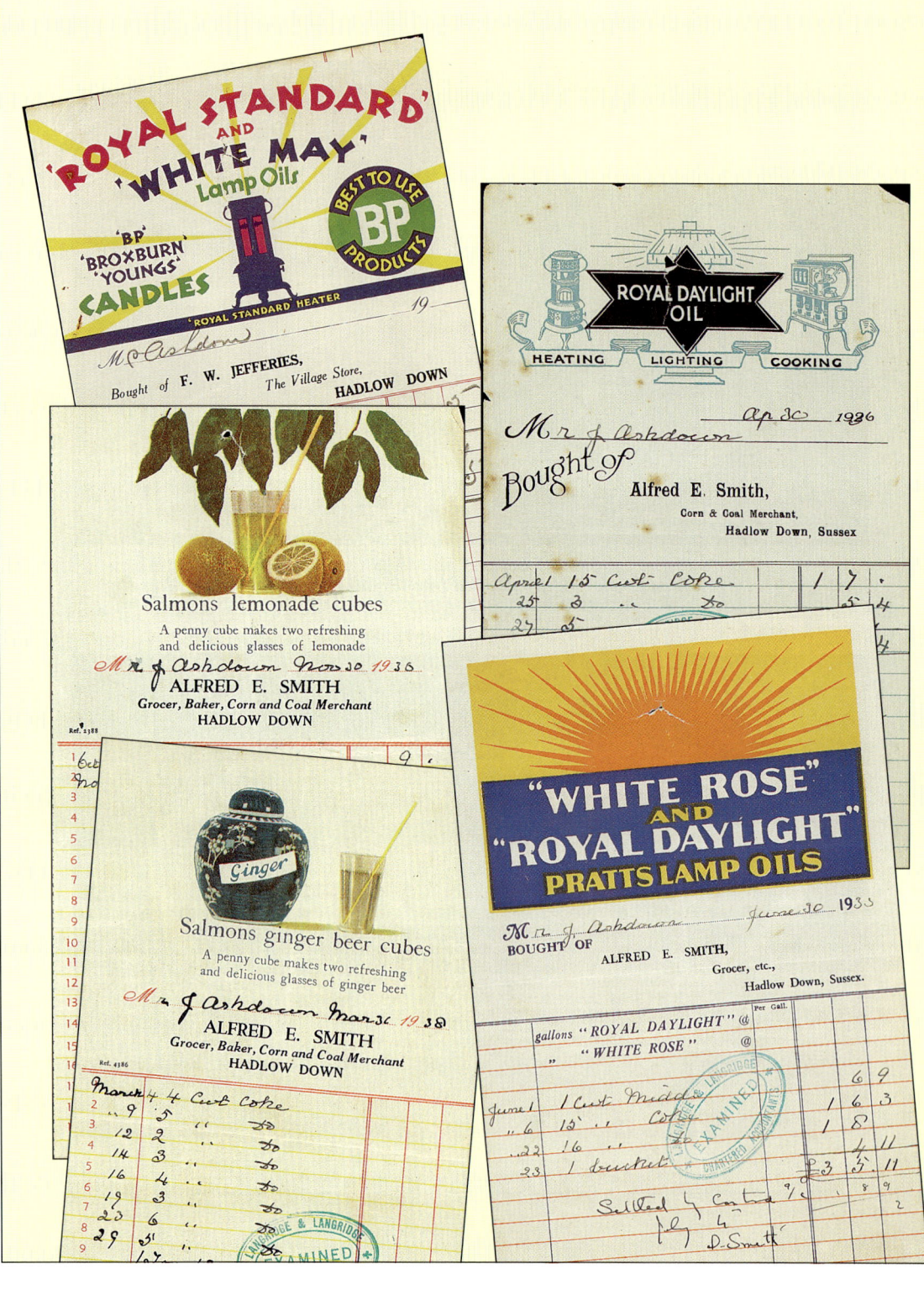

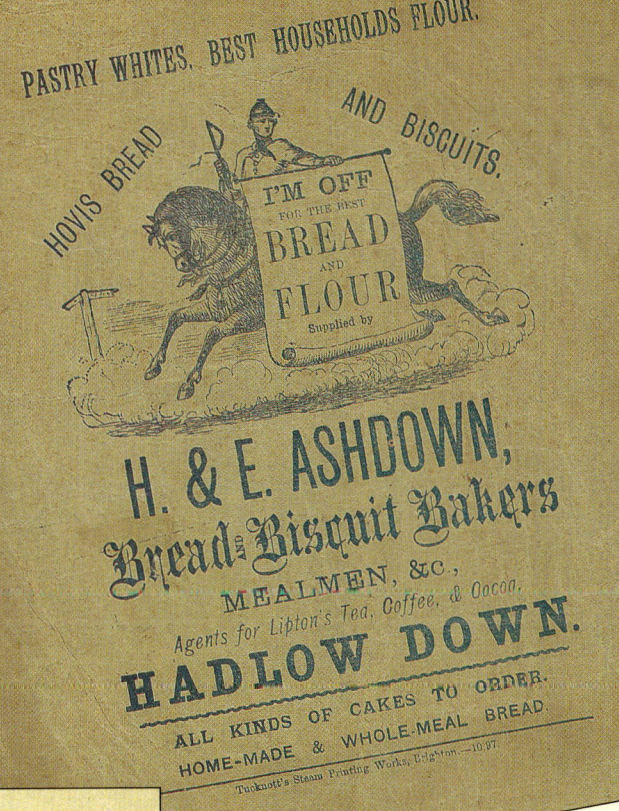
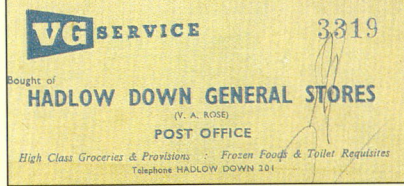
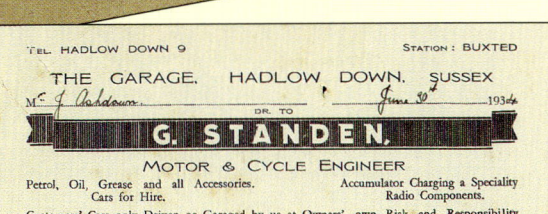

Watercolour by Mr Edward L. Laurenson R.A. His wife, Charlotte, was also a distinguished artist. They lived at Nurney, now Wildwood, in Wilderness Lane during the 1930s.

DRAWN ON STONE BY C. HENMAN CLERK OF THE WORKS.   W. MOSELEY ESQ.R ARCH.T   HENRY JOHNSON BUILDER.

WEST · VIEW · OF · MARKS · CHAPEL · HADLOW · DOWN

BUXTED · SUSSEX

1836

Hastingford. Mr Hoath the farmer, centre. James Walters behind.

Hastingford House as two cottages, one with two bedrooms and the other three, both with kitchen, scullery and earth closet. Alfred Walters is pictured in his mothers arms.

Hop picking at Hastingford. Back row Winifred Walters, Lily, Nellie, James Walters, Alfred. Front Jack and May, sitting

Colonel Coode haymaking at Curtains Hill Farm, during the War.

The Fry family, Nashes Farm. From the left Jesse, Robert, Albert, Henry, Charles and Joe

Henry Fry haymaking.

Joy and Gordon Long's cows going to grass. Cecil Godley is helping because of illness.

For many years the twice-daily sight of the Long's cows ambling along the A272 from Fir Tree Farm in Wilderness Lane was commonplace enough. The cows' placid and unconcerned journey took no note of any annoyance to motorists, stressful though it may have been for Joy and Gordon. A most effective form of rural traffic calming.

Alf Smith's wood cutting gang in Waste Wood, 1914/18.

Guides and Brownies led by Joy Godfrey-Faussett, third from the left, centre row.

Brigadier General Godfrey Faussett

Taken from '70 years of Scouting in Uckfield District', by Faith Lee.

"The Brigadier came to Scouting late in life after retiring from the Army. Inspired by his son's enthusiasm he quickly became a leading light in the movement, respected by all who came into contact with him. "He was a gentleman who gave many Scouters vision and drive to go for the boy. His actual rank I do not know, you never bothered with such matters when he was around." "He was great on discipline and the trainees would do anything for him"

You could lead a horse to water
And Godfrey could Faussett to drink.

1st Hadlow Down Scouts, started in 1924. Brigadier General Godfrey Faussett far right.

He retired from Scouting due to ill health in 1941 and died in 1942 aged 73. Interestingly the Brigadier fought in the Boer War and later in his career came up with the idea of laying telephone lines in war zones. The Army clearly found the idea fairly outlandish but gave him permission to conduct experiments. The lines frequently didn't last very long but were quickly replaced and the initiative led to the formation of the Royal Corps of Signals. Lord Baden Powell who also fought in the Boer War founded Scouting, partly at least, because of the boy runners that he had used there to carry messages around. So the Brigadier who became such a champion of Scouting and a supporter of Baden Powell actually moved the foundations of scouting and wartime communications forward in the name of progress.

Luther Godley, Proud father

Sussex Express

12th February 1914

"THE BIRTH RATE-In another column we allude to the report of the Medical Officer of the Rural Council for this part of Sussex wherein he makes mention of a decline in the birth rate. Hadlow Down has, judging by recent events, not laid itself open to a charge in this respect, for during the past six weeks three pairs of twins have arrived, the last of which two girls, were presented to Mr Godley on Tuesday. [Bertha and Kitty Mitchell]"

Stewart Grainger and his children

Elspeth March his ex-wife lived at Annes in Wilderness Lane and he visited them from time to time. Circa 1954/56

"The young prince wearing jersey and slacks, strides out manfully behind his mother on a visit to watch a meet of The Eridge Hunt in Sussex. The country air brought the colour to his cheeks. But should he have gone? Is this really healthy fun? Or is it as some critics say organised cruelty".

from Illustrated Dec 1956

Sussex Express

30th November 1956

> "The Queen and Duke of Cornwall spent the week end at Uckfield House, the residence of Lord and Lady Rupert Neville. On Saturday morning The Queen and Prince Charles visited Hadlow Down to watch a meet of the Eridge Hunt. The Marchioness of Abergavenny is one of three joint masters. Villagers were surprised and delighted when The Queen and Prince Charles got out of the car and took up a vantage point on a piece of rough ground."

This "piece of rough ground" is the field behind The New Inn!! some folks have no respect. A letter to the now Prince of Wales produced the reply that he couldn't remember the occasion. Most of us in the parish would be amazed that he could forget it. At the time there was a lady living in a caravan behind the pub. She saw Gerald and said "I saw The Queen today she walked past my window". Gerald replied "yes and I am the King of Siam" a little later, learning more, he had to apologise.

Tea Ladies at The Fete. Circa 1956.
From the left. Florrie Camshall, Nancy Lucas,
Bertha Stevens and Nellie Packham.

Henry James William Bray
who confuses us by signing his work
J.W.H. Bray

Mr Bray was a professional photographer who
lived with his wife and family in Cherry Tree
cottage from 1919 to 1926, before moving to
Seaford. We are grateful for the legacy of pictures
he left, many of which are included in this book.
His shop and studio was on Mutton Hall Hill,
Heathfield.

Extracts from a W.I. competition entry written by Grace Greenwood from Fairlight Glen Farm, in the mid 1960s:

"Hadlow Down was the 4th in East Sussex to start a Women's Institute, the first meeting was held in the Gate House Chapel. It was soon found that there was quite a lot of talent among the members and a choir and drama group were soon going strong.

During the 19th century Hadlow Down was a farming community. As usual in those days the pay varied from as low as 9 shillings to 15 shillings per week, with cottage rent, milk and 100 house faggots free. People with large families found it hard to manage, but with rabbits for the trapping and where they were able a pig kept to be sold, or the best cuts and some good fat pieces left hanging up for dumplings and frying, well it all helped. Then in September came Hop–picking. Mum and the children would be off each day for a fortnight or so and in good years earn enough to set the children up in clothes for the winter and some coal for warmth.

WI drama 'Snowed Up With a Duchess'

What distances the men used to walk to work; often from Hadlow Down to Isfield. Of course they knew the short cuts and the rights of way, but they must have been tired at the end of the day. Never the less some of them found time for practical jokes. On seeing a neighbour late one night asleep and thoroughly drunk in his donkey cart outside his cottage. Some young men lifted him indoors, then took the wheels of the small cart, took that in , reassembled it, put the donkey back in the shafts, the old chap still out to the world back in the cart and left him. One can just imagine his amazement when he awoke in the morning."

Grace was not the only author in the family. Husband Bert tried his hand a few years later in the parish magazine March 1987:

Home Guard Duty

"Colonel Coode of Five Chimneys was Platoon Commander when I joined the Home Guard in 43/44. I remember we had a very mild winter that year. We had to 'sit in' at Old Boot Cottage - Miss Barrow lived there in those days - on telephone duty. The phone only rang once while I was there and that was just the Colonel making sure we were awake.

We were very well armed – at first we had 1st World War rifles and ammunition, but they took those away and gave us new ones but no ammunition. Perhaps we were supposed to club the enemy to death with them."

SMALL HOLDINGS

HADLOW DOWN, MAYFIELD, SUSSEX

ABOUT 3 MILES FROM BUXTED AND HEATHFIELD STATIONS, L.B.& S.C.R.

VALUABLE

FREEHOLD INVESTMENTS

BUILDING SITES, PLEASURE AND POULTRY FARMS,

TO BE SOLD BY AUCTION, BY MESSRS.

H.J.AUSTEN&SONS

AT THE SWAN HOTEL, TUNBRIDGE WELLS,

ON FRIDAY, MAY THE 8TH, 1896,

AT FOUR O'CLOCK, P.M., IN 3 LOTS, BY ORDER OF MR. GEORGE LARKING, COMPRISING

LOT 1.—Part of

SPOODS FARM

Containing about **10a. 1r. 13p.** of Hop, Arable, and Woodland, together with the
FARM HOUSE, STABLE, COW LODGE, &c.,

In the occupation of Mr. James Winter, together with Lot 2 at the rental of £35 per annum

LOT 2.

TWO ENCLOSURES OF GRASS LAND

And a piece of Woodland adjoining Lot 1, containing 4a. 1r. 20p. in the occupation of Mr. James Winter.

LOT 3.

ANOTHER PORTION OF SPOODS FARM

Containing **6a. 0r. 7p.** of GRASS LAND with a piece of Garden Ground, and inter-
sected by a stream, together with the Stable, Cart Shed, Cow Lodge, &c.,

In the occupation of Mr. John Packham, at the rental of £14 per annum

Each of the above Lots possesses good road frontages with choice Building Sites for the erection of Residences, and
are well watered and timbered, and also form admirable small holdings for which there is now such a demand.

*In spite of the auctioneer's hype in 1896, evidently no roadside residences were built
or smallholdings created*

This poster is thought to refer to Upper Spoods as long before 1896 Spoods was part of the Abergavenny Estate. George Larking was a Miller and Game dealer who lived at Moons Mill Farm, now Broomfields, just over the border in Blackboys.

Hadlow House Circa 1949

The origins of Hadlow House fall into the dim and distant past although it is believed to date from Henry VII, around 1485. For some 200 years from the late 1600's it was home to the Day family and at this time the house was most likely a very substantial farmhouse. It is thought to have undergone some alteration and enlargement before the 15th August 1871 when the Hadlow Estate, then 893 acres was bought by the Abergavenny Estate for £42,950. Possibly further work was required to establish the Dower House, which it duly became. The Duncanson family who were resident during the second war are remembered by many as supporters and benefactors of the village. For one year only the annual flower show combined with a Fair was held in the field opposite. The present conversion dividing the Mansion house into two plus old Hadlow House was effected in 1962

Tom Dummer, who occupied No. 1, now deceased, wrote...

"With such history extending back over the centuries the presence of a family ghost is hardly unexpected. The identity of Uncle George, is not clear. Quiet and gentle in disposition but not without a mischievous bent, George, it is said often appears when someone is in trouble. Notwithstanding, he has nevertheless a penchant until quite recently for banging drawers, taking down pictures off the wall and putting holly in shoes. Moreover, he always appeared more frequently around Christmas time. Who was he? We will never know, after a gentle and compassionate exorcism ceremony in 1990 his presence is no more and peace and tranquility now reign throughout the entirety of Hadlow House."

Displaced persons enjoy a drink together in Hadlow House gardens. Circa 1948

Peter Zenka remembers…

"During the last war the Army took over Hadlow House, firstly for Canadian Soldiers and then between 1947 and 1949 a contingent of 50 to 60 displaced persons [POWs] mainly Latvian but including a couple of Ukrainians and one Polish moved in. The house was run by a couple who were employed by the council with residents housed 6/10 to a room. The age range was 21 to 45 and all men. The POWs enjoyed being there because we were free of the Russians and knew if we returned to Latvia we would be shot by the Soviets under Stalin. There were no problems integrating into Hadlow Down and the council found us work on local farms."

On the road to Buxted

Toll Farm was for many years occupied by Colonel Lambert and his family. He ran a business producing a product called 'Lawnsand' a dressing designed to improve garden lawns. The recipe, no doubt a closely guarded secret was rumored to include mercury. Certainly one man who worked there claimed that his teeth went black and he had to buy a new pair of boots every month because they just fell to pieces on his feet. The firm had a stand at the Chelsea Flower Show where the product was much acclaimed and on one occasion a member of the Royal Family took a leaflet.

Although no research for this publication has been carried out some have claimed that The Toll was originally a Toll Gate. This is hotly denied by Heather Kirkley, who was brought up there. She maintains that in 1926 the remains of an old snow plough dumped on the side of the road was mistaken for the decaying gate post of the toll and gave rise to the myth.

A piece of local mythology which, it must be said, is unsubstantiated, tells the tale of how during the last war around the time of D-Day, General Eisenhower, who was a friend of Colonel Lambert, used to visit the Toll and regarded the haven as a bolt hole in times of stress. However, it was a little more than that, for at the time he was supposedly conducting a clandestine relationship with his lady chauffeur and the Toll provided the venue for a discrete liaison.

Interior of the Toll circa 1914

Five Sisters Corner, opposite Spotted Cow Lane. So named because it was part of Toll Farm and owned by Samuel Hammersley, of Saxon Court. During the 1950s Samuel gave the green to the council and at the same time planted five Whitebeam trees, one for each of his daughters: Penelope, Jill, Priscilla, Jenniver, and Phillipa. Two of them blew down in the Great Storm and were subsequently replaced by Jenniver. There are other trees on the green, origin unknown, probably self-seeded.

Tinkers Lane cleared at last

Ray and Jean Campbell lived at Loudwell Farm in the winter of 1962/3. Snowed up, with the milk tanker unable to get in for 16 weeks proved tiresome. The milk was taken out by tractor over the horse field opposite and through the garden of the Brooms to the main road. The army at Maresfield offered help and sent four men with two shovels for the day. As by the next morning the snow had drifted in and you couldn't see where they had been working, the initiative was abandoned. Jean bred Airedale Terriers which compounded the problem, so eventually a phone call to the R.S.P.C.A. to report the dogs were starving brought instant help in the form of three council bulldozers. They cleared the lane and made a mountain of snow in Claude Jessett's field. Once again people could walk in the road, instead of on the tops of the hedges.

The Great Storm which hit this part of the country in the early hours of Friday 16th October 1987 brought havoc to the village and surrounding parish, but it was a time when villagers pulled together and supported each other. The scars of that terrible and terrifying occasion are still visible within the rural environment of East Sussex. The whole county, along with other parts of the south-east, suffered immense damage in just a few hours, unfortunately it was a catastrophe endured by many. The spirit shown then by people with a common problem, resurrected the neighbourliness of bye gone days.

The Brooms. Just one of the six million trees lost in Sussex.

There were few, if any, properties that escaped damage on that fateful night, although fortunately there was no loss of life. Telephone and electricity lines were damaged right across the south-east. For most, electricity was restored within two weeks, the telephone often taking much longer especially in outlying areas.

Most roofs lost at least a few tiles or gutters, trees however caused the biggest display. The Brooms, pictured above, lost sixteen mature trees which was a common story, whilst Wilderness Wood sitting on the ridge was devastated.

Tony Honess and family contemplating the clear up. Root plates like this were a common sight for many months.

With no electricity for fourteen days, cooking food presented the biggest challenge. At the time Mavis Farrar worked for the County Schools Meal Service and managed to obtain permission for the school canteen to be opened and used as a communal kitchen. People brought their food along for Mavis to cook, she appraised the situation and told them when to return. One lady arrived with a brace of pheasants and the request, "perhaps you could sort these out for me". To their credit they did!

113

The Huggins family December 1912

Standing from the left: Betty Huggins, Rupert Huggins, Gilbert Huggins, Christine Huggins, Elsie Huggins, Kitty Costello, Eddie Costello V.C. Sylvia Costello nee Huggins, Basil Huggins, Cuthbert Huggins. Sitting: John Maffey [Lord Rugby] Mrs C.L. Huggins, with grandaughter Penelope Maffey, Charles Lang Huggins, Dorothy Maffey nee Huggins.

Chapter Nine

THE FOLKS IN THE BIG HOUSE

by Meg Rostron and Peter Gillies

"people say falsely that there was no link of affection between the families of squire and labourer".

For well over 100 years the eyes of the village were trained on The Grange and its occupants. The family is reputed to have taken up residence in the late 18th century. The first name we have is Benjamin Hall, who was master of the house early in the nineteenth century; the family continued right up until 1934 when the remaining portions of the estate were sold. They provided a solid mainstay of leadership and direction for the village.

No evidence has been found that either Benjamin or his Great Nephew, Charles Lang Huggins who succeeded him, assumed the title of Squire. It has been suggested that the children in the school were taught to curtsey or touch their caps and say good morning to Squire Huggins but as no newspaper reports of the period appear to use the title it would suggest the children were merely learning respect for their elders in the time honoured fashion. At its height the estate was quite extensive occupying much of the High Street, Wilderness Lane (Grange Road, as it was then called), in addition to several outlying farms. The extent of the estate was testimony to wealth and also gave rise to power, which always seems to have been constructive and benevolent.

When Benjamin moved in the house was called Buxted Lodge and indeed was situated in the parish of Buxted. His main claim to fame was his vision for the church and school along with the energy he expended in campaigning for and orchestrating the fulfillment of his idea.

"There are very many poor children wandering about the lanes in ignorance of almost every duty, moral or religious".

So wrote Benjamin in 1834, towards the end of William IV's reign. Life, always hard for the dwellers in the Weald, with its poor draining soil and atrocious roads, was made more difficult still by the uncertainties brought about by the corn laws. In the circumstances the "Torrents of infidelity", which Benjamin complained of were not to be wondered at. Fired with enthusiasm he and his wife contributed £20 "earnestly wishing it could be more", and expressing the hope that the proposed facilities would help to "subdue the general dissatisfaction among the lower orders at this time so prevalent".

Although the new chapel was consecrated in 1836, plans for the school were lagging behind, it was not until April 1837 that the Rev. Edwards was able to write: "I am happy to inform you that on Monday last the first stone of the house and school were laid by the fair hands of my wife". A tattered fragile old book, now in the East

Bucsted Lodge Sep. 1885

Charles and probably his mother,
before the commencement of his building mania which saw the transformation into The Grange.

Sussex Records Office with the words 'Dr Saunder's Will and Parochial Memoranda' written in spidery copper plate on the brown suede cover records:

> 18th April 1838 the school was opened at Hadlow Down for the admission of children'

Four years of tenacity, overcoming all the frustrations and difficulties had at last borne fruit. On 25th April the official opening took place with a service in the Chapel at 11 o'clock. It is not too difficult to imagine the bright modern buildings gleaming in the April sun, and the excitement of the children at the new world that was opening up before them. A new Queen in London and a fresh beginning in Hadlow Down…, although there would be some regrets to come at the loss of freedom to roam the lanes.

The house that Charles took over from his Uncle looked nothing like the monument he finally left to be sold on his death. It is said that on the birth of each child he extended the house and as his family rose to nine children it helps to explain the ultimate size of the property. By the time he had finished it was nearly one hundred

The drawing room at The Grange, circa 1910

yards from the kitchen to the dining room, which might have been manageable if trolleys could have been used all on one level, unfortunately there were sets of steps in the way, producing a steeple chase for the servants in full livery!

Property appears to have been an abiding passion for Charles. He built Chestnut Cottage in Grange Road in 1891, firstly occupied by the butler and later as a retirement home until her death in 1920, for the family retainer, Nurse Hansford. Buxted Lodge, subsequently renamed Hadlow Lodge also in Grange Road was built for Charles's mother to live in. Corner cottage which used to stand between The

The new wing added in 1905 and Corner Cottage on its original site.

Grange and the main road was moved to its present site on the other side of the cross roads. Presumably this was to make room for more children and yet more extensions. The Lodge to Wilderness Farm, School Lane Cottage, Bermuda Cottage, now Albury House and Holiday Home, now Marlow House were all undertaken as part of the empire he created.

For lesser mortals this would have been more than enough but the village was

Buxted Lodge, Grange Road, now Hadlow Lodge in Wilderness Lane.

faced with the chapel in none too good a state of repair, added to which it was felt to be too small and architecturally rather unfashionable. Prompted no doubt by the memory of Uncle Benjamin and driven by his own devotions, he undertook the rebuilding and remodeling of the Church entirely at his own expense. Clearly financial life in the city and with stockbrokers Huggins and Clark in particular was rewarding. Bearing in mind that Charles had his own private chapel in The Grange, the only benefit to him, if it can be described as such was that a new much quieter bell was hung so as not to disturb those in The Grange. The benefit of the rebuilding to the village must have been considerable.

In the grounds below the house there was a water pump powered by a stationary engine which used to supply not only The Grange itself but also all the estate properties with running water, Coachmans was the site for a header tank, to serve Chestnut Cottage. Properties on the main road evidently had their own storage tanks. It was in the early 1930s that Luther Godley lost his job of looking after the engine and pump

119

Swimming bath picnic

when the mains water came through the village allowing everybody to enjoy the luxury of taps and running water.

A great many of the houses had electric plants, usually a stationary engine and small generator, if you were lucky there might be a bank of accumulators which meant that when the light was switched on the engine started automatically. In Nurney there was a superior lighting system using a special highly refined unleaded petrol which was then pressurised down the pipes and burnt with mantles! The Grange enjoyed gas lighting supplied by their own plant. This was situated opposite the church in a corrugated iron shed, water was dripped on to carbide to make acetylene gas which was then piped to the house for lighting. The village benefitted from mains electricity around 1930 although many parts of the parish had to wait another twenty years or more for such luxury.

The intricate web of employees at The Grange and estate tenants together with Charles's involvement as a J.P., school governor and provider of a venue for many events, must have helped to create the framework of social life and customs in the village,for all concerned.

Sussex Express

September 1914

FOUR SONS SERVING

"The village has contributed no mean quota to the number of sons of Sussex who have responded to the call of their country in her need and they have been set a good example by the inhabitants of "The Grange". Mr Lang Huggins has four sons , all of whom are serving in some capacity. One is a Captain in the Gordon Highlanders, another a Lieutenant in the 3rd Hussars, a third is a Lieutenant in the Hon Artillery Company and the fourth is attached to the aeroplane section of the R.N.V.R. "I have no more sons to send", he told our representative. "but if I had, both Mrs Huggins and myself would gladly let them go. I believe that all single men should go. It is a real patriotism that impels men to join and it knits all closer together. I believe that after this war things will be very much better".

Happily all four sons surived, although war is never discriminatory:

Sussex Express

May 14th 1915

"Mr Charles Arthur Dingwall brother of Mrs C L Huggins of The Grange was on the Lusitania returning from America when it was torpedoed, it is with great regret that his name does not appear on the list of survivors and it is feared that he has perished."

September 1914

SOLDIERS HOSPITAL

"The holiday home where each summer a large number of town workers, by the kindness of Mr C Lang Huggins, spend a recuperative period is being converted into a hospital for convalescents for whom there will be accommodation for twelve. Mr Huggins is having the home suitably fitted and the patients will be sent there by the Soldiers and Sailors Society."

July 1919

PEACE DAY CELEBRATIONS

"By the kindness of Mr C. L. Huggins J.P. the festivities were held in the grounds at Hadlow Grange. The proceedings opened with a dinner to service men, ex-servicemen and their wives, the company numbering nearly a hundred. The discharged men were issued with an ounce of tobacco or packets of twenty cigarettes each. The bonfire and firework display under the direction of Mr Scriven followed and afterwards dancing on the bowling green was kept up till midnight."

The clock on the Stables provided a useful service for those within hearing distance of its chimes. Initially the task of weekly winding fell to the carter but he wasn't much good so the job passed to the chauffeur who wasn't very interested. Like pass the parcel, the task moved on to Luther Godley whom his son Cecil described as "Head Muck in the garden". Luther kept the clock going well but was shrewd enough to realise a younger man was needed so pressed Cecil in 1937 at age 15 into training. There then followed an unbroken 61 years of service until ill health forced retirement.

Whether things were better after the war as Charles had hoped, is, like beauty, "in the eye of the beholder", for Charles at least it must have been a sad time because in 1919 the Huggins family abandoned Hadlow Down and went to live in Eastbourne. An initial sale of the furniture which lasted two days probably satisfied them financially, although today reading the catalogue it appears like an antique dealers dream. The first day made £1886 14s. 6d. and day two a further £1688 17s. 11d. making a grand total of £3575 12s. 5d. which now wouldn't be a quarter enough to buy:

Lot 337

A German 20 H.P. six cylinder Laundaulette, Vandenplas body. SOLD for £425

A month later in April 1919 some 200 acres was sold notably Waghorns and Pigsfoot farms together with farms in Buxted and Blackboys and some properties on the main road. Even after the sales, there were responsibilities to be attended to in the village and possibly the wrench was just too great. Whatever the reason Alf Long the chauffeur continued to take the Rolls down to Eastbourne and bring Charles back to Hadlow Down as frequently as possible until his death in April 1933. Kitty and Bertha Godley remember being given the job of running round the empty house opening all the windows, to air the place, which must have been a major operation in itself.

The balance of the estate, 154 acres and all the properties were offered for sale by auction in September 1933. Those which did not sell, notably The Grange itself, were offered again in April 1934. Mr Ron Ticehurst and his partner Mr Watson from Heathfield bought the house and realising it was far too big they demolished the centre third leaving two very substantial properties.

The family links with the village were not to be finally severed as Charles's son Gilbert and subsequently his grandson Ulric living in the Wilderness, continued as supporters of village life.

FOR SALE
Handsome modern residence with seven reception rooms and billiard room, 30 bed and dressing rooms. Four bathrooms excellent stabling and well established grounds.

Apart from the school and church, there is little left today to provide a direct link with the family. On August 23rd 1907, daughter Dorothy married John Loader Maffey and a small bone china cup and saucer embellished with their initials, was produced. How many there were and how they were distributed is a mystery; at least one survives today (see colour section). The church sports three memorials. The four very attractive windows in the Lady Chapel were given by Charles and Agnes's nine children, as a memorial to their parents after their mother's death. John and Dorothy Maffey's son was only four months old when he died and was buried at sea, they dedicated the stained glass window behind the font to his memory. Sadly Basil Huggins and his wife Rhona, lost three sons during the second world war, and there is a plaque erected to their memory in the Lady Chapel.

Charles died on 15th April 1933 in Eastbourne. A requiem was held in St Peters Church before bringing him back to Hadlow Down. St Mark's was packed and floral tributes abounded. Among them was one from the W.I., one from all the local traders and one from The Grange employees. Representatives from every aspect of his life were there: The Court of Saddlers Company, of which he was a member, and his church and city colleagues adding to the throng of local people. His grave in the south-east corner of the churchyard was 'lined with yew and studded with daffodils'.

For the first time with the obituary of Charles Lang Huggins, and then only in the headline, did the *Sussex Express* use the term which many might feel he had earned, BENEVOLENT SQUIRE.

Chapter Ten

THOMAS FARROW

by Peter Gillies

"Won't it be nice when everyone has three acres and a cow."

Why Mr Farrow consistently quoted his address as Blackboys is a mystery. The house Dewbrook as it was called in the 1920s [now Moons Mill, at the bottom of Tinkers lane] is well inside the parish boundary, although the bulk of the estate may well have stretched into Blackboys and Framfield. He lived here with his wife and family for about nine years from 1909 to at least the end of 1917 and there can be no doubt he must have been the talk of the parish. Only three years later at the end of 1920 he was the talk of the nation.

The late Charlie Leeves who remembered Thomas Farrow well said succinctly,

"He thought he was pretty much of a swell".

Certainly judging by reports that appeared in the *Sussex Express*, Thomas liked to be in the forefront of all that was happening and apparently wanted to be a benefactor and possibly something of 'The Squire'. By the time he arrived in the village Farrows Bank had been established for two years and was to the onlooker a very successful and thriving business with an equally successful and confident Chairman.

The following *Sussex Express* report provides us with a clear picture and even leaves us wondering if Mr Farrow's press officer wrote the article and submitted it on his behalf.

11th November 1910

SPLENDID FIREWORK DISPLAY

"Mr Thomas Farrow Chairman of Farrows Bank Ltd who resides at the beautiful estate known as 'Dewbrook' near Hadlow Down has since his residence there done much to relieve the hum-drum and monotony of village life. He has patronised and organised outdoor and indoor functions of all kinds giving special prominence to sports and pastimes. The Dewbrook cricket team which was raised during the present year and played its matches in Mr Farrows grounds had a victorious career and with one exception defeated every London and local visiting team. On November 5th last year Mr Farrow gave a firework display for the especial benefit of his family and friends and found to his pleasure that a number of local residents put in an appearance.. He promised them that in the following year he would repeat the experiment and on Saturday last upwards of 300 persons visited 'Dewbrook' to witness a display which by universal consent was acknowledged the most brilliant ever seen in the neighbourhood. The fireworks were supplied by the famous firm of Brock and Co and were under the superintendance of a special representative of the firm. After a series of childrens and miscellaneous fireworks had been discharged a reproduction in miniature was given of the well known Crystal Palace display programme including the illumination of the grounds. The fireworks being over a huge bonfire was made, over which sat a majestic Guy Fawkes, while the Hadlow Down Drum and Fife band rendered choice selections of music. Mr and Mrs Farrow were accorded a special vote of thanks by the visitors."

Early in 1911 Thomas embarked on a new venture which was soon to embroil him in controversy. The launch of 'The Sussex Land Bank' to be run on Mutual Credit and Co-operation principals must have seemed to many like a slice of heaven. This was a time of tennant farmers and smallholders when the national economy was still very agriculturally based, cheap credit would not only have been commercially welcomed but thought to be socially desirable by the far sighted patrons.

Problems first appear in a letter to the *Sussex Express* from Mr Henry Devine, a Banker and Author of a book called 'Peoples Co-operative Banks'. Henry complains that Thomas is not providing a Mutual Co-operative Bank for the benefit of its members at all but is merely opening another branch of Farrows Bank for the benefit of the bank and its shareholders. The difficulties were compounded further because Thomas had enlisted the support of over 70 county gentleman as patrons. One of these, Sir William Grantham wrote directly to Thomas and sent a copy to the *Sussex Express*.

Mr and Mrs Farrow and family

"your letter of April 8th in which you repudiate altogether the idea of its being a Land Bank in the usual acceptation of the term and say it is an ordinary Joint Stock Bond carried on for the benefit of the Co. running it. Under these circumstances I must ask you to withdraw my name from your list of Patrons."

The cat was really out of the bag now. Thomas had been publicly exposed for at the very least misrepresentation, at worst fraud and was now being rejected, by his influential friends as others removed their names from his list. Whether it had much commercial impact on him is difficult to tell. The bank had 74 branches and clients who were known as 'Farrovians' received their annual copy of the 'Farrows Bank Gazette'. In November 1911 extracts of letters from grateful customers were printed.

A Farmer writes: "I wish to thank you very much indeed for the prompt and thoughtful way in which you have carried out my business for me. Had I not been able to obtain the assistance you have so kindly offered me I should have sold up and gone to Canada before this".

130

A Smallholder writes: "I thank you and also Mr Farrow for the kindness you have shown me by lending me fifty pounds. It has enabled me to buy some stock and tools to work with and given me a good start.It will be a good thing for smallholders".

A Smallholder writes: "I thank you very much for accepting me as a customer of the Sussex Land Bank. I have found a great benefit from the same in being able to get in my hay harvest and also to be in a position to purchase stock at a bargain price.I wish you success in your project".

A Poultry Farmer writes: "I greatly appreciate Mr Farrow's efforts in promoting a Land Bank. I have obtained financial assistance [at a small percentage of interest] which has enabled me to increase my stock.I intend to do what I can to support the movement".

There being no reason to suppose the letters were anything other than genuine we can only hope they remained as optimistic and supportive in later years.

Further troubles beset Mr Farrow during the year, this time in Hadlow Down itself. Plans were being prepared for Coronation festivities, so in true form Thomas made some suggestions complete with an offer to "defray the greater part of the expense". Bearing in mind his sumptious November 5th celebrations the previous year this should have been an offer for the parish to grab with both hands. However in a letter to the *Sussex Express* on June 20th he complains that his offer although handed to Mr Huggins by the clerk, was then witheld from the committee. Possibly Mr Huggins resented what he may have perceived as a challenge to his unofficial position as Squire of Hadlow Down or perhaps the recent controversy over the Sussex Land Bank was taking its social toll, the truth will probably never be known. The matter spurred Thomas to send a copy of his letter to every resident in the parish! In spite of his efforts the official committee closed ranks and managed to provide a very full and active days celebrations without any competition from Dewbrook.

For the next six years at least Thomas continued in ebullient form to dispel the "Hum-drum and monotony of village life". Charlie Leeves remembered seeing his first ever moving picture at Dewbrook when Thomas brought the equipment down in his car and set it up in a barn for local people to watch. Also with typical Farrow flamboyance the bank had a motor vehicle constructed to look like a money box which drove around the towns promoting the bank allowing people to post their cash deposits through the slits. Mr Winter of Upper Spoods Farm suffered considerable loss when lightning struck his only horse, so in true fashion Thomas started a collection and raised £25 to replace it which probably saved the smallholder from ruin.

The Dewbrook cricket eleven continued to be successful in most of its matches. In June 1912 Mr Farrow basked in glory when he celebrated his Jubilee with a big party attended by family friends and local guests. For once the inevitable cricket match seems to have been given a miss but the Hadlow Down Drum and Fife band provided a selection of music. The Rev Wassell from the Gatehouse Chapel thanked Mr Farrow for the life he had brought into the district and expressed the hope that he would continue to reside at Dewbrook for many years. The last known date for our hero still to be in Hadlow Down is when his address appears in an advertisement for the bank dated November 1917.

There had never been any suggestion that the Bank was anything other than sound and in 1920 an approach was made from an American finance company to take over Farrows Bank. It seems to have been a fairly sloppy deal with Mr William Read, the representative of Norton Read and Co. accepting everything at face value. They were presumably further heartened when at the A.G.M. Mr Farrow announced the dividend was to be increased to 6.25%. Eventually the books were checked properly followed by the bombshell announcement that the balance sheet was a complete sham. The inevitable happened in December 1920 when the bank's operations were suspended and Thomas Farrow along with his assistant William Crotch were arrested to appear at the Old Bailey charged with conspiracy to defraud. The balance sheets showed the value of the bank had increased from £640.000 to nearly £4,800,000 in ten years but it was all lies. Thomas had been engaging in 'imaginative property valuation' simply massaging the figures in order to make the books look good. There was little support for them either in court or in the country as so many of the customers were people with small savings who could ill afford the loss, the very people Thomas had championed and declared he wanted to help. They were each sentenced to four years in prison.

It is interesting to note that in 1910 when The Mutual and Co-operative movements were considered so important and receiving the support and patronage of many influential people, Thomas may well have been contributing to his own downfall in trying to exploit the system by misrepresenting the Sussex Land Bank for personal gain. Today the position has evolved full circle and there are those trying to convince us that the system is out of date and should be dismantled for personal gain.

Thomas Farrow has been described as "a mixture of a well meaning booby and a scheming deceiver". Let the *Sussex Express* have the last word.

Sussex Express:

November 1910

MR THOMAS FARROW'S GENEROSITY

"He forwarded a cheque for 100 guineas towards the relief fund which has been started by Sir William Dunn M.P. on behalf of the unfortunate depositors in the now defunct Charing Cross "Bank".

Dewbrook staff circa 1911
Frank Leeves, Under-gardener is standing on the left. The others are unknown.

AUSTRALIA

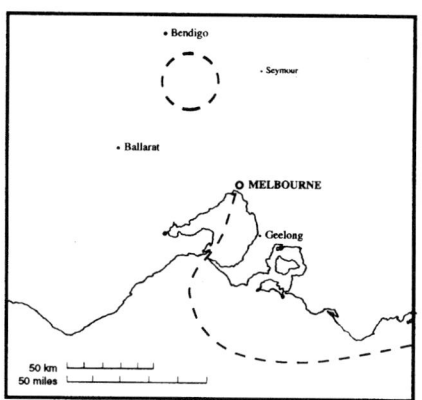

- Bendigo

- Seymour

- Ballarat

○ MELBOURNE

Geelong

50 km
50 miles

USA

NEVADA

LAS VEGAS

ARIZONA

NEW MEXICO

CALIFORNIA

- Flagstaff

- Gallup

Santa Fe .

ALBUQUERQUE

• PHOENIX

•TUSCON

Nogales
Nogales
Nogales

TEXAS

150 km
150 miles

MEXICO

Chapter Eleven

THE BLACK SHEEP

by Rosemary Alexander

"… made up my mind I would leave home."

[Every effort has been made to replicate the spellings used in the original letters]

Martha Austin bought her house [then called Ivy Cottage, subsequently The Bakehouse and today called Cobwebs] in Wilderness Lane for £3 in 'lawful English money', but that was in 1821. Though unable to sign her name on the Will which was witnessed by Maria Anne Stone, William Olive, and Owen Stone in 1826, she was obviously a woman of substance, being the owner of a tenanted cottage in Robertsbridge as well. The fact that she was a spinster, with two natural sons, John and William, hints at a colourful history. When Martha died in December 1839, John inherited the property in the Manor of Robertsbridge, and William now with a wife named Emmis brought up a family of eight children at Ivy Cottage. Their third born was a son called Thomas, The Black Sheep.

William and Emmis Austin's family papers lay undisturbed in the loft of Ivy Cottage for nearly 100 years and now provide us with a snapshot of Thomas' life, after he left Hadlow Down never to return.

Was Thomas Austin born restless, or were the neighbours surprised when, in 1850, he ran away to sea? Subsequent adventures indicate the urge to seek wider horizons was not the result of a single family quarrel. Whatever his failings, he did not lack

135

courage. The voyage to New York, in a wooden sailing ship, huddled in darkness below deck for a large part of the time, breathing an odour compounded of stinking ballast,

Ivy Cottage

unwashed human bodies, and the cows, sheep, and goats which provided food on the voyage, must have been far from comfortable. He'd be lucky to get a bunk to sleep in. Performing natural functions entailed squatting in the heads. And on top of everything else there were the rats... rats by the hundred, swarming everywhere.

His first letter home, dated May 5th, 1850, simply told his parents he had arrived safely.

"Dear Father and Mother

I left London on Friday March 15th and we went quite sharp all the first week and then we had very bad wether all the rest of the time, at two days before Good Friday we had it very ruf and on Good Friday there was a vessel wracked just by us, but not nere a one life lost and we lay in sight of land three days before we could get in."

The second, more than a month later, betrays an aching homesickness, and goes some way to explain the sudden departure.

**TO
PARTIES DESIROUS OF EMIGRATING
TO AMERICA.**

18 **48.**

THE GOOD

BRIG CREDO,

Of *Aberystwyth, John Humphreys, Master,*

WILL SAIL FROM THAT PORT (WEATHER PERMITTING)

FOR QUEBEC DIRECT,

On the 4th of April next,

And will take PASSENGERS upon the following terms and conditions :—

	£	s.	d.		s.	d.	
Adults, 14 years of age and upwards -	3	0	0	with	5	0	head money
Children, 1 year and under 14 of age -	1	10	0	,,	2	6	,, ,,
Infants, under 12 months				- Free.			

Passengers to find their own Provisions, &c., and the Ship will find Water, Fuel, and Bed Places.

As a limited number only will be engaged, the Passage should be secured by the 13th of March at the latest, at which time a deposit of £2 for each Adult, and £1 each Child must be made, which will be forfeited in the event of the Passenger declining the Voyage. The Passengers to be on board not later than Monday, the 3rd of April, when they will be required to pay the remainder of the Passage Money, and the Head Money.

☞ *Any further information that may be required, can be obtained on application to Mr. Thomas Jones, at the Ropewalk, or to the Master on board.*

J. COX, PRINTER AND STATIONER, PIER STREET, ABERYSTWYTH.

Although we have no information as to where Thomas embarked, a poster like this may well have been instrumental in luring him to the Colonies.

137

"you both said you would never have no peace whilst I were with you so I should think you would have plenty now I am away.. if Father had let me go to Plumpton that Thursday I should not have come to America."

Repeated requests for news of old friends in subsequent correspondence show how much he missed Hadlow Down, and how many villagers travelled overseas in search of adventure. He asks after:

"...old Harssell...that yoused to be a Baker at Mayfield town opposite the Oak as I saw him...just before I got your last letter and he tolde me he woode call and see you..."

"...tell olde Fumbele foot Samuel Sands that I live next door to his neighbour. Chas Potter not five steps aparte."

Mr. Sands was the lame occupant of Old Boot Cottage, pictured in Alice Day's 'Glimpses of Rural Life in Sussex', father of ten, and husband to the formidable Ann. There are enquiries of Mercy Mugridge who may have been a former girlfriend. and 'Butcher' seems to have been a brother's nickname.

There was clearly no shortage of work, soon after arrival:

"a man come to me and asked me if I wanted work on a farm for he woold give 18 shillings a week and board and logings, that is about 9 or 8 of our english money. So wen you hear abowt money you just ask if it is english or yancka"

By November 1850 he had reverted to his roots in the building trade, working for a Mr Alonzoe Fairchild, in Schenectady, State of New York.

"Dear father

now I wright a little sketch of their forme of houses and living here. They build theire houses thus, all houses have got a seller six or eight feet deepe and thirty two feet by twenty two for a common house with a kitchen and bedroom and small hall on the bottom floure, two roomes upstairs but the master and mistres of the house mostly have a bed in the corner of the kitchen or the small bedroom downstairs with no fireplace nor oven but they have a large stove with four hobs on the top for a pot or a kettle and a oven in the middle of it so convenient for whomen. Shooerly I wish you could see it.

Now theire plans of building here, they donte build a scaffold here as you do on both sides the wall but from the inside and lay all the owtesiders over-handed and they lay five coarse of brick stretching and then a header and I have built a chimbelmey fourty feet high without any scaffold it was five feet square with two foot walls".

During the next three years he mentions...

"travelling about from one plaice to another, this is a bewtiful contery with shouger a growing and orrangies etc."

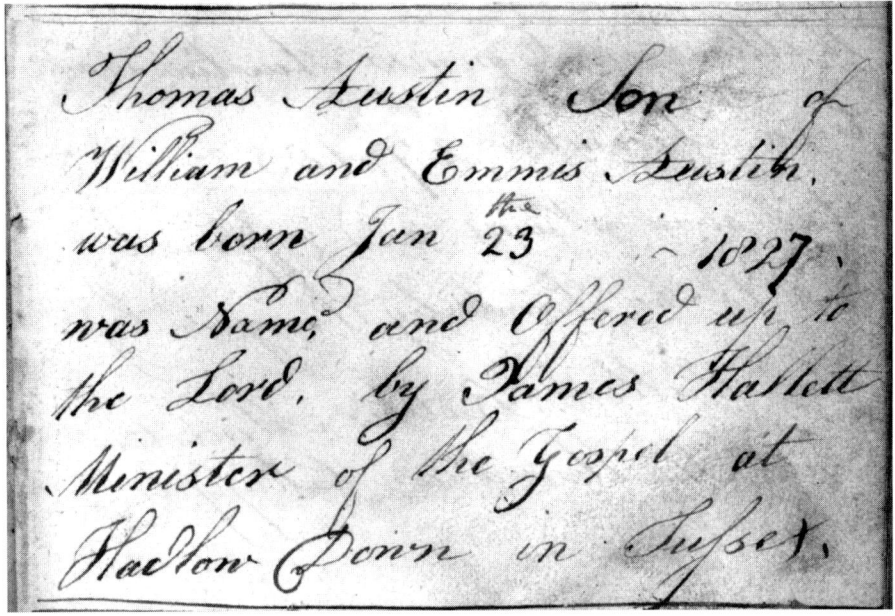

Thomas Austin's entry in the family book

January 1853 from California he writes:

"I have been travelling. I have not seen a house for eight months sometimes on snow and ice ten feet thick and at other times 150 miles without water but then amongst all this there is pleasure at all times seeing all kinds of wild animals such as Buffalowes, Dear, Elcke, Antilope, Bearse both Grisely and Brown Bearse and the Buffalowes as many as two thousand or three thousand at a time and I did have sporte with them I tell you. But the fourth of July last I was almost frose to deathe and wrapt up in two pairs of blankets a crossing the Rocky mountains. California is a butifull country with unexhaustiable supply of gold and if a man can make his self at home here for a yeare or two he can make something to lay up.

Thomas evidently did not settle in California because a letter dated November 1853 is posted from Creswick Creek, New South Wales, Australia. He mentions having visited Peru, Mexico, and the South Sea islands, these countries were probably included in the itinerary. Finally, he joined the gold prospectors:

"I am on the gold fields again and digging the precious mettel from the earth. How often doo I wish I had someone here I new to cook my grub for me wen I have don my days work I woold be so happy. You dont no wat it is to be in a foren country without any friends or relations near you so I have got pretty well used to baking damper and cooking meat and tea now. I have put in a small speciment of Gold...if you get this safe I will send a bigger piese..."

In another letter he writes:

"I have been very unfortunate lately, I sunk a hole threw the rock 100ft. In all 260 ft deep lost six months time and spent about £100 and have lost it which ould of turned me out from 15 to 20 hundred pounds then I shud of come home but now I must wait until I can get another goulden hole before I can come home I cannot say how long that will bee but I hope I may get one soon."

January 1855 Geelong Victoria New South Wales he writes:

"The next letter you will receive your Australian daughter that you have never seane will write then you may expect more news than I send you".

Now married to Ann, he is still bedevilled by the lack of friends and relations.

"I found out where my grandfather is in Sydney about six months ago. He is living at Richmond near Sydney he has a public house and a brickyard he was then quite well considering the advance age of 98 years."

Meeting a former villager '...James Addams, the Wheale Wright' provided little consolation. They only had time to exchange a few words. The following May his wife asks

"If there is anyone from about Buxted or Hadlow Down emigrated to the coloneys, Tom would be glad to see them."

She,too, mentions James Addams, who 'he saw one Sunday night but not since'. Thomas takes over the pen to ask about John Brooks, the carpenter, how many children he has, and sends love to Mr. and Mrs. Ashdown... the first mention of a family destined to play an important role in the Austin's history, as one of Thomas's sisters married John Ashdown at the age of twenty-four.

William Austin's remaining sons left home in 1856, by which time, far away in Australia, Thomas had a boy of his own, named William Alonzo.

"Born last Christmas morning about half past severn o'clock so he came in time to have a bit of pudding for his dinner, he is a nice little thing you ould like to see him. His hair has been falling of or I ould send you a bit but I will send you a bit in my next letter".

Another undated letter obviously written during this period refers fondly to his son, and begs his mother to 'tell Mrs. Bennett to write and asks whether old Harry Bridges is still alive'. The longing to show off his children to the Sussex relatives is plain. In the same year that Thomas's mother, Emmis Austin, followed her husband to Hadlow Down graveyard, poor Thomas suffered yet another blow, the death of a 6-month-old baby.

As the eldest son, much responsibility falls on Thomas and he tries to care by proxy for his two youngest sisters who were under age. With the help of a friend in the village, he poses the question of whether the girls would like to join him in Australia.

August 8th 1859 Thomas writes:

Dear friend

"If the girels come out here the best way wold be to come out under goverment if you wold plese to see about it. For in a government ship there is everything provided for them in first rate stile and if they are sick there is a Docktor and nurse and then there is constables to keep the sailors from interrupting on them".

Though he doesn't mention the fact it seems likely that his brother William then aged thirty, probably emigrated to join him in Australia but no mention is ever made of the girls. There was no reason to keep in touch with the Old Country, now his loved ones were dead. Nothing more is heard of the 'black sheep' until January 1st, 1884, when an inquest was held on William Austin, bricklayer, drowned in the river Campaspe. Thomas Austin gave evidence that, because forty years ago the deceased met with an accident, he began to drink, a weakness which may have accounted for the ultimate tragedy.

What happened to Thomas, Ann, and their children ? How many Australian descendants are unaware of their links with Hadlow Down?

Some years later in 1907 the entire Funnell family emigrated to Canada; only one letter, also found in Ivy Cottage roofspace, has survived.

"Dear Mary and Harry   12th July 1907 SS Victorian Belle Isle Straits.

I am begining this letter before we reach port as I believe there will be a chance to post it where we leave the mails on Saturday. We are well and jolly had to have the baby vaccinated today as no one is allowed to land unless they have been done. I will give you just a brief summary of our journey from Liverpool. We sailed at 5pm on Friday and went by the Northian route, we passed the Isle of Mann just before dark and on Saturday morning when we got up we were passing the north of Ireland, and the sea was getting very choppy and people begining to be sick, and during the morning all the family were bad with one exception, myself. I never had a twist in my little Mary, and had a busy day looking after the rest. My gum she did toss and roll something Hawful on Saturday but afterwards the sea was as smooth as a gals bottom, there were about 1,000 bad some for three days there was spue Heverywhere, a funny thing some of the ladies were sick at both ends and then knelt down and kissed and cuddled it, it was a sight believe me.

Wednesday evening, when about 100 miles from Belle Island we ran into a fog and at 9.30pm we had to stop as we had been told the previous night by S.S.

Virginian that there were icebergs about. We steamed past one very large Iceberg about a mile away and have seen 9 altogether. This morning it was bitterly cold, but now as I am writing we are in the Gulf of St Lawrence and it is getting quite warm. By the time we get up tomorrow morning Saturday it will be hot and we shall be in the river St Lawrence, had it not been for the fog we should have reached Quebec on Thursday night but now it will be Sunday."

Unable to post the letter as he had hoped it continues

"21st July 1907   Toronto.

We landed at Quebec on Sunday last about 2.30pm [that would be 7.30pm at Hadlow Down]. I had to go to the shed and find our baggage we had 9 lots and I found them in 8 different places and got them checked and passed by the Customs Officer. We boarded a train for Montreal which place we reached at 5.30am on Monday morning and reached here at 7.30pm. I guess it was hot we slept at a Government Hotel and in the morning I and Stan went to the imigration office, we had plenty of offers for farm work but the pay was too low not near as much as we were given to understand at home. At 11am I went to the office of The Grand Trunk Railway and saw the foreman. He said, "what do you want" I replied "Work". He said "Come right here in your working clothes at 7 tomorrow morning". I went the next day and was put in the Bonded shed, and have been there since, at $40 a month. Elsie also got a crib on Tuesday a large sell everything stores she is on piece work, her money will run to about $25 a month. Stan has not got anything yet, he had an offer to be bound to a jeweler for 4 years at $3½ a week but that wont do I want him to get a temporary job and then learn telegraphy and go on the railway as there is a great demand all over canada for them. Toronto is a lovely place all the streets are from N to S and E to W.........every 3rd each way the trams run they do..........miles an hour. If you dont get out of the way they will go over you. Oh I forgot to tell you all we did on Tuesday. Elsie went out and got three rooms, we are living in now they are $3 a week. We are trying to get a house, a decent one in the town with 6 rooms costs about 18s per week. I know one party who has a seven roomed house at 28s per week and sublets 4 of the rooms for 55s per week. We have got one chap who wants to lodge with us and will bring a friend, they will pay $4 for board and lodging. Taken all round living as we did at home costs about the same.

I suppose you have seen the papers about the accidents to other ships where we were fog bound, we were lucky. I think this is all this time with love we remain

All the lot of us

A Funnell
Emily Funnell
Stanley Funnell
Dorothy Funnell
Bertie & Joyce"

CANADA
WANTS MEN
TO TILL THE SOIL

Farming in Canada
means
100% Annual Profit.

Get a piece of the earth — in the Empire — under the Flag. Canada's land is freehold land. Two years' rent of a British Farm will purchase improved land of equal area in Canada — Britain's nearest overseas dominion. 160 acres Government land free for farming. Work for all farm labourers and domestic servants guaran-

IN THE EMPIRE. UNDER THE FLAG.
GET A PIECE OF THE EARTH.
CANADA'S LAND IS FREEHOLD LAND.
TWO YEARS' RENT of a British Farm
will Purchase improved land of equal area in
CANADA
BRITAIN'S NEAREST OVERSEAS DOMINION.
160 ACRES GOVERNMENT LAND
FREE FOR FARMING.
Canadian Wheat realised this year
60/- an acre for an expenditure of 30/-
WORK FOR ALL FARM LABOURERS
AND DOMESTIC SERVANTS.
Canadian Institutions are Built on British Model
For free maps, pamphlets and full particulars
apply to Mr. J. OBED SMITH, Assistant Super-
tendent of Canadian Emigration, 11 & 12, Charing
Cross, London, S.W.

VICTORIA
THE GARDEN STATE OF AUSTRALIA.
THE LAND OF SUNSHINE AND OPPORTUNITY.
THE GOVERNMENT OF VICTORIA
OFFER TO
SMALL CAPITALISTS,
FARMERS,
MARKET GARDENERS,
FRUIT GROWERS,
DAIRY FARMERS, etc.,
Blocks of IRRIGATED LAND on EASY
Crops all the year round. Magnificent
Splendid climate (300 days of sunshine).
passage £6.
DOMESTIC SERVANTS also red
wages. Passage £3. Employment
The Victorian Government Represen-
in your district shortly, to give all in
(There is also a big demand for
Tradesmen for Melbourne). Writ
in first instance to
BEAVER JONES, CHAN
Authorised Agents for the Vict
Etc., 26, DRURY LANE.

iculars,
sistant
11 and

50,000,000
ACRES

LAND FOR THE MILLION.
50,000,000 Acres of LAND
open for SETTLERS in
WESTERN AUSTRALIA
FREE GRANTS of 160 ACRES.
Assisted passages offered to Farmers,
Farm Labourers, Vignerons, Orchardists,
Market Gardeners and Domestic Servants.
For Illustrated Pamphlets and further particulars apply to the
Agent-General for Western Australia, 15, Victoria Street,
London, S.W.

Turn of the century advertisements
encouraging emigration

143

Chapter Twelve

ONE MAN AND HIS ENGINE

by David Skinner

"I was trusted to drive a team of oxen to Lewes market...
They went up hill as fast as down."

If you go a few paces South West from the West door of the Hadlow Down Church you may notice a distinctive black marble headstone in the form of a wheel. Engraved upon it are a builders trowel, a sickle, a set of engineer's callipers and an anchor. This is Claude Jessett's grave and the symbols represent his interests in life. Claude was better known in latter years for his steam engines than for his farming, fishing or building, his most enduring legacy being the annual Tinkers Park steam engine rally which he started in the sixties.

Claude the grandson of George Bracher, the Hadlow Down Village blacksmith was born in Hastings but after the death of his father the young Claude and his mother moved back to her family home of Bracherlands at the East end of Hadlow Down. When he left school Claude was apprenticed to the forge engineering works at Cross in Hand who in those days were still repairing the council's steam rollers. It may have been this that kindled his interest in steam engines.

In 1942 while still in his early twenties, Claude bought his first steam engine. This was a Burrell Gold Medal Steam Tractor named 'The Tinker'. He found it parked on the Ashdown Forest where it had been used for timber hauling but he had to go to London to purchase it for £25 from its owners.

Claude's interest in steam engines grew and in the 1960s he bought a steam roller named Daisy from a scrap yard in Newhaven on the day that it was to be cut up. Claude and his friend the late Bob Douglas, who at that time lived in No 2 Beech Villas steamed it back to Hadlow Down from Newhaven. Bob was normally employed as chauffeur to the Huggins family in the village. Later Claude acquired 'The Pensioner' which was once owned by Jimmy Jupp a well known employee of Benjamin Wares brickyard in Uckfield. He also acquired a Wallis and Stevens 'The Golden Queen' an Aveling and Porter roller called 'Topsy', a Tasker 8 section roller, a small portable engine and another larger portable from the saw mills at Isenhurst.

In the 1960's Claude started on the construction of a light railway to run round his land adjacent to Tinkers Lane . His first locomotive was a diesel then in the 1970's he added steam.

For a number of years in the early sixties Claude and his wife Joyce visited a steam rally at Elham near Canterbury and people pressed them to have something

1999 Rally. Tractors, cars, lorries, auto jumble and steam.

similar with their engines at home. So in 1966 they held the first Tinkers Park Traction Engine Rally on the fields adjacent to Tinkers Lane, which gave the event its name. This Traction Engine Meet, as the first one was called, was intended to be a low key affair held on Saturday afternoon only. A special Constable was allocated to control the traffic in and out of the field. When he arrived he said he was not expecting much to do as most people would be attending the Heathfield Show which was on at the same time. By mid afternoon the same Constable was telephoning for assistance!

In addition to Claude's engines 5 or 6 others attended. John White, one of his several names, arranged for a number of engines to attend on their way to the Polegate rally which was to be held the following weekend. Unfortunately Mr. White did not tell the engine owners about this diversion! On the day of the rally no drivers for these engines turned up so Claude, wishing to be helpful, lit up the engines and people drove them around. It was only later that this prank came to light. The Harrises, famous for their travelling fairground rides, were also there with two of their smaller rides. At the end of the day they asked Claude if he intended to repeat the event the next year and if so could they come again. Now Claude knew that the Harris family had a very nice old set of gallopers, roundabout to us normal folk. These were last used

1999 Rally. Steamers and Harrises gallopers

147

in 1952 for the coronation celebrations after which they had been put into storage. This was too good an opportunity for Claude to miss so he said that they could only come to the next year's event if they brought their gallopers.

That first event was a great success. The entrance charge was 2s.6d and that covered the costs. People around the site with collecting tins raised £100 for Cancer Research Campaign, in today's money that would be around £800.

With so many things to look after Claude could not manage alone. There were many local and not so local volunteers whose help made the early events possible. Luther Mitchell looked after the small portable, which ran a threshing drum demonstration, and Arthur Mantle who came from Robertsbridge, drove The Golden Queen. Owen Mitchell cared for Topsy which he and Claude converted back to its original form, a tractor, but with the addition of twisted brass a dynamo and lights around the canopy to make it a Showman's Tractor. On completion of the conversion in 1967 they renamed it 'The Southern Queen'.

The second rally and all subsequent ones were two-day events. The Harrises did attend and so did their gallopers. Additional attractions in the arena were added. Over the years these included The White Tornadoes motorcycle team, Clown Paddywack and his comedy car, a Juggling Act, Sheep Shearing, a tightrope Act, The Southdown Highlanders Junior Pipe band, The Rainbow Steel Band, The Crawley Corps of Drums, Wright Brothers Motor Cycle Stunt Team, Chris Julians Gyrocopter Display, Leone and Tanya a swaypole and trapeze act, J.C. Diamond escapologist, The great Blondini and his exploding coffin, The amazing Magnus a strong man, The Battling Cumberland Giants and Vera Mcleod and her Dancing Horse Sorrell. Vera was the wife of Tex Mcleod a cowboy film star in the late 1920s.

Most people would have found such a collection of steam engines quite enough to cope with, but not so Claude and Joyce. They also collected fair ground and dance band organs. The first to arrive, in 1963,was a 48 key Limmonaire called The Silver Cherub. This was followed in 1966 by an 88 key Bursens dance organ then in the early 70s a Mortier and a 52 keyless Ruth in 1974. In 1976 they obtained two further organs, a 60 key Richter and a 72 key Marenghi fair organ. Others arrived in the late 70s. The 1990s saw the addition of an 87 key Gavioli and a 35 key Bursens to the collection. Some of the organs were in poor condition when they arrived and some deteriorated further in storage but over the years work has been done to bring them

Kevin Meayers adjusts the Gavioli, July 1999

back to playing condition. Initially this work was undertaken by Victor Chiappa from Clerkenwell but the majority has now been done by Kevin Meayers from Hemel Hempstead.

The organs in the Jessett collection have always played an important part in the steam engine rallies and for a period in the mid 70s a separate Organ Festival was held in September to raise additional funds to support the traction engine rally.

Peter Gillies remembers…

"I recollect Claude saying he wanted to include a barbecue and roast a pig or bullock [always had big ideas did Claude] but couldn't find anyone to take it on. Like walking into a well sprung trap I said "I couldn't see a problem all that was needed was a spit with some means of turning it and a fire". "You're on" said Claude with considerable enthusiasm. I didn't think much more about it until next time I saw him, whereupon I was treated to a conducted tour of 'The Spit', complete with a reduction gearbox to obtain the right speed, driven by a Lister D stationary engine and a fire basket underneath. Undoubtedly I was 'ON'. Fortunately my wife, Delia, was game to give it a try so my big mouth found some moral support. The whole escapade settled down to a slightly more reasonable level when Tottingworth Abattoir, in Heathfield suggested a Pony of beef which they boned and rolled ready for the job and we decided to start the cooking off in Joyce's oven. I don't know if it was cheating or cowardice, but it was certainly wise; at least we didn't get any complaints. When the great day arrived I discovered there was another surprise, a chef's outfit complete with a silly hat, freshly laundered and snowy white, all ready to wear! Everything was going really well when somebody asked, "When will it be ready?" It was a very good question but pretty pointless asking us, we hadn't got a clue. After much ponderous consideration, apparently careful thought and with great aplomb three o'clock was announced; that gave us a couple of hours of peace and quiet. What we hadn't reckoned with was the queue that started forming well before-hand and was growing at the same rate as my confidence was fading. Finally with both meat and queue gone we sighed and relaxed; whether it was a financial success I don't know. If Claude had stopped to think about how many portions we needed to sell, I'm sure he didn't tell me and I certainly didn't even think about it. We did it for two years before the Organ Festival was abandoned."

Over the years an affinity has grown up between the Tinkers Park rally and the New Inn. On the Saturday evening many of the steam engines leave the rally field and steam along the main road to park outside the pub. Regular visitors to Tinkers Park know this happens and wait around for the engines to arrive. The atmosphere is noisy but good natured. The bar is crowded usually to the point of overflowing, but there is probably more talking than drinking going on. As dusk approaches the engines leave the pub and return to the rally field for the night, whilst under cover of darkness their drivers return to the pub for the evening session. This follows a fairly predictable pattern each year. It starts with more drinking than talking then engine problems are discussed and technical matters are aired in progressively louder but less coherent voices. The same old legends are retold, probably with more embellishments than the previous year and soon Dave Young dressed in his old top hat gives in to very little pressure and sings the Thigh Knacker song. Late in the night, often too late, people wander back to bed on the rally field.

1999 Rally. What else are pavements for?

Although the site at Tinkers Park is a lot smaller than those used by many other steam engine rallies it is still very popular and usually attracts between four and five thousand people each year. One year it achieved ten thousand. In the early years parking was not too well organised and very long tailbacks developed along the main road. One year Joyce was watching some of the more inconsiderate actions of motorists and said to an AA man standing nearby: "I just can't understand some people". His reply was to foretell the coming of today's road rage problem, "Madam" he said, "they are not people they are motorists".

From the mid 70s the 3rd Haywards Heath Boy Scouts took over running the car parking and things improved greatly but as ever in this country even the best made plans can be confounded by our weather. One year it was so wet that no cars could get out of the field without a tow from a tractor or other four wheel drive vehicle. The result was mud everywhere. All over the field, the entrance and exit gateways and worst of all the main road. The policemen on duty were looking decidedly displeased so people with shovels, spades and brooms tried to clear it up but it was a lost battle. The conversation was just turning to the cost of a council cleanup operation coming out of that year's takings when Alan Stiller, from Upper Spoods arrived with a mechanical road sweeper and saved the day.

1999 Rally. Early on Saturday morning. Add two thousand people and stir.

Ever since the first rally in 1966 all the profit, with the exception of a small contingency fund held to cover loss making years, have been donated to The Cancer Research Campaign. By the end of the 1998 event the total donation had passed £100,000.

It would not be fair to omit from this account the voice of a tiny minority in the village of Hadlow Down whom would rather do without the inconvenience of delays on the main road for two days a year or those who complained about the terrifying explosions that came from Clown Paddywack's comedy car. However I do not expect that it stops them basking in the reflected glory when our village is mentioned for its magnificent contribution to a good cause.

And what of Claude? He died in 1987 one day after the great storm of that year. Like his rally he was not universally popular in the village, but then no one who does anything significant ever is. Joyce and her band of helpers continue the rally and most would agree that it is a very good thing. Alongside Claude now are his two old engine mates from the village, Owen and Luther Mitchell. God Bless them all.

1977 Organ Festival
From the left Dave Smith, Reg Packham, Alec Moore, Arthur Mantle, Jim Blades, Owen Mitchell, Tony Reene, Andrew Reene, John Pullen, Stephen Epps, Robin Neale, George Epps, Anthony Pullen, Sid Moore, Harry Urben, Joyce Jessett, Brian Gent, Claude Jessett, John Blades, Norman Hobbs, Bertha Mitchell, Graham Arding.

ROLL OF HONOUR   GREAT WAR 1914 18

HARRY EARL ALCE	CHARLES HEASMAN
LAURENCE ARTHUR BACKHURST	FRANK HOATH
LEWIS JOHN BALDOCK	ARCHIE HOLDING
HARVEY MORRIS BEALE	ALBERT GEORGE HUMPHREY
WILLIAM THOMAS BOTTING	JOHN JARRETT
WILLIAM CARR	FRANK RICHARD KIDD
JOHN HENRY CARTER	ALBERT KINGSLAND
HENRY THOMAS CARTER	GILBERT J LAING
CHARLES CORNFORD	HARRY G S LAING
GEOFFREY CORNWALL	FREDERICK H LANGRIDGE
GEORGE REGINALD DANIELS	FREDERICK LEE
GILBERT JOSEPH DANIELS	FRANK LEEVES
HERBERT DANN	WALLACE LEEVES
CHARLES STANLEY DANN	FREDERICK HAROLD MITCHELL
HERBERT DAWSON	HENRY FREDERICK NOAKES
LEONARD DAWSON	ARTHUR CHARLES PACKHAM
FRANK DIVALL	HENRY WILLIAM POPE M C
CHARLES EDWARD EASTWOOD	FRANK SAUNDERS
FRANK EASTWOOD	EDMUND SPENCER SMITH
THOMAS WILLIAM FENNER	JACK SMITH
HERBERT GARTON	WILLIAM WICKENS
PERCY HALL	CHARLIE WINTER
SIDNEY HALL	ERNEST WOOD

1939 — 1945

ANDREW BAILEY	THOMAS PARDOE
CYRIL DABSON	FREDERICK ROGERS
JEROME DUNCANSON	THOMAS SIVERS
FRANCIS HAZELDEN	EDMUND THEOBALD
ALLAN KINGSLAND	JOHN WOOD

IN HONOURED MEMORY OF THOSE WHO HAVE GIVEN THEIR LIVES FOR THEIR KING AND COUNTRY

Chapter Thirteen

FOR KING AND COUNTRY

---

by Gerald Standen

*"reminds me of his great grandfather, Sargeant Martin, who
served in the Battle of Waterloo under Colonel de Blanc, a great
uncle of my own".*

My Father once said to me on joining the R.A.F. "Never volunteer for anything without knowing what you are letting yourself in for". However when this book was promulgated I did undertake to deal with the war history of the village not realizing how much there was. Fortunately I have a good memory and an interest in history, particularly military.

The second part of the chapter is mainly concerned with World War 2 from my own recollections but cross checked with many other publications. It is time all this should be documented before being lost in the mists of time and failing memories. I make no apology if I have omitted anyone's bomb story or any other subject. My answer is to do a better one yourself. I dedicate this chapter to the diminishing numbers of "those who were around at the time".

A brief glance at the map will show that this part of England could not fail to be affected by wars on the continent particularly those in France and the Low Countries. As an instance the Romans landed comparatively close [Pevensey] and settled, building villas [traces were found at Howbourne Farm some years ago] and iron foundries in this parish. Traces have also been found i.e. coins and artifacts believed left by the Crusaders on their way to embark for the Continent. Two beacon sites South Beacon and Hardly Beacon are also marked on old maps covering Hadlow Down. No doubt the Ironmasters and Gunmakers in the parts of Mayfield and Buxted

MRS. OWEN PACKHAM

Nurney Cottages, Hadlow Down

This worthy Sussex mother has contributed a noble share to the Empire's Forces. She has seven sons in the Services and an eighth would also have been doing his bit but for the fact that he has been medically rejected. Two sons-in-law of Mrs Packham, who is a widow, are also serving.

PTE. A. E. O. PACKHAM Home Service

PTE. H. PACKHAM The Buffs

PTE. A. C. PACKHAM Middx Regt

PTE. J. PACKHAM Royal Sussex

STOKER F.W. PACKHAM HMS Hindustan

DRIVER T. R. PACKHAM A. S. C.

PTE. G. PACKHAM A. S. C.

DRIVER H. MARTIN R. F. A.

DRIVER G. HILLS A. S. C.

*Sussex Express
1917*

which later became Hadlow Down prospered very well from the wars of the sixteenth and seventeenth centuries.

Apart from the lighting of all the beacons at the threat of the Armada [Macauly], the villages of this area had a long period of peace, there seems little or no reference to the English Civil War.

This changed greatly at the start of the nineteenth century. The Napoleonic Wars brought a very serious risk of invasion to South East England; among the many precautions taken was a survey of the Rape of Pevensey which covered the parishes of Buxted and Mayfield.

This was to include:

> "To remove from an invader, all livestock Horses, Oxen, Cows, sheep and wagons and carts.
>
> The countryman between fifty and sixty years of age for removal of the above.
>
> Local men to assist the army in defence plus all useful implements ie. Spades, Shovels, Pick axes, and similar items of equipment".

Fortunately the invasion threat was averted at the time thanks largely to Trafalgar and the victory at Waterloo. One villager known to have fought at Waterloo was Serjeant William Martin (see following pages).

For the parishioners of Hadlow Down, by now a parish in its own right, a century of peace had followed until August 1914 when World War 1 [The Great War] broke out. Many of our young men soon joined the army and sadly never returned, the casualties for a relatively small population being very high indeed. This was because many volunteers joined at Uckfield into the 5th Battalion Royal Sussex Regiment and in common with the 'Pals' Battalions of our Northern towns, were slaughtered at the same time. On the home front work went on as usual; much of the local woodlands were cut down to satisfy the almost insatiable demand for pit props to help the war effort.

On many days the villagers were reminded of the war by the rumble of gunfire from France, [I remember experiencing the same thing from the battle of France in mid May 1940]. Older people in the village had lifelong memories of all the doors and windows rattling as several hills such as that at Messines were undermined and blown up. There was a total black out, but not much air activity although one Zeppelin was seen, and the nearest bomb dropped was at Frant.

One Canadian soldier who was recuperating at a military hospital in Kent wrote to his sweetheart in this parish saying:

A 26—1 *953086.*

ROYAL HOSPITAL, CHELSEA,
11 April 1870

William Martin _____ by whom an application is preferred for a Pension

is required to answer the following Questions.

Questions	Answers
Where were you born, and when?	at Mayfield, Sussex in 1792
When, and at what place, were you attested, and for what Regiment?	attested for the Militia at Tunbridge Wells in 1813. attested for the Line at Brighton April 1814 for the 95" Regiment (now Rifle Brigade)
Did you enlist for a limited or unlimited period, and how long did you serve in the above Corps?	for seven years — serve 6 years 227 days counting 2 years for Waterloo
Have you served in any other Regiment? If so, state the particulars of such Service	Served in no other Corps.
If you have served abroad, state in what parts of the world, and how long.	in France and Belgium. nearly 4 years
On what account were you discharged? if for disability, state the particulars thereof.	on account of the near expiration of the limited term of service
If you have been wounded or disabled, state in what part of your body, and in what Action, and to what Hospital you were sent in consequence	slightly wounded at Waterloo

William's applications to the Royal Hospital, Chelsea for a pension as a Waterloo veteran.
He enjoyed 9d a day for nearly eight years until he died on 31st March 1878. His wife died ten days before him.

Questions	Answers
Did you sign your Discharge, or only affix your mark thereto? If the former, write your name opposite	*Wm Martins*
State your present age	In my 79ᵗʰ year
State your height	5 ft 6½ inches
Colour of Hair..................	Brown hair but now grey
Colour of Eyes	Blue eyes
Colour of complexion	fresh complexion
State your trade or occupation at the time of enlistment	Labourer on a small farm
State your present trade or occupation..........	I still work at farm work as far as my broken health permits ~~~~~
If you were present at any Capture, Battle, &c., for which Prize Money has been granted, state the name and date thereof, and the Regiment in which you were then serving	I was present at Waterloo, 18ᵗʰ June 1815 in the 95ᵗʰ Regt. 2ⁿᵈ Battalion, Captain de Blanes' Company – Colonel Norcote, and he being disabled,
State the name of your Commanding Officer on that occasion; also, the names of the Captain of your Company, Adjutant, and Quarter-Master, and of any other Officers who were present	Colonel Wilkins, and he being wounded, Major Miller, and he being wounded, Captain Logan commanded The Regiment – The adjutants name was Smith Quarter-Master's name was Ross
State the names of the Serjeant-Major, Quarter-Master Serjeant, and any other of the Non-Commissioned Officers or Privates	Serjeant Major (in 1815) Harris Serjeant Major (in 1819) Fairfoot Serjeant McGrotty acting Quarter Master Serjeant
State the names or numbers of the several Regiments or Corps that were present on the above occasion	The Light Brigade consisted of the 52 Regt 71ˢᵗ Regt 6 Companies of the 95ᵗʰ Regt 2ⁿᵈ Battalion 2 Companies of the 95ᵗʰ Regt 3ʳᵈ Battalion
State the amount of Prize Money you received, and when, where, and by whom it was paid to you..	about 3.13.0 paid in France in 1817

Questions	Answers
If the Applicant served in the Royal Artillery, he is to state likewise the several places at which he served with his Troop or Company...............	
State for what Actions you received Medals	*Waterloo*
State your precise address, adding the nearest Post-town thereto, and the County in which you reside	*Hadlow Doan near Mayfield, Sussex* *but Uckfield is the Po. Town*
Are you in receipt of a Pension from any source? If so, on what account, and did you receive any Gratuity at your discharge	*No*
If discharged without Pension or Gratuity, state on what account	*Time of service having nearly expired* *Wm Martin*

I Certify that the Individual, whose answers are inserted against the above questions, has declared in my presence that he is the actual Person whose services, &c., are described herein; and has exhibited to me the aforesaid Medals.✗

Reginald R. Kirby

for the　　　　　　Staff Officer of Pensioners for the

Brighton District.

(Date) ✓ 29th day of *April 1870*

✗ *medals not pro-duced but can perhaps be certified to ✗ by reference to the Register.*

"The Zeppelins paid us a visit but they got a hot time of it and soon cleared out".

The *Sussex Express* April 1915

A NARROW SHAVE

"Miss N Packham of Hope Farm has received an interesting letter from her brother Private J Packham who is at the front with the Uckfield Company 5th Battalion Royal Sussex Regiment. Private Packham relates how one night they had a hot quarter of an hour, blazing away to such an extent that their rifles got so hot they could hardly hold them "Of course we were getting returns all the time, but I am glad to say that I came out without a scratch and so did all the Hadlow Down boys. I can tell you I had one very narrow escape. I was with a Waldron fellow when a shell burst beside us and blew a part of the other fellows coat away, but neither of us was hurt. You can hear the shells coming through the air but cannot see them. The only thing we can do is go down on the ground and hope for the best."

Alf Smith (6th from left) and his team cutting pit props in Waste Wood

It is believed there was a similar survey to that of the Napoleonic War carried out in 1915. One lighter aspect of the otherwise grim four years was that it brought the villagers into contact with the Canadians who were stationed at Crowborough and ventured this way on their days off, mainly Sundays.

An entry in my mother's autograph book:

Sapper K.C. Keddy 505619 Canadian Engineers

"He was mutt enough to walk seven hundred miles to join up. But would walk twice as far again to get out of it".   Xmas 1916

The 1914/18 war ended with many village people laid low at the time of the Armistice by the 'Spanish flue' epidemic at its worst in October/November 1918.

Peace Day Celebrations at The Grange

Most of the surviving men from the war were back in 1918 and peace day celebrations for the end of the war to end all wars, took place in July 1919

By 1938 the land fit for heroes had not materialized and war clouds were again looming on the horizon. In the Spring of that year a meeting was held to form a village A.R.P. [Air Raid Precaution] squad. At the time of the Munich crisis in late September, gas masks were issued along with details of the accommodation for Women and Children if and when evacuated from London or other threatened cities. This was

Peace Day Celebrations, July 1919.
Entrants for the fancy dress competition outside the Post Office

assessed by 'the Powers that be' to be a fairly safe area.

The evacuation of London took place on September 1st 1939. My father took me to Buxted station "to see the biggest train you'll probably ever see in this part of the world". It was enormous with two locomotives and at its second stop at the platform the front engine was in the cutting by the recreation ground.

Editor's Note – The platform is approx 150yards long and the distance to the cutting is the same, thus accounting for the second stop in the station.

The Mitchell twins entry, Kitty as Mary had a little lamb, whilst Bertha portrays Little Boy Blue, in the garden of Cherry Tree cottage

163

Hadlow Down took over 100 evacuees, apart from those evacuated privately. All those villagers who had cars turned out to ferry the children back and more volunteers arrived at the school to help give them something to eat and drink while they waited for the billeting officers to make the necessary arrangements. I well remember how tea was late that day because everybody from the pub had turned out to help feed the new arrivals. At the time the war broke out on September 3rd quite a few of the village men were already in service being Reservists and members of the Territorial Army. On one occassion, when I was on the train going to school in Lewes, an old lady remarked "When I was a young girl in the last war I sent white feathers to lads like you".

Editors note – In his usual colourful language he explained the situation! The practice of sending white feathers to young men considered to be shirking their patriotic duty, was rife in the Great War.

On another journey being fairly tall and blonde, I was mistaken for a German. This time adopting a strong gutteral accent I explained that my Dornier plane had crashed over Framfield! A stunned silence followed this revelation.Gradually the village affairs settled into a wartime footing, accepting the black out, and with petrol and food rationing gradually increasing, but no real war.

Local Defence Volunteers
Back Row Minnie Coates, Fred Sands, Stan Henton, Unknown, George Standen, Miss Hughes.
Seated Sid Smith, Jim Ashdown, Captain Davies.

On May 10th 1940 the expected Blitzkrieg commenced with the German invasion of France and the Low Countries; such was the rate of the German advance that continental gunfire as in The Great War was heard here on the 18th May. I remember commenting to Father that it was strange to hear thunder on such a fine day but he told me it was the guns in France if I put my ear on the road I would be able to hear and feel the vibrations. I did and he was quite right. With the Dunkirk evacuation the number of Army movements through the village increased greatly. The main road, then the B2102 was the most important route between the channel ports and the military bases around Salisbury Plain. Several village men had become casualties or taken prisoner in the Battle of France.

The Royal Observation Corps bunker at Mayfield. John Tyrell with the binoculars identifies and estimates the planes speed. John Paget calculates the height and Ernie Asdown relays the information to base

This had now become far from a safe area, there was much frantic digging of Air Raid Shelters[mostly crude 'dug outs'] or strengthening of cellars or hopefully strong rooms, with sandbags and boxes of earth.

A Local Defence Volunteer force, later to become the Home Guard, was established here as soon as Anthony Eden announced its formation. There was no shortage of volunteers [the oldest being 73] and the first men turned up with Shotguns, Clubs, Pick axe handles indeed whatever could be found. One man, served loyally if stubbornly throughout the conflict, he refused point blank to sign any papers put before him, steadfastly maintaining that he couldn't write. This only confirmed the old adage of Sussex man "We wont be druv". They were soon to be equipped with Canadian Ross rifles, followed by army uniforms and the LDV armband was replaced, by that of the Home Guard. A practice Rifle Range was set up firing across the driveway into an earth bank at Hole Farm in Wilderness Lane.

By now the threat of invasion was taken seriously; during June and into the Autumn the river from Huggets Furnace through to Buxted and beyond was deepened and widened by John Mowlem and Co. Tank traps and pill boxes were built, many of which still remain today. This was thought to be known as the G.H.Q. line, intended to reinforce the coastal approaches and act as a second line of defence. It must be said that the village was mentioned with others along the ridge, in the plans for operation Sea Lion [The German invasion of Britain].

The first German aircraft seen over here, a Dornier, appeared in the early evening of July 3rd reconnoitering the defence line, another appeared about a fortnight later at midday and later that afternoon the first bombs in this area were dropped, just outside the parish at Jarvis Brook. Surprisingly by then most of the evacuee children had returned to London.

The main events of the Battle of Britain during 1940 as far as we were concerned were.

August 15th the first aerial dogfight when a raid on Croydon Aerodrome was intercepted over here, some bombs were dropped but not in Hadlow Down.

August 16th another raid intercepted; as a result bombs dropped in the east of the parish causeing considerable damage and the two brothers [James and Alfred Berry] who were milking at the time were killed along with thirteen cows at Scocus Farm. Cattle killed on Hadlow Park other bombs in the woods nearby.

August 18th large number of German bombers [Dornier 17s] flew very low over the village returning from a well documented attack on R.A.F. Kenley.

August 30th Heinkel 111 shot down at Roy Hill two crew members killed buried in Uckfield Cemetery. Two crew members baled out and were captured.

September 6th Dog fight approx. 9.00am spitfire shot down at Howbourne Farm, pilot killed.

September 7th Luftwaffe turned their attention to London's docklands, enormous conflagration and reflections lit up the night sky.

September 15th [Now Battle of Britain Day] Dog fight am and pm. Dornier 17 seen shot down near Argos Hill.

October 1st Bombs dropped near Five Ashes school mid afternoon and near Little Broadreed around midnight.

October 7th Messerschmitt BF109 shot down at Mayfield, pilot killed and buried

Heinkel 111 crashed at Roy Hill

in Hadlow Down Churchyard. After the war the body was exhumed and taken to The German Military Cemetery at Cannock Chase.

Editors note – This grave was cared for by a villager all through the war. At the time, few if any, knew who was responsible but there were various rumors of ladies who had lost sons over Germany. Perhaps one found solace in caring for another.

October 27th Bombs dropped at Pigsfoot Farm [now Claylands] slight damage and cattle killed. Later many incendiary bombs dropped near river defence line. By now most of the air activity was at night, odd bombs were dropped but luckily did no damage and there were no casualties.

Every night the bombers of the Luftwaffe could be heard on their way to bomb London or the midland cities. Some days the contrails of high flying fighters could be seen. At night with the total blackout, if the sky was clear, it was possible to see from along the ridge the glow in the sky from a large raid on London. From Curtains Hill a glow in the sky from raids on Portsmouth and Southampton and flashes in the sky from the Cross Channel gun barrage at Dover. Towards the end of the 'night blitz' one could hear that there were even more R.A.F. night fighters in action, to all intents and purposes the 'night blitz' on London ended with a massive raid on May 10th 1941. With the bombing effectively over, because the Luftwaffe had largely moved to Russia, a period of consolidation as far as the village was concerned set in. The Home Guard under Colonel Coode set up their Guard Room in a shed in Dabson's Builders Yard [now Greenacres] with an improved rifle range in the woods down Moon Lane, below Little Hadlow.

Had the invasion ever materialised no doubt Colonel Coodes military experience would have stood the village in good stead. As an indication of his thorough forward planning he was reputed to have got out of bed one night climbed through the window and shinned down the drainpipe before mounting his bicycle and timing the whole journey from bed to the guardhouse.

Stirrup pumps were issued to many houses along the Main Road with a P marking painted on the walls, fence or gate. The army moved into Hadlow House and the Wilderness and were a major part of the daily scene with their movements and 'schemes'. Hardly a day passed without increased air activity nearly all on our side by the RAF and later the United States Air Force. There was not much evidence of the enemy although the south coast suffered almost daily 'hit and run' raids on the coastal towns but they very rarely penetrated this far inland. The army units, nearly all Canadian, were generally well liked and would invite the villagers to their weekly film shows in the hut with very up to date films provided by the Canadian Legions.

The army units in the parish were:

The East Lancashire Regiment [recently returned from India]	Roy Hill
The Royal Army Service Corps. Toronto Scottish Regiment	Hadlow House and The Wilderness
The 2nd Division Royal Canadian Ordnance Corps.	Hadlow House
The Cape Breton Highlanders	Hadlow House
The Royal Sussex Regiment	Hadlow House
Canadian Ordnance Corps.	Hadlow House and The Wilderness

The 1st Division Royal Canadian had a vehicle workshop at Hadlow House and a gun workshop at Five Ashes garage

The Toronto Scottish were probably the best liked. An amusing incident took place in February 1942 when two very drunk soldiers shanghaied Miss Pollocks donkey [Miss Pollock lived at Hyders and the donkey's field was on the southern side of the main road where "Lawton" is now] and coaxed the unwilling beast down to the Wilderness and upstairs!! The C.O. was not amused and for a month the two men had to perform a nightly picket on the gate of the donkey's field.

From January to March 1944 what was later known as the mini blitz occurred. Although the Luftwaffe were over here in some force very little happened. On one occasion a very large object was heard to drop but not discovered until the following September when a 1000 kilo parachute mine was found in Waste Wood, it had to be defused and removed by the army bomb disposal squad. A Junkers 188 bomber was shot down just outside the parish boundary on the night of February 24th . Many people watched this from the main road,

Tom Malloy and Charlie Sayer, Toronto Scottish Regiment. The soldiers were not permitted "civvies" so when they helped out behind the bar villagers provided Hadlow Down uniforms!

fortunately for us the enemies attrition rate proved too high and the so called mini blitz had fizzled out by April.

At about midnight on June 15th the first V1 or popularly named doodlebug went over here on its way to London. An uncanny sight with flaming jet pipes and the peculiar note of its jet engine which when it cut out, caused the bomb to fall to earth with a very high blast explosion. Owing to the fact that Hadlow Down was towards the western edge of what became known as doodlebug alley, we were spared

Captain Geoffrey Cartwright-Dale of the Scottish Toronto Regiment married Miss Prudence Coode from Five Chimneys. The happy couple walked to their reception in The Grange where they and their guests were greeted by the regimental band playing in the garden.

169

the intense concentration. A mere twenty or thirty miles to the east of us, known as 'the fighter area', had a considerable number from mid June until the launching sights were overrun in late August. Three V1s fell in the parish, the nearest to the centre of the village being on the main track in Waste Wood. Fortunately there were no casualties and damage was comparatively slight. The next generation of flying bombs V2s came later and just one fell close to the parish at Inchreed Farm.

In the meantime the last of the Canadians, The Algonquin Regiment, went across to France in late July. They were stationed at Possingworth but made many friends in Hadlow Down as they used to frequent the New Inn and park their Bren Gun Carriers in Wilderness Wood.

On September 17th at about two pm. a vast armada of aircraft towing gliders passed over us, presumably reinforcements for the battle of Arnhiem. The first Meteor jet fighters had by now made an appearance in the skies over here. By the Autumn of 1944 the war in Hadlow Down was entering a quieter period with hopes for its end. The RAF and the USAAF carried on passing over head and at night the flashes and rumbles from the V2 rockets hitting South London could be seen and heard. Some of the village men even came back home on leave from abroad. The winter was quite depressing with shortages and fairly stringent rationing and the disappointment that followed for the many, who thought the war would be over by Christmas. The long awaited end came with the defeat of Germany [V.E. day May 8th] followed by Japan [V.J. Day August 15th]

The celebrations here were fairly low key owing to the small population and so many still in the forces. Fortunately there was not such serious loss of men as in the 1914/18 war because they went into so many different services, instead of their county regiments. Food rationing actually worsened after the armistice and continued until 1954 but the basic petrol ration for domestic use was restored in June 1943 after an absence of three years. Demobilization was much slower than in 1919 and men were still being called up. Many of the young men in the village continued to be seen in their service uniforms well into the 1950's but what they did and where they served is another story.

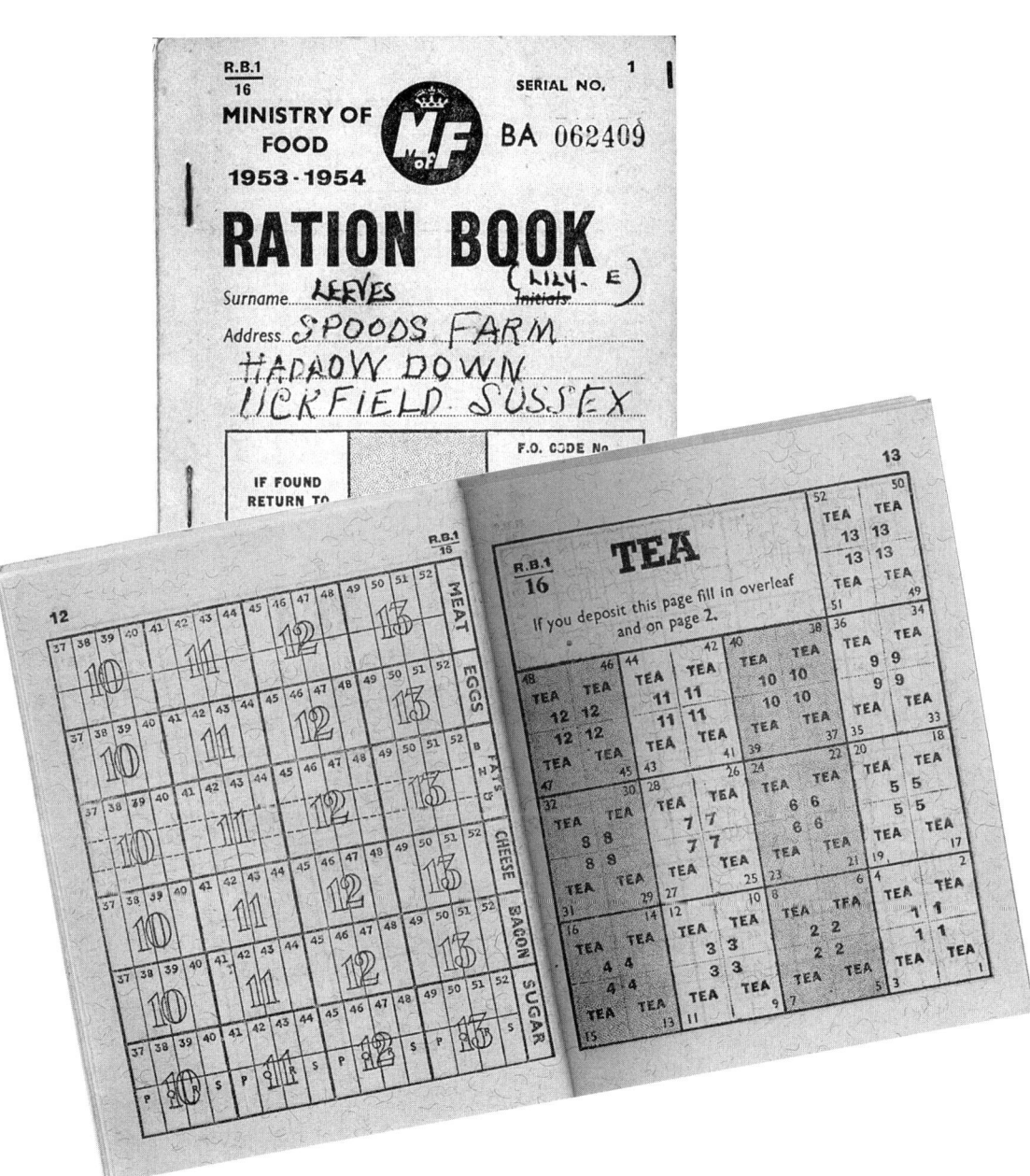

171

8th June, 1946

TO-DAY, AS WE CELEBRATE VICTORY,
I send this personal message to you and
all other boys and girls at school. For
you have shared in the hardships and
dangers of a total war and you have
shared no less in the triumph of the
Allied Nations.

I know you will always feel proud to
belong to a country which was capable
of such supreme effort; proud, too, of
parents and elder brothers and sisters
who by their courage, endurance and
enterprise brought victory. May these
qualities be yours as you grow up and
join in the common effort to establish
among the nations of the world unity
and peace.

George R.I.

Chapter Fourteen

THE CHILDREN'S WAR

by Meg Rostron

*"... and the Bible reading in the day school had helped her
all her life"*

In September 1939, 101 years after the school was founded, it faced its greatest challenge. On April 25th, Miss Gladys Clark, the headmistress accompanied by Miss Hollingsworth the pretty young infant teacher had taken sixteen of us to the Lewes Musical festival where we sang a rather twee school song called Nymphs and Shepherds. Five months later we were singing a very different tune.

> Underneath the spreading chestnut tree,
> Mr. Chamberlain said to me...
> If you wanna get your gasmask free,
> Join the local A.R.P.

To be strictly accurate, it wasn't Mr. Chamberlain who supplied us with gasmasks, but Major Gilbert Huggins and Mr. Jimmy Ashdown, in their capacity as Air Raid Wardens.

Although we didn't realise it then, our closed little world was about to change. The days when as in 1935 we celebrated Empire Day with an "Address on the Empire by General Godfrey Faussett, followed by the singing of national songs, saluting the flag and a hearty rendering of the National Anthem", followed by an even more enthusiastic consumption of buns and lemonade... were gone forever.

In June, Col. Reid M.C., A.R.P organiser for the district, had visited the school

and suggested digging a trench beside the churchyard wall, as a precautionary measure. This was never carried out, but a slit trench was dug in the field opposite, at a later date, but it soon filled with water, and was never used. Later on soldiers of the East Lancashire Regiment sandbagged the north wall and applied yards and yards of sticky tape to the large windows. However the sandbags soon began to leak their contents onto the asphalt, helped by an occasional schoolboys boot and were eventually removed, leaving us with the sole protection of the criss cross patterns of tape on the window panes.

Miss Clark's entry in the log book for August 31st read ' Opened school 9 a.m. Closed school at the end of the afternoon session in accordance with Government instructions. Evacuation scheme comes into operation on September 1st'.

Later that day she attended an Extraordinary General Meeting of the school managers, and said, "If only 100 children were sent it might be possible to fit them in..."

She was concerned, however, about the inadequacy of the sanitary arrangements for such a large influx of children. Her worries were well-founded. In 1936 Pastor Halford, representative of the Baptist chapel, had complained of the state of the lavatories, and after interviewing the cleaner, had arranged for new pails and disinfectant to be purchased. The managers agreed that "More frequent emptying was desirable, twice a week instead of once as before!" It was not until 1940 that the old pails were replaced by Elsan chemical closets, and the cleaner got a wage rise, as he now had to go once a day to empty the one earth closet used by the teachers, as well as once a week to empty the six Elsans.

In the meantime, on September 1st 1939, the children of Gordonbrock Road School, with luggage labels tied round their necks for identification, were marched to Ladywell Southern Railway station to embark on the strangest adventure of their young lives. Norman Johnson, then six years old, recalls how long the journey seemed, and that the train stopped continually. When they finally arrived at Buxted, they were issued with a brown paper carrier bag with some rations to take to wherever they were billeted. Frantic preparations had been made to receive them. At a meeting with the managers, Miss Clark's response to Father Warlow's query as to "whether the present provision for feeding the influx was sufficient", produced the unsatisfactory reply, "all that could be managed was to warm up some milk or Bovril". Father Warlow then suggested that "the Baptist authorities might allow the use of their chapel within 100 yards of the school".

By the 18th September the school was reopened with, as Miss Clark reported, in her laconic manner, "the evacuated children also being taught in the building". In real terms this meant Miss Hollingsworth struggling to teach her infants in the same room as the evacuees of a similar age, plus five teachers and assorted helpers. We older children were crammed into a tiny room along with Miss Clark and Sally the big black curly coated retriever,which was her constant companion. The large room we had occupied before was filled to overflowing with three schoolmasters and an enormous number of kids with strange accents, who made no secret of the fact that they regarded us as country bumpkins. No wonder we stayed at opposite ends of the playground for the first day or two, regarding each other with suspicion.

At least we who lived at a distance were to be liberated from boring sandwiches which the fortunate carried in Oxo tins, whilst the less fortunate had to bear the all-pervading flavour of school satchel with a subtle undertone of gym shoe. We were soon to be able to enjoy the privelege of moaning about school dinners.

The Baptist chapel, always known in the village as the Tin Chapel because of its corrugated iron roof, was a good deal further off than the 100 yards estimated by the vicar. It was a strange venue for a canteen, with its pulpit and walls lined with Biblical texts in the lurid colours beloved by printers of religious books of the times. A local lady, Mrs. Funnel, helped by a lady called Eva did the cooking on oil stoves. Betty Cruden nee Cherryman, now living in Polegate, remembers being waited on by Lady Hamilton from The Grange, Mrs. Hammersley from Saxon Court and Mrs. Eckersley from Five Chimneys. Her favourite days were when we had sprats followed by summer pudding. She recalls Christmas parties arranged by the Baptists, where each child received a present and a huge plate of goodies. Considering these took place in wartime, the generous spirit amongst the congregation left a great impression, particularly as her family were not members of that denomination.

Nothing tickles the nostrils quite so much as the smell of freshly-baked bread on a cold morning. My mile-long walk to school, with our three little boy evacuees trailing along behind, took us past the Ashdown's bakery, where the delicious aroma wafted across the road. In the early days of the war, before rationing really began to pinch, Mr. Ashdown did a nice line in fancy cakes. One little evacuee gazed open-mouthed at a particularly attractive pink iced specimen that Mum had bought, and said innocently,

'We don't get cakes like that in England...'

The same five-year-old, watching my Dad doing the milking, asked,

'Do you have to pour it in at the top first?'

Betty Cherryman who had to walk all the way from Howbourne Lane, used to buy a hot roll for a ha'penny from Bill Ruff's bakery behind Mrs. Smith's sweet shop. Old Mr. England, who lived in Grange Cottage opposite, was usually in there getting the daily pinch of yeast he took as a tonic to keep him young. In palmier pre-war days we could buy all kind of sweets from Mrs. Smith's shop. Now, we had only a measly ration we would buy one of Mr. Ruff's spicy scones to share between two of us. Some boys even bought Oxo cubes to suck as a substitute for sweets.

Back at school, a ha'penny bought us a 'seat' for Mr. Hall's film show. The bearded teacher from London had a film projector and some silent Charlie Chaplin and George Formby films. We thought they were great, but I expect they seemed pretty tame to sophisticated townies!

Although we were expected to walk to the canteen in some sort of order, hardly to be graced by the term 'crocodile', the return after the meal was a glorious free-for-all, with boys swinging from trees and getting up to all kinds of mischief. We girls had a craze one summer for picking seeds of parsley and hog weed plants, and throwing them at each other. They were dreadfully messy, getting stuck in our hair, and down our necks. Unfortunately for Betty, a teacher spotted her putting the seeds in her gasmask tin, and she was sent to The Grange for a telling-off by Sir Robert Hamilton, a very stern-looking man, who resembled King George V. She was understandably terrified, and it certainly put a stop to that particular game.

There are sad memories too. Alan Kingsland whose father was a gardener at The Grange had joined the Navy a year after leaving school. One morning in 1941 we heard that he had gone down with his ship, he was seventeen years old. Another poignant memory is of an Asian boy, an evacuee, who suffered total amnesia after a bomb fell on his home, killing his mother, grandmother, and baby sister. Memory loss was so severe he had to be taught everything from scratch, which made him a target for bullies, who Miss Clark soon 'sorted out'.

Sheila Seaton nee Blackford, who now lives in Bishop Stortford, recalls the day when she almost missed her canteen dinner. A British plane was shot down that morning, and the two airmen baled out. We all stood in the playground watching their slow descent, a world away from sky-diving. One man drifted out of sight. The other hung so limply from his parachute we couldn't tell whether he was dead or alive. As he disappeared behind the trees, Sheila and a few other girls, decided to try to find where he landed. After about half an hour, they discovered him at Stocklands Farm, caught

Tommy Long and the gardening class

177

up in a tree, and watched as villagers arrived to get him down, and carry him to the farmyard on a gate. The girls got into an awful row for that escapade.

A 750-pound bomb made a crater behind the hop gardens at Hastingford that turned into a nice pond, when it filled with water. Sheila remembers an incident much later in the war, when a Spitfire fell victim to 'friendly fire' from ack-ack guns which were sited in a field just below Gatehouse. She and her brother, Tony, watched them firing at a doodle-bug. Unfortunately, the gunners didn't notice the Spitfire on its track, and hit it instead of the real target. Luckily, the pilot managed to bale out, and landed safely. An exceptionally nasty air battle started one day as we walked back from the canteen. It was very noisy with machine gun fire and a quantity of bombs jettisoned. June Coates shepherded us into her garden at The School House, and six of us crowded into the Anderson shelter with her Mum and Dad.

My husband, Derrick, saw plenty of V1s passing over, launched from ramps outside Paris. Several came down near Blackboys. One that dropped on Crowborough, killing I don't know how many Canadians, sailed about 50ft over his head. His family lived opposite the Canadian camp, at Possingworth where they had almost every Canadian Division except the 5th. Their forage caps had a long thin decoration worn on one side of the head, and a few of the men stitched a razor blade to the front. If the French Canadians got into a fight in Heathfield, locals learned to keep well clear. But it was not all blood-and-guts. The troops put on films and concerts in the old Hadlow Down village hall. Derrick enjoyed the Andy Hardy films, and the drag artists who a small boy didn't recognise as men until friends enlightened him. The majority of the Canadians were decent fellows, and were never any threat to us children. We could go anywhere in safety in those days...apart from the threat of the Luftwaffe.

Two chaps were killed whilst milking at Scocus farm in 1940. A German plane dumped its load on the shed. About 150 bombs dropped between Five Ashes and Cross-in-Hand during that incident. Our planes had intercepted the raiders, and they paniced, and loosed their loads. One field in the area was pitted with about 19 bombs.

Apart from these occasional dramas, the usual sounds were nothing more than 60 or so spoons scraping plates, as we downed Mrs. Funnell's stew and semolina pudding. RAF dog-fights with the enemy were not the only hazard. The arrival of Londoners brought a strange blossoming of purple to many young faces, and the previously unheard word 'impetigo' was bandied about. The nasty sores spread like wildfire, and were treated by a substance called Gentian Violet, hence the brilliant purple patches. Our family was stricken with scabies, brought by two evacuees who

Scocoes (sic) Farm, Five Ashes, after the raid on August 16th 1940.
Two sons of the farmer, Messrs. J.W. Berry and A.A. Berry, were killed, together with 13 cows.

arrived later in the war. The skin disease had been treated in London, but broke out again in spring. The Medical Officer from Lewes inspected us with a magnifying glass, and declared us all infected. To my mother's great horror, my young brother, Chris, two evacuees and me, were whisked off by ambulance to a secret destination. Whilst Mum's imagination ran riot, this turned out to be a large house in Rotherfield where such delights as dysentry and, of course, scabies were treated. By an odd coincidence, a friend's brother had helped develop the cure which superceded the lengthy treatment with sulphur. We were given hot baths, and painted all over with something that looked like whitewash. The nurse slapped it on with a large paintbrusbh, and it was freezing cold. Then we had to stand in front of a fire to dry, and the whole process was repeated the next day.

Poor old Mum was busy at home washing and airing every scrap of bedding. She and Dad had to use the same treatment but, as the only paint brushes they had were covered in creosote, they used a toothbrush. Luckily this treatment worked very well and, in 48 hours, the cure developed for use in the armed forces, proved effective.

179

No Names, No Pack Drill

Some will be forever grateful for the fact that boys will be boys, others of course are just relieved if and when at last, they grow up. The following tales have been related and perhaps it is best, no matter what their position is today, if the miscreants remain anonymous.

School life for all of us is a mixture of new experiences, anticipation, fear, excitement, fun, reawakening of old horrors and many more. For one young lad playing in the school playground it may have been the feeling of importance that possessed him upon seeing the visitor enter the gates to rush around the yard shouting the news to all and sundry. Now he could have broadcast the fact that "The Bug Nurse is here, the Bug Nurse is here" as it turned out it was "The Cock Doctor's coming, The Cock Doctor's coming". So preoccupied with his role of Town Crier was he that on rounding the building at top speed and in full voice he ran straight into the visitor and fell over. Picking him up the Doctor said "Yes laddie and your little cock will be the first".

Considering attendance at Church was much more common years ago it is inevitable that some tales will surface. Palm Sunday is a very important date in the church calendar and in order to celebrate this festival with some panache, a Mrs Abbott from Cross in Hand used to bring her donkey along to the service. The boy whose job it was to carry the incensory, discovered that the poor beast didn't like the smell of incense. He then contrived, by giving it an extra long swing as the procession walked past, to give poor old dobbin a really good whiff which set him off braying in full voice.

Hadlow Down Church used to be considered quite High. Consequently there was a stoup on the wall inside the door of the church for a small supply of holy water which the visitor could use to bless themselves with, upon entering. On one occasion some boys discovered that the water level was rather low and they naturally felt it was their duty to top it up. Clearly this was no easy task as in the normal way the bowl would be at head height for such small boys. With considerable effort they managed to lift one of the team up in order to refill the bowl!!

Again the incensory caused some merriment. Normally only a small amount of methylated spirits would be necessary to ignite the charcoal, but on this occasion the boy in charge overfilled it. As he walked up the aisle swinging it from side to side so the flaming meths spilled out leaving a trail of fire and possibly damnation behind him. The congregation must have wondered if certain Biblical predictions were coming true, eventually a Canadian soldier decided the pyrotechnic display, although very enjoyable had gone on long enough, he stood up grabbed the container from the rascal and ran down the aisle, into the churchyard throwing the whole conflagration into the water butt.

One lad who attended the Tin Heaven was given a very warm and genuine welcome. He found himself sitting next to an old lady who did her best to make him feel at home. When it came to singing they all stood up and she held out her hymn book for him to share. Sadly her hand trembled so much that he was quite unable to read a word. As we all know when you aren't supposed to laugh and try to suppress it, that's when the giggling starts. The only hope was for the organist, the tremble and the giggle all to be in time together, this they never managed to achieve.

During the summer of 1942 an idle boy happened to discover a very old cricket ball that had been lost under the hedge, it was in a very dilapidated condition and quite beyond further use for cricket. Without much thought he threw it right up in the air as high as possible, grabbed the bat with both hands and swung for all he was worth. W.G. Grace would have recruited him on the spot. The ball soared into space, the casing falling off as it went and the string inside began to unravel. The huge parabolic curve ended behind some trees so the last of the flight was only heard as it crashed through The Providence Chapel window. In time honoured fashion it was time to make yourself scarce and lie low. During the war there were constant references in the papers to keeping a lookout for strange objects that may have been dropped either deliberately or accidentally from enemy aircraft. In the Chapel at the time was Emily Fenner who obviously thought this strange object was another diabolical German invention. So she wrapped it up in newspaper and took it hot foot to Luther Godley, who was an elder of the Chapel. He obviously recognised it as a cricket ball and guessed where it had come from. The culprit continued to keep his head down but knew he had been rumbled beacause of all the heavy hints that were dropped.

COMMENDED ANECDOTES

Sent by Selina Locke aged 12. Hadlow Down National School. November 10th 1911

Singing Teacher: "Now children we'll have 'Like little drops of water' and put some spirit into it".

Principal [whispering]: "Careful, sir, this is a temperance school. Say put some ginger in it".

HADLOW DOWN VARIETY CLUB
PRESENTS
ENCORE
AND MORE...

FRIDAY 20TH AND SATURDAY 21ST
OCTOBER 1995
DOORS OPEN 7.30PM
LICENSED BAR
ADULTS £3 / CHILDREN £1.50

TICKETS AVAILABLE FROM THE GENERAL STORES HADLOW DOWN
OR BOOK BY TELEPHONE: 01825 830201

Chapter Fifteen

VILLAGE DELIGHTS

by Peter Gillies and Joan Wiltshire

"Our Sussex folk had much dry humour, …"

There seems always to have been plenty going on in Hadlow Down. Certainly without the influence of television we can see how villagers made their own enjoyment and exploited every opportunity, as a diversion from daily work. The main change is the venue. Prior to the opening of the school in 1838 there was no community building in the village. The introduction of such a facility must have had quite an impact on everyday life, by expanding horizons and providing new opportunities.

The *Sussex Express*

1909

"Concert in aid of funds for the football club was given in the schoolroom… The financial result was very satisfactory and a most enjoyable evening was spent."

"Conservative Meeting – There was a big attendance of Politicians from all parts of the Parish and beyond which filled the main schoolroom to overflowing and many who could not avail themselves time for the supplementary accommodation afforded by the adjacent classroom had of necessity to turn their steps regretfully away."

1910

"Concert – a very enjoyable and successful concert was given at the schools... Programme of recitation, banjo and mandolin, song, pianoforte and comic song."

"Another Social took place in the schools when about 80 were present… Dancing to the accompaniment of Mr E Shoosmith formed the principal amusement. The proceedings commenced at 8.00 and continued until 4.00am."

Back Row: Bert Day, Lee Fry, Charlie Bishop, George Peckham, Unknown, Ernie Bowin
Middle Row: Walter Foord, Sid Duce, Frank Barden, James Ashdown, George Peckham, Bert Peckham, Jesse Moon,
Stephen Divall, Dud Simmonds Sr. Front Row: Jim Smith, Harry Alce, Henry Ashdown, Rev. Bowen, Mr Scribbins
and daughter, Tommy Long, James Packer, Horace Sewell. Children: Dud Simmonds Jr. and Jim Smith.

There were other events taking place, away from the confines of the school, and in various venues, some were primarily educational:

Sussex Express

January 1914

"The housewives of Hadlow Down owe a debt of gratitude to Mr W.E. Durrant L.A.C. chef who on Wednesday afternoon commenced a course of lectures combining the art of good plain cooking and economy. The numerous company assembled in the play room at The Grange which had been kindly placed at their disposal by Mrs Lang Huggins who graced the proccedings with her presence. Assuming that the average family comprised six Mr Durrant based his demonstration accordingly. He showed them how to prepare and serve an appetising and wholesome three course dinner for half a dozen people at a total cost of 10½d or only 1¾d each. The dishes were sold to cover their initial cost and found ready purchasers."

The Annual Hospital Parade whilst having a very serious purpose always managed plenty of music and the traditional 'tea':

Sussex Express

July 1910

"HOSPITAL PARADE – The annual effort of the local Hospital Sunday Parade Society takes place next Sunday when the committee hopes to eclipse all previous records in the matter of financial success. The procession will this year in addition to the various Friendly Societies and their banners and the Five Ashes contingent of the St Johns Ambulance Corps, be accompanied by three bands. The long march will commence from the Schools at 1.15pm to Five Ashes and after tea, on return to the village, Buxted will again be visited and at the conclusion of the journey a special service will be held at St Mark's."

Sussex Express

August 1910

> "The grand total of the collections on behalf of the Hospitals amounted to £36. 6s.7d. and the committee met at the New Inn on Thursday last to decide on the distribution of the money."

The annual Flower show was an outdoor event.

Sussex Express

September 1910

> "The annual exhibition of the result of local horticulture and the prowess of home athletes took place on Wednesday in the field lent by the kindness of Mr A.E.Smith. The entries were well up to average numbering over 400".

Still the school was required:

> "The Prizes won at the recent flower show were presented at the schools on Monday evening by Mrs T.J.G. Duncanson who gracefully performed the pleasing duty. Owing to the Hop Picking and other calls on the time of land workers the attendance was not very large".

Sussex Express

August 1912

> "ANNUAL SCHOOL TREAT – The annual treat given the children attending the schools took place on Thursday last when in spite of threatening weather the participants were only once driven to shelter by rain. A short service was conducted by the Rev J.A. Warner. Tea was then partaken of and the children did ample justice of the many good things provided for them. During the day the Heathfield Brass Band played selections which were much appreciated. After tea the party adjourned to The Grange where amusements in the shape of swings etc and sports were freely and fully indulged in, and the parents were entertained to tea in the play room."

Use was also made of the loft above Preston shop as a meeting place, sometimes with a gramophone to enliven the proceedings. The building of Holiday Cottage, now Marlowe House, in the early years of the twentieth century, by Mr Charles Lang Huggins of The Grange and the subsequent use of the property by the village for community recreation, was the first real taste of a village hall.

Sussex Express

November 1912

> "READING ROOM RE-OPENED – The room at the holiday cottage which every winter is kindly placed at the disposal of the villagers by Mr Charles Lang

Huggins has again been opened, and on Wednesday last, the first evening of the season, there was a good attendance of members who participated in billiards, cards and other games."

November 7th 1913

"GIRLS' FRIENDLY SOCIETY – Through the energy of Mrs Lang of Wilderness a branch of this excellent society has been formed here. The inaugural meeting took place at the Holiday Home [which will be its headquarters] on Saturday last. Nearly 20 members were enrolled and these with future members will meet there every Saturday when they will, in addition to spending part of the time in recreation, ply the needle for the benefit of the various missions which the parent society seeks to aid."

Marjorie Jarvis remembers… if you wanted really exciting entertainment it was necessary to travel to Heathfield where in the State Hall, Station Road, there would be a dance or silent movie to enjoy. The only trouble was travelling by bicycle, with the potholes in the road to contend with and when the acetylene lights were good they were excellent but so often they were awful, making it quite an adventure.

Perhaps this gave the village the idea that it would benefit from a proper purpose-built community centre, so a committee was formed under the chairmanship of Mr

Awaiting the arrival of the royal party.

Mr Harboard accompanies Princess Marie Louise down Hut Lane for the opening ceremony.

*Hadlow Down Guides and Brownies provide a guard of honour
under the auspices of Joy Godfrey-Faussett*

LOT 22.

(Coloured Pink on Plan).

THE RED TRIANGLE HUT SITE

The plot of land being part of O.S. No. 610 extending to about .131 of an acr[e]
by an unmade track opposite to the New Inn on the Hadlow Down Road, and form[s]
the Red Triangle Hut.

The Hut is used as a Village Hall and a nominal rental of 5s. per annum is p[aid]

Hadlow Down Estate auction catalogue, September 1949

Harbord from Five Chimneys. Fund raising had to be addressed and villagers helped.

The land which belonged to the Eridge Estate was made available to the village and the Hut obtained from the YMCA hence its nickname for ever more The Red Triangle Hut, mimicking

Their aim is to collect 52,800 pence

Part of an old lamp standard has been converted into a collecting box for the Hadlow Down Village Hall rebuilding fund appeal which is to be launched at 11 a.m. tomorrow (Saturday).

The box is being erected in the garden adjacent to the Village Stores and the Hut Committee are hoping that it will be the means of raising a mile of pennies. A map of the village will be put up to indicate progress.

The mile has already been started by Mrs Pullen of Council Flats, School Lane, with a collection of bun pennies. She has been invited to launch the appeal.

Footnote: Ten pennies represent one foot.

Fund raising for the hut's replacement, circa 1962
Mrs Pullen (centre), Mr Elkington, General Watson, Rev Gibbs and his daughter.

George Standen, Ron Knights and Fred Harrison, a few of the many volunteers who helped concrete The Lane.

the red triangle badge of the YMCA.

The hut was opened by Princess Marie Louise on June 8th 1921 amid considerable celebrations.

The task of making up the road came later and the village rallied round to achieve this with their own labour.

The life of 'The Hut' came to an end in July 1965 when demolition made way for the replacement to be opened in November the same year. Its status raised to that of 'Village Hall', the facility continues to serve the village well.

Entertainment in the Village 1923-99

By Joan Wiltshire

When the Hadlow Down Variety club started in 1982 I had no idea that we were following in the footsteps of another amateur theatrical society in our village. I learnt about The Pied Pipers of Hadlow Down from their intriguing minute book loaned to me by Gerald Standen. It contained their press cuttings, photographs, programmes and, of course, the minutes of their meetings.

The Pied Pipers were formed in 1923 to "entertain and interest the village" and to "obtain money for objects to be decided upon from time to time" It was minuted not to give performances for any political reason. Most of the performance proceeds were given to local organizations, particularly the newly formed Girl Guides, the Scouts, the football club and their own village hut. Charitable donations were also given to the Uckfield Cottage Hospital and the Uckfield Nursing association.

Founder members were Mr and Mrs Verpilleux and their daughters and Brigadier-General E Godfrey Faussett, his wife son and daughter. Altogether there appeared to have been about 20 members.

Rehearsals were mostly held in Wilderness Lane at Nurney Cottage [then the home of the Verpilleux family], and Annes with final rehearsals at the Red Triangle Hut. Stage curtaining proved to be a problem which was partly overcome by the cast

lending their own curtains for performances. Lighting was supplied from batteries installed by Rupert Huggins. The Police were apparently very concerned that the Hut doors were not blocked during performances.

Their costumes look spectacular. Trademark outfits were Pierrot which they wore to start off every performance, other characters include the Punch and Judy Family and an impressively armour-clad Henry VIII with Catherine and Cardinal Wolseley.

The minute book declares that their songs, dances and sketches were well received, with the only drawback being complaints from the audiences when they had to sit on benches instead of

In aid of the Royal Sussex County Hospital.

THE PIED PIPERS OF HADLOW DOWN.

DECEMBER 17th, 1924.

Produced by Mr. MURRAY N. PHELPS.
Lighting by Mr. C. R. HUGGINS.

chairs. Their surviving programmes included one-act plays such as 'Give it a name' by Mr H C Harbord, a cast member and comedies such as 'A Storm in a Tea Shop' by one Stafford Hilliard. The troupe also sang many popular songs of the day including 'Widdicombe Fair', 'Mother's Darling' and the song cycle 'The Jackdaw of Rheims' by Herbert Bath. Frequently present within their programmes are joke advertisements and notices including 'Don't go elsewhere to be cheated, walk in here – Potash and Perlmutter Co' and 'Wanted – a donkey to do the work of a country parson – Payne Puddlecombe-on-slosh'.

The company frequently took their shows to other venues, such as Horam, Mayfield and Uckfield. The Pied Pipers continued to give twice yearly performances until 1930 when their minute book stops. Perhaps they disbanded then.

In the mid-seventies a choral society was organised by a composer, Norman Kay, who lived in Hadlow Down. The singers were called The Downlanders. Many happy hours were passed practising in the New Inn and Norman really put us through our paces. We gave a carol concert one Christmas Eve in St Mark's Church, where the acoustics are outstanding, plus performances in the Village Hall.

The Hadlow Down Variety Club was formed in 1982 and the first performance was 'Autumn Follies'. Seventeen shows followed until the present day, including cabarets and a mini pantomime. Rehearsals were fun but concentrated. Several of the

Variety Club costumes sold in the Village Hall 30th May 1998 Joan Wiltshire and Anne Zenka

club members have been involved right from the beginning, notably Anne Zenka, Fiona Bickerton, Geoff Humphrey and Reg Hunt. Club members usually total about 30. Joy Moore from Framfield has supplied us with live music for many of our shows and latterly Barbara Hart [at that time living in the Burwash area]. Lavish costumes are the Variety Club's trademark and until recently we ran a costume hire service.

Proceeds from the shows went to the Village Hall, Macmillan Breast Cancer Research and St Wilfreds Hospice to name a few. The new flame retardant stage curtains were donated to the village hall. We went joyfully 'on the road' to the Horder Centre, residential care homes in Uckfield, Mayfield and Five Ashes.

The most important thing about the Variety Club was that it brought so many people together whose paths may never normally have crossed, in an atmosphere of laughter and congenial community spirit.

Variety '86
Back Row :Mavis Farrar, Reg Hunt, Anne Zenka, Nigel Harrison, Shiela Willson, John Humphrey, Fiona Bickerton, Joan Wiltshire.
Kneeling: Jill Levide, Josephine Lawson, David Hunt, Ginny Harrison, Dorothy Makepeace.

Kent and Sussex Courier

1948

"From Riga Opera House to Hadlow Down is a long way measured in miles but for 70 Latvian agricultural workers [housed as displaced persons in Hadlow House] who sat listening to a concert in the Village Hut on Sunday the miles were rolled away.

The vocalists were a baritone and soprano from the Riga Opera House Co., singing songs and arias in the Latvian tongue. The Baritone Edvins Krummins who is now working at a London Hospital, and the Prima Donna Lidza Marsalka received a great ovation from their compatriots as their recital ended."

Cast as St Trinians 1992
Back row: Jo Dummer, Jim Dixon, Joan Wiltshire, Carol Hoddinott, Louise Pitcher, Reg Hunt,
Anne Zenka, Ginny Harrison, Glenis Pitson
Kneeling: Dwayne Zenka, Mavis Farrar, Anthony Wiltshire

THE HADLOW DOWN HERALD

5p

November 1973   3rd Edition

AUTUMN FESTIVAL CELEBRATES HISTORIC EVENT

This month the traditional autumn festivities of Hadlow Down take place
and excitement is growing to fever pitch as the great moment draws nearer.
Following the outstanding success of past festivities, this year's
occasion has been considerably extended and now covers two days.   November
3 and 4.   On Saturday, November 3, there will be a packed programme of
events including a Dutch auction in the morning, children's tea party and
fancy dress parade in the afternoon,
bonfire spectacular in the evening, and the
day will culminate in a dance at the Village
Hall.   The autumn festival ends on Sunday,
November 4, with a specia' "Son...
service at St. Mark'...
will be...

THE STAND-

THE HADLOW DOWN HERALD

5p

FIRST EDITION

London 5th November 1971

London 5th November 1605

November plot against the King's life

from our Political Correspondent ... London 5th November 1605

A YOUNG MAN giving the name of Johnson and
describing himself as a servant of Thomas Percy,
was arrested at midnight last night in one of the
cellars under the House of Lords. This arrest was
made after suspicion had been aroused by Lord
Mounteagle today. After the arrest the cellar was
searched and found to contain
barrels of gunpowder and fuse
devices under piles of firewood.

Conspiracy

Lord Mounteagle had inspected
the room yesterday morning and
in a statement from him early
today, he said he was working on
a "documented warning submitted some ten days ago". Lord
Mounteagle continued, "I believe
from my source of information

conspirators efforts tp murder
our King and Parliamentary
figures and to blow up the Houses
of Parliament.

Opening of Parliament has
this year been postponed twice,
the original date being February
7th. This delay must have been
beneficial to the conspirators
who secreted into the cellars
many barrels of gunpowder approaching two tons in weight.

GUNPOWDER

THE inventor of gunpowder is
unknown, but Roger Bacon a
Franciscan friar (1294) and Ber-
thold Schwartz a German monk
of the late fourteenth century,
share the honour of giving the
first scientific account of the
composition of gunpowder.

The modern recipe is approxi
mately:
   75% saltpetre
   15% charcoal
   10% sulphur
This mixture is ground into a
fine powder, mixed into a moist
paste, dried and then crushed
again into varying size grains.

Treason and Plot

"Creeping, creeping, creeping
goes Guy Fawkes,
Creeping through the tunnels of
the cellar
On Bonfire night", said
Mrs. Keller.
"If that had not happened we
would not be here."

The school of St. Mark's Church, Hadlow Down

"This Indenture made the twenty
seventh day of January one
thousand eight hundred and
thirty eight between the Reverend
William Edwards, Minister of the
Chapel of Hadlow Down in the
Parish of Buxted in the County of
Sussex East of the first part, The
Right Reverend Father in God,
William by Divine permission
Lord Bishop of Chichester, Bishop
of the Diocese wherein the said
Parish is situated of the second
part and The Incorporated Na-
tional Society for promoting the
Education of the Poor in the
Principals of the Established
Church throughout England and
Wales of the third part. Whereas
the piece or parcel of land or
ground herein after particularly
mentioned and intended to be
hereby bargained and sold, is
part and parcel of the glebe land
belonging to the said William
Edwards as Minister of the said
Chapel of Hadlow Down".

Thus starts the document that
one hundred and thirty three
years ago was drawn up to
facilitate the building of a school
in Hadlow Down. The Incorporated National Society mentioned had been set up as the
document later says, "for promoting the education of the poor
in the principals of the established
Church throughout England and
Wales for the purposes of an Act
passed in the Session of Parliament
held in the sixth and seventh

celebrated but our school had
been established a full thirty
years before. The original building was erected on a gravel pit
and consisted only of what is now
known as the junior classroom.
This apparently was divided into
three sections, each part occupied by a seperate class. It is
still quite easy from the outside of
the building to distinguish the
old part of the building with its
sand-stone walls and until the
recent re-decoration the rods and
rings that supported the curtains
dividing the classroom were still
in position.

The other sections of the building have been added over the
years starting with the infant
classroom, then the kitchen (both
of which were originally used as
extra school rooms) and finally
the toilet and cloakroom block.
Pupils have at one time exceeded
a hundred and fifty, the children
ranging from school entrants to
school leavers as of course there
were no secondary schools.

Unfortunately the original
school log-book has been mis-
laid and full records only start
when the book begun in eighteen
eighty eight. Since then many
interesting and amusing inci-
dents have been recorded in the
log-books. These are occasionally
related in the school section of
the Parish magazine.

Numbers are now higher than
they have been for many years

Chapter Sixteen

AUTUMN MADNESS

by Chris Purser

"The school treats were heald on the lawn. When four years old I trotted around with the cake "Take some more", I said to a boy. "Please, Miss, I can't, I have eaten seven pieces and my pockets are full"".

The tradition of Autumn Festivals has long been established in the county, particularly associated with November 5th and the Gunpowder Plot. This tradition, practised in Hadlow Down over many decades, significantly developed during the first half of the 1970s into a whole village celebration. This culminated in a week long 'Autumn Festival' in 1974. At the time the school was in desperate need of additional accommodation having grown from a handful of kids [about 18 in 1969] to an amazing 65 in 1973. In order to secure the required capital funding from the Department of Education the school had to provide a proportion of the money [17.5%], what better incentive could there be to organise an event that would assist the village in acquiring better school accommodation for its children.

A handful of very enthusiastic parents, members of the Parent Teachers Association [P.T.A.], in concert with the head teacher and the vicar, Lewis Hollowood, set about the task of developing what was already an established Bonfire Celebration into a seven day event that would attract interest from people outside the village and provide a variety of activities for villagers to enjoy. Three years previously, in 1971, the first copy of the *Hadlow Down Herald* had been published as the advertising vehicle for the Bonfire Celebrations. The *Herald* had been published once a year every year since then and was to form an important attraction for the proposed festival week.

Whilst it was an unintended consequence, that regular publication which was later produced as an A4 magazine, was the forerunner of the *Parish Magazine* which is now distributed free on a monthly basis to all households in the parish.

The thorough advanced planning, started in March 1974, paid dividends. The programme for the festival week lengthened into ten days and was advertised on the back of a mock election flyer encouraging villagers not to vote for Conservative, Labour or Liberal but for the Hadlow Down Autumn Festival. A box office was established in the grounds of Hyders alongside the A272 for advanced booking. The programme advertised was:

Friday 11th October Festival Dance
        8.00pm to midnight Village Hall 75p per ticket

Saturday 12th Sponsored Womble Hunt
        9.00am School

Saturday 12th An approach to Ballet [Elizabeth Nelson School of Dancing]
        2.00pm and 4.30pm Village Hall 25p entrance.

Sunday 13th Harvest Festival Eucharist
        11.00am Church

Sunday 13th Parish Luncheon
        12.30pm School Adults 75p, Children 30p

Sunday 13th Organ Music
        2.00-5.00pm Church

Monday 14th Jigsawtium
        8.00pm Village Hall Spectators 5p

Tuesday 15th Piano Trio/Downlanders
        8.00pm Church 45p

Wednesday 16th "Everyman" [The Aquarians]
        8.30pm Church 40p

Thursday 17th Bingo session
        8.00pm Village Hall 5p per card

Friday 18th Henderson Brass Consort/Prodigal singers
        8.00pm Church 45p

Saturday 19th Auction
        10.00am Village Hall Entrance free

Saturday 19th Torchlight procession
> 7.00pm from Village Hall Lane Torches 15p

Saturday 19th Bonfire and Fireworks
> 7.45pm Hidden Cottage Meadow Free

Saturday 19th Grand Prize Draw and Clock Raffle result
> 9.00pm approx Village Hall free

Sunday 20th Festival Eucharist
> 9.30pm Church

Sunday 20th Songs of Praise
> 3.00pm Church

Autumn Harvest Festival of Flowers and Fruits
> 12th, 13th, 14th in Church

Apart from the amazing prices charged compared with today there are one or two other points particularly to draw to the attention of the reader.

The Wombles were very much in vogue at that time. The Womble Hunt challenged the children to find a specific number of items within a short space of time. Apart from a prize for the most successful children they were also sponsored in order

to raise funds for the school.

The world's first Jigsawtium was completed in Hadlow Down. Waddingtons provided the jigsaws, all unopened, all of the same picture and containing 500 pieces. Teams of four competed to build the puzzles in the quickest possible time. Whilst contemporary records have been lost indicating the winner's time, memory suggests that the winning team completed their jigsaw in less than three quarters of an hour beating fourteen other teams.

The Downlanders, who gave a concert on the Tuesday of Festival week, were a group of villagers, singing a variety of music in four part harmony and conducted by the music critic Norman Kay who lived in the village. The group which existed for several years and only drew on villagers was surprisingly successful and always consisted of at least twenty singers.

The high spot of the week for many was the torchlight procession and fireworks. Hot food was available after the fireworks and a sing-song was conducted around the dying embers of the bonfire. Some may still remember the rendition of the teapot song, performed with actions by the head teacher.

> "I'm a little teapot short and stout
> Here's my handle, here's my spout
> When the water boils you hear me shout
> Tip me up and pour me out".

The festival was a great success in the way that the village co-operated and resulted in substantial funds being accumulated. It must be remembered however that the week long festival was a development from previous years' activities and although it never quite aspired to the same heights something similar was repeated a few years afterwards. The ultimate aim of securing finance for school accommodation was achieved and in 1976 the 'temporary' prefabricated building was erected. As this piece is being written that accomodation still exists but the school is looking to replace it as it has now finished its useful life. Would the village rally again?

1999 now 23 years old and due for demolition

Chapter Seventeen

THE SCULL WOOD AFFAIR

by Rosemary Alexander

"Surrounded by the beauty of the Weald they grew up to love nature."

Disaster tends to unite people, and for many years Hadlow Down residents were united by a disaster which today still affects part of a lovely hillside. The first hint of danger came in 1967 when Trevis Johnstone, of Stocklands Farm, applied for planning permission to use part of his land for waste disposal. The Parish Council opposed the scheme, and Wealden District Council turned it down until a new owner, Mr Leppard took over and his experience as an estate agent enabled him to find a way through the labyrinthine paths of officialdom. He installed a tenant, and leased an area known as Scull Wood to East Sussex County Council, for a sum reputed to be more than the average villager could expect to earn in a lifetime. [Reliable rumour stated £20,000 per year for ten years!!] From that date, the fate of the land was sealed. By the mid 1970s, despite vigorous protests from villagers, E.S.C.C had granted itself permission to use the ground as a landfill tip for seven years.

As things turned out, seven years became rather longer... an additional eight years, in fact. From the day the tip opened in 1976, its activities were a constant source of trouble. In 1978 the owner of Stocklands Farm was reprimanded for obstructing a right of way. Traffic restrictions had to be imposed on roads in the area. Negotiating narrow, winding lanes is a hair-raising experience at the best of times, and extremely difficult when outsize vehicles suddenly appear round corners, travelling in the opposite direction.

When two giants meet...

Stocklands Lane was banned to refuse lorries. Drivers were instructed to use Waghorns Lane and Five Chimney's Lane in order to avoid the school. Both roads had to be widened, and passing places created. Predictably, impatient employees did not always stick to the authorised route. Locals became accustomed to heart-stopping near-misses, and unavoidable accidents.

Life became intolerable for householders in what had been a peaceful rural setting. As soon as construction work started, noise increased steadily throughout the years. Reversing lorries emitted loud warnings , and revved-up engines rose to a thunderous roar as they moved up and down the site. Mud spread on roads created another hazard, but not everything was annoyed over the state of affairs. Seagulls welcomed the new 24-hour restaurant. On a single morning, a distraught mathematician counted 15,000 screeching birds picking through the rubbish for tasty titbits, The interior of nearby houses

... the inevitable happens.

were hung with tapestries of flies. Clouds of dust cast malodorous 'nets' across gardens, and filthy papers swirled like ballet dancers across lawns, when the wind was in certain directions. Sickening smells doused the scent of flowers.

The burner flaring into the darkness transformed quiet country nights into a foretaste of hell. E.S.C.C denied methane gas seeped through the earth to poison the atmosphere but, on misty mornings, fumes were only too horribly apparent.

Month after month, the Parish Council had to deal with a string of complaints,

particularly over the very real possibility of injury to children. Councillor Mrs. Foster suggested 'Danger' notices be
provided at the entry in Stockland Lane to warn people
against straying onto the tip, but E..S.C. Councillor Logan
argued that warning signs merely incite curiosity. Maybe he
was forced to count pennies. By March 1979, his Council
admitted the site had cost more to develop than antici-
pated.

Villagers drew comfort from the thought that the
blight was not permanent, and stoically counted the weeks
left before the contract expired. Little did they realise how
optimistic was that belief. In 1982, the Parish Clerk, E.C.
Beard, heard from the County Engineer that, 'the County
Council has no plans to extend the area of land known as
Scull Wood'. On December 12th, 1985, a new Parish Clerk, John Palmer, wrote to
E.S.C.C pointing out that the landfill rubbish tip had been in operation for ten years,
and seeking an assurance ' there will be no attempt to prolong this most unsatisfactory
intrusion into the life of our village'. A bland reply assured him the land would be
handed back to the owner by the end of 1989.

But confidence in officials had been badly damaged. Ugly rumours began to
circulate, and fears proved valid when, in May 1987, the P. C. formally objected to a
request for an extension to the tip, 18 hectares of prime agricultural land. In August
that year, W. D. Councillor, Norman Buck, wrote to E.S.C.C, deploring the manner
in which the matter had been handled, and John Palmer circulated letters to individual County Councillors making clear 'the anger and frustration felt by villagers'.
Subsequent correspondence accused E.S.C.C of back-tracking on an agreement, and
officials tried to evade the issue by claiming the terms had been misunderstood.
Relations with the authorities worsened. By the end of 1987, John Palmer received an
arrogant letter from the Chief Executive expressing annoyance over a public meeting
arranged by Hadlow Down P.C. without consulting his officials.

In January 1988, tired of struggling with officials apparently indifferent to
Hadlow Down's plight, the Parish Clerk was instructed to contact the Secretary of
State for the Environment. On the 6th, E.S.C.C's Developement Control Committee
met to discuss the problem, and on the same day Michael Fox of the D.o.E. confirmed
that the views of the P.C. would be taken into account when 'a material departure from
the E.S.C.C. structure plan' was debated.

Eventually a compromise was reached. At a heated meeting in the village hall on February 2nd, those present reluctantly approved a resolution that the P. C. ' will not object to a reasonable time extension (say to January 1st 1990) to the existing landfill site subject to adequate safeguards, on condition the East Sussex County Council withdraws its current planning application to extend the site', and agreed to dump only W.D.C. household refuse. Accordingly on February 10th, after an emergency meeting of a sub-committee of E.S.C.C's Highways and Transport department, the planning application for an extension was withdrawn, but land-filling at Scull Wood would be changed from 8.00am-3.30pm Mondays to Thursday to 8.30am-2.30pm Mondays to Fridays, with no activity over the weekend.

The armistice was brief. In March, a thousand chickens, which had allegedly died of fright, were deposited at Scull Wood. Admittedly, the carcases were removed for burial at Pebsham, another E.S.C.C. tip, but it was an unpleasant interlude. In October the press highlighted worries over landfill gas, and leachate seeping into ponds and streams. Lorries laden with earth from construction work on the Maresfield by-pass meant the predicted forty vehicle movements per day increased to thirty per hour.

Just over a year after the 1988 agreement, rumours started to circulate again. E.S.C.C denied any intention of reneging on the deal but, on August 10th, W.D. Councillor, Norman Buck, pointed out in a letter to County Councillor Colonel J.D. Richards O.B.E., 'This does however leave the door open for private and industrial dumping'.

The land-owner, who wisely did not live at Stocklands Farm, denied there had been substantive negotiations with a commercial company, but on August 31st 1989,

Methane and leachate bubbling to the surface

the Assistant County Engineer wrote to Hadlow Down P.C., 'It is correct that approaches have been made by a number of waste disposal companies' interested in using Scull Wood. By February 1990, Wimpey Waste Management had staked a claim.

In March 1990 E.S.C.C closed the tip, but that was far from the end of the matter. Determined to continue operations, Wimpey applied for planning permission on a further fifty acres, and a ten year licence to continue its waste disposal use. The conditions were even harsher than previously. Lorries weighing 30 tons, would make 30,000 trips p.a, and longer working hours, from 7.30 am to 6 pm, plus another two hours for covering-up and spraying refuse, would increase activity by 72.4%. The crowning insult for residents in Buxted, Five Ashes, Rotherfield and Maresfield was that rubbish would be transported from far and wide across South East England.

The fight reached its climax throughout the summer of 1991. Hadlow Down P. C. led the onslaught, and Crowborough residents, formed a vocal protest group, CAW, Crowborough against Wimpey under the leadership of Ian Brigden. The first combined meeting packed Crowborough Town Hall. Every available seat was occupied plus the aisles and the steps to the platform, Tom Ryan, a former chairman of Hadlow Down P. C., conducted the proceedings, and outlined Scull Wood's history. Tempers were kept in check, and a construtive attitude was maintained towards a situation which threatened communities for miles around. A second demonstration took place inside and outside the W.D.C's offices, where John Steel, Wimpey's barrister painted an idyllic picture of how the site would look, when the company finished operations. Elaine Batchelor, whose land at Marlaines included a Site of Special Scientific interest, cast doubts on his love of nature by disclosing that the company's advisers had already tresspassed on her fields, and pollution posed a threat to the ponds, and their Crested Newt occupants.

Rumours and wild gossip was rife that summer when, sadly, Mr Leppard committed suicide. Naturally Scull Wood was felt by many to be the root cause but there was no evidence of that. Later, villagers learned he'd been found dead in his car, but very little appeared in the newspapers, despite the fact that he was a person of some importance in the district. People asked why the tragedy had been hushed-up. Secrecy merely served to encourage speculation.

A public enquiry on the future of Scull Wood opened in August 1991. That autumn the seasonal colours brightening the hedgerows were supplemented by showers of orange and yellow posters pleading, 'Don't Let Wimpey Waste Our Village'.

On the first day, Wimpey's barrister repeated his description of the Eden planned to replace the tip at the end of twelve years, and a Mr. Stubbs gave an optimistic estimate of the decibel levels expected to be reached during operations. Throughout the next few weeks, residents presented a rather different scene based on past experience. The Kit Wilson Trust claimed animals at the sanctuary risked serious illness from the noxious substances released from an area just beyond their boundary fences. Lambs in the fields round Hastingford had died of mysterious illnesses. Tongue in cheek, Bob Spencer, who farms in Stockland Lane, asked whether he should ignore ADAS advice and allow cattle to graze in fields next to the site, and Buxted Parish Councillor, Ron Giddens, launched a witty attack, whilst acknowledging the fact that E.S.C.C 'fought with one leg tied behind its back'.

The proceedings, including nit-picking evidence from experts, seemed set to go on for ever but, at 6.30 pm on November 22nd, after a final session reminiscent of a family farewell party, every line of enquiry had been exhausted. The long period of argument and counter-argument had made the characters familiar as old friends. The Inspector , Chris McDonald, looked weary, but was still alert to every nuance, every misinterpretation of the law. Until he reached a decision, Hadlow Down must wait in trepidation for the result of his cogitations.

In February 1992, the verdict was announced., and the village celebrated victory. Churchwarden Ian MacDonald, who regularly won first prizes in the Domestic section of Horticultural Society shows, baked a special cake, and Jim Dixon wrote a song...some of the verses of which were not exactly complimentary to the villains of the piece. But yet again, that did not end the matter. The aftermath of that long-drawn-out ordeal still causes trouble. Foul drainage pollutes the soil, the burner continues to flare alarmingly, fires break out, and the fire brigade had to be summoned to deal with a threatened explosion. Tankers pay regular visits to remove contaminated water which means, in rainy weather, several huge vehicles rumble down Waghorns Lane just as in the old days. According to E.S.C.C 's original estimate clearing the accumulated leachate would take 25 years. Judged by previous over-optimistic forecasts, this means around the year 2020

Tom Bridges who as chairman of the Parish Council, fought so hard on Hadlow Down's behalf has the last word.

> "We should all remember that multinational companies and arrogant local authorities can be beaten. One should never hesitate to take on the giants in this world because while there's life, there's hope and the little man can win."

The Thorpe family celebrating.
Benjamin, Harriet (in pram), Hannah and Christopher

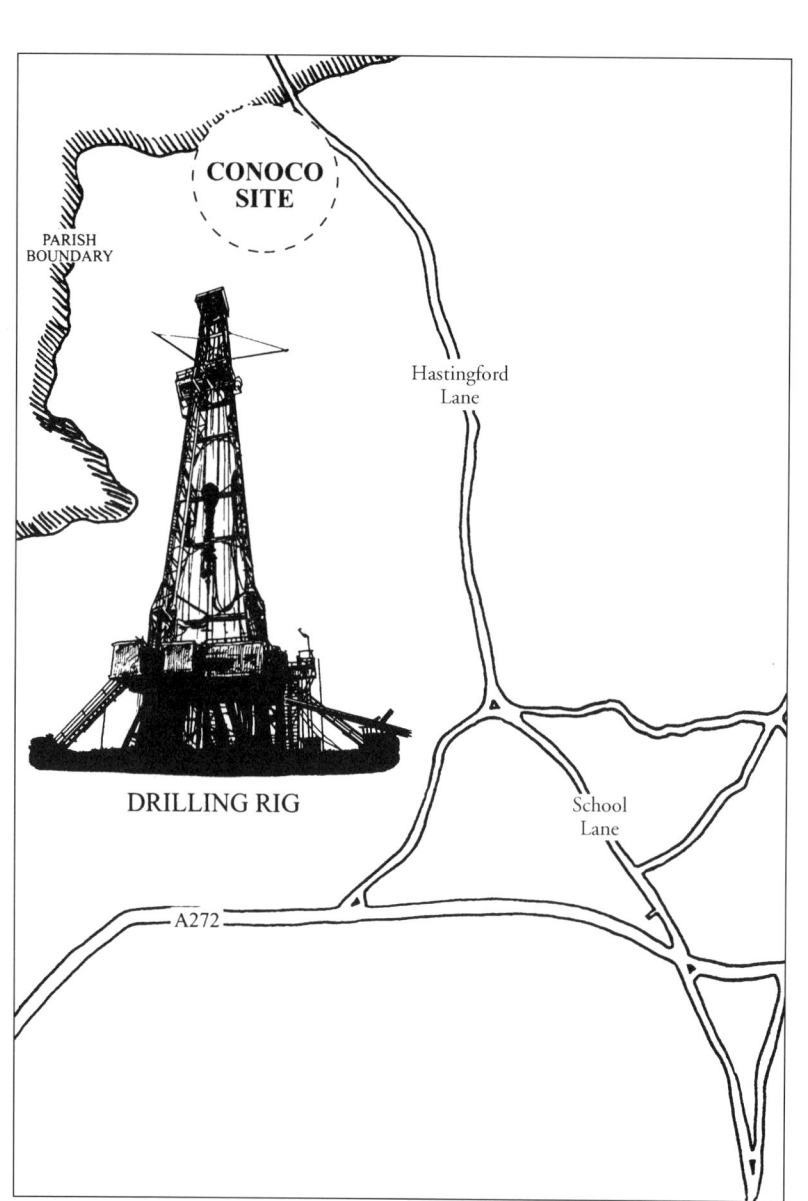

CONOCO
SITE

PARISH
BOUNDARY

Hastingford
Lane

DRILLING RIG

School
Lane

A272

Chapter Eighteen

CONOCO

---

by Peter Gillies

"In those days we burnt no coal"

It was during 1980/81 that Hadlow Down became the epicentre of the western world, with the shattering news that Conoco the oil company were about to start exploring for oil. Initially only a geophysical survey was envisaged and for several months large vehicles could be seen parked around the lanes with miles of electric cable draped along the hedges and verges linking metal pads together. The lorries would rev and vibrate for considerable periods, we were led to believe they were sending shock waves down into the ground which were picked up by the pads and relayed back to operators in the control room on the lorry, magically constructing pictures of the sub-strata way beneath our feet.

As is so often the way in the country if you leave them alone they go away eventually and true to form, this proved to be the case. It clearly took time to analyse the data because, in 1984, when we had all but forgotten about it, much to everyone's surprise and fuelling long dead rumors about fortunes waiting to be made, a second geophysical survey was carried out.

No fortunes, no nodding donkeys no oil drilling, the old maxim held again and peace returned, when once again they packed up and went away. Not for quite so long this time, early in 1986 on a site just over the parish border [strictly in Rotherfield] Conoco moved in to start drilling! This was serious: there would be noise, pollution, massive lorry movements, rubbish dumped, strangers wandering about, economic upheaval etc. etc. The Parish Council were monitoring the situation and held a site meeting It was generally felt that Hadlow Down would bear the brunt of the problems and Rotherfield would reap the financial benefits. The spectre raised was aggravated by the rumour that the drill did not even go down in a straight line but a huge curve under the parish boundary back into Hadlow Down. "Just as we thought, they are sneaking OUR oil all the time".

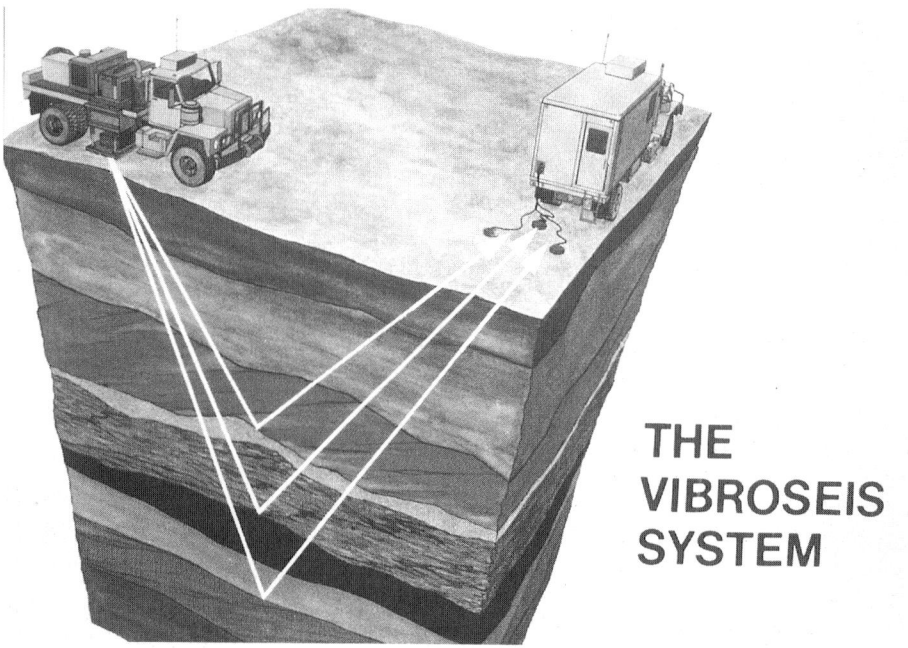

THE VIBROSEIS SYSTEM

The timetable went as follows:

Early February 1986	the first team moved in to prepare the site by levelling, laying hardcore and erecting the guard hut.
24th March	25 lorry loads of equipment were brought in.
27th March	drilling commenced.
15th April	drilling ceased.
18th April	the site was cleared.

At the time rumour had it that the quantity of oil found was uneconomic at present so the well is capped off for future exploration.

The official explanation now is as follows:

After 20 days of drilling a depth of around 5,000-ft had been achieved with a shaft diameter of 9". The top section was lined with a steel tube so that local water levels were not affected in any way and below that a perforated tube was used in order to allow water found in the strata along with any pumped down the shaft to be used for lubrication and help the spoil back up the pipe. The only oil was in the engineers oil can. No oil at all was found, not even an encouragement for future exploration. Consequently the well was 'Plugged and abandoned'. Asked about the rumour circulating at the time the company spokesman said "Put it down to the oilman's eternal optimism and fear of bad commercial news". The well was optimistically called Rotherfield One.

The old maxim had come right again, albeit after some narrow squeaks.

A Vibroseis truck in action
Sound waves generated by the pad on the road surface travel through the ground and bounce off underground geological formations. Analysis of the signals can indicate potential oil and gas bearing rock.

HADLOW DOWN SPORTS CLUB.

ANNUAL DINNER

IN

The Village Hall, Hadlow Down.

ON

SATURDAY, MAY 22nd. 1954 at 8 p.m.

PRICE 6/6

Each Member may invite Paying Guests to the
DINNER.   R.S.V.P

Mr. D. COATES,
SCHOOL LANE COTTAGE,   HADLOW DOWN.

AN ARTISTE IS BEING ENGAGED TO ENTERTAIN THE ASSEMBLED
COMPANY.

Chapter Nineteen

ELEVEN-A-SIDE

by Gerald Standen

*"... the men used to meet in the large meadow in front of the
house and play cricket till dark."*

First published in the Parish Magazine October 1990 with later additions.

With the recent drought order, its attendant hosepipes ban and the consequent discussion amongst the local cricketing fraternity, my thoughts went back to the days of the late 1930s and the state of the art then.

Older inhabitants of the village will possibly remember that the cricket ground in those days was down Tinkers Lane where the Vineyard is now. It was an idyllic setting for a playing field, peaceful, secluded and with excellent light but with no facilities or utilities just a wooden shed for a pavilion or the scorers, a bell tent for the cricketers to change in with the toilets being behind the numerous rhododendron bushes.

I well remember the summer holidays from school with the time spent at the above ground being utterly bored while my father and one or two others enthusiastically acted as groundsmen. At about midday, father would cheerfully abandon the Pub [much as I do now], remove the rear seats from his Studebaker car and load up with 5 and 10 gallon drums filled with water, garden forks, and the odd knife discreetly nicked from my mother, then proceed to the cricket ground.

Access was gained either by climbing the bank about 100 yards down the lane; rough steps cut into the bank took one onto the field beside a large beech tree, then to the pavilion and the end of the rhododendron grove, or there was a stile in the hedge further down the lane, finally there was the gate, as now; this was the one used by cars and was good for most of the year.

On arrival, the whole dreary procedure started. The water was tipped at either end of the crease, the ground being aerated by gently digging with the forks, the hallowed pitch then being scrupulously rolled. The knives came in for methodically removing all daisy and plantain roots over the sacred 22 yards. Mowing would then start with a decrepit clapped out Atco Motor Mower probably one of the most diabolically temperamental machines I have ever known. I must say that I certainly did not enjoy those mornings of my summer holidays.

All this brings to mind another thought - the cricket teas. After the Pub closed, a massive sandwich making session was carried out by a Mrs Markwick. A large fruit cake was cut into portions and fancy cakes supplied by Messers Weeks of Uckfield. The car usually driven by my father, Luther Mitchell or Frank Barden [if they could be spared from the game], was sent to collect these goodies along with a ten gallon urn of tea. On arrival at the ground, the scorers were turned out and their place in the pavilion was then used for serving the teas.

Hadlow Down had an excellent team in those days with a superb ground. The games were taken relatively seriously under the autocratic captaincy of Arthur Collins, a retired Brighton business man, who had played for Sussex as an amateur around the period 1895-99 which made him a very dedicated man. The club had the patronage

Hadlow Down Cricket Club in the 1920s.
Harry Alce standing on the left, and on the right, Tommy Long. The Packham brothers are
holding bats.

of the wealthier members of the community and most of the tradesman along with many young and not so young, eager members.

The village 'officially' only played their Home Matches here on Saturdays. In deference to the Vicar who was a Patron of the club, Sunday matches were spuriously in the name of Mr —————-XI versus whoever. This of course was a complete 'con' but helped to maintain the status quo. Sunday matches usually finished by 6.30pm so that players could get to the Church, or more likely the Pub. Football had also been played on the field from shortly after World War I until the early 1930s.

Sadly these halcyon days were to end in 1939 with most of the players joining the forces or called up as Territorials, some of whom were reported missing at Dunkirk and Calais. With the sound of the Battle of France within distant earshot and largely in respect of and for those taking part it was decided to suspend cricket for the duration. With the decision to 'wind up' there was the question of what to do with the ground. Should poles and cables be erected to prevent the possibility of a German landing by gliders, or even Junkers 52s, but these devices were not erected, instead old rollers and other tackle were left on the outfield and the sacred square well roped off.

This was the end of the use of the ground for the war years apart from two informal Regimental football games, The Toronto Scottish Regiment in 1942 and the Cape Breton Highlanders in 1943, both were Canadian units being stationed in Hadlow Down.

With the return of many of the men from the services cricket resumed and the ground came back into use in 1946. Very little work was needed to restore it and both cricket and football were played until 1949. As a former part of the Eridge Estate it was sold on behalf of the Metropolitan Railway Country Estates by Messers Strutt and Parker in 1949.

FOOTNOTE.... The oldest form of the game is probably 'Single Wicket' which consists of one batsman defending one

Colonel Coode and his grandson John McKenzie, teammates, with the 'pavilion' behind

Back row: Brian Hemsley, George Standen, Albert Packham, W. Markwick, G. Rich, T. Smith, B. Hoad.
Middle row: Jim Vigger, C. Packham, G. Cheesman, D. Rich. Front row: C. Lade, Bert Swift, F. Wickens.

wicket. This was very popular when matches were played for money with only one or two, but possibly as many as four or five, players on a side. Played a great deal in southern districts especially in Hop Growing districts and at Hop Fairs, on occasions County matches were arranged. The chief players were more or less retainers of the noblemen and other wealthy patrons of cricket at the close of the 18th century. It was the custom to play the first game of the year on Good Friday.

Sussex Weekly Advertiser

20th April 1778

> "CRICKET...this is to give notice that on Saturday 2nd May A match will be played on Hadlow Down in the parish of Mayfield. Between three of the East and three of the West of Sussex for five guineas a man. The wicket to be pitched at 12.00 clock."

Following the demise of the Tinkers Lane field, village sport was transfered to a pitch behind the Red Triangle Hut. Whilst this was obviously very convenient in many ways, it had the disadvantage of being <u>very</u> wet, so bad in fact that it was neccessary to lay a concrete strip with coconut matting on top for the wicket. The club was only allowed to stay there from 1950 to 1953.

We appear never to have been without a football team although being a small parish, putting up a team has on ocassions presented a problem. The Junior football team, which was started by Ron Barden, had to register their players with the League and as it was a case of if you turn up you will be playing; all sorts of strangers found themselves team members. Sometimes a new face would be queried. The conversation would go something like: "Is he registered?" "Yes of course." "What's his name?" "Bill Smith." "Oh no, we know what Bill Smith looks like." Somehow the team kept together and name changes helped. Hadlow Down became Hadlow Down and Five Ashes when somebody from that village joined. It wasn't long before Hadlow Down, Five Ashes and Mayfield was deemed necessary and eventually the unequal struggle was abandoned in favour of Ashdown United.

The problem was no easier for the senior team: during the 1950s and 60s

Junior Football Team circa 1971
Back Row David Green, Simon Briggs, Jonathon Allen, David Fenner, Stuart Valentine, Mickey Barden.
Kneeling Terry Luck, Derek Lefroy, Unknown, Derek Roman, John Da-Silva, Keith Southern

Hadlow Down had rather a bad name in the football world. The Captain came from Uckfield and he worked at the Crowborough Army Camp so frequently brought soldiers to make up the team numbers, even to persuading the Military Police to let a man out of detention for the afternoon. On one notable ocassion there were only four men from the parish and seven soldiers in the team. It was hardly surprising, when we played Magham Down and won 26–nil that our popularity waned somewhat.

For 24 years the village was without a sports field of its own. Various grounds were used on Waghorns Farm, Wilderness Farm and for a while Ashdown played in Five Ashes. During the late 1960s a steering committe was formed to remedy the situation, by providing a village sports field. Once again the parish responded and eventually the money was found to purchase the existing ground at the bottom of School Lane. Much work needed to be done before play could commence, including the building of the pavilion. A new era dawned with the official opening of our own village playing field in 1977. Pat Reid of 'Colditz' fame, who lived at Possingworth, Blackboys then, performed the opening ceremony.

Pat Reid and Ulric Huggins opening the Pavilion in 1977

Probably the last remaining cricket cap from the 30s.

St Mark's School Summer 1999

St Mark's School
July 1999

Head Teacher
Verity Poole

Teaching Staff
Christine Clarke, David Gordon, Margaret Kent, Sue Smirthwaite

Support Staff
Janis Hughes, Judy Cowling, Sally Hand, Doreen Newman, Neil Kempson, Anne Chilton, Sarah Skinner

Class 1	Class 2	Class 3
George Beale	Dominic Bartleet	David Cannings
Tyler Birt	Rosie Bourgoin	Keaten Coppard
Joseph Butler	James Nathan	Quin Coppard
Samantha Gilbert	Louise Mackay	Hayley Gilbert
Ryan Clingo	Sam Pearson	Alexandra Delmage
Kieran Foley	Tara Allen	Donna Loan
Alastair Mackay	Megan Blowey	Ben Mortimer
Emma Nelsen	Colette Foley	Ben Sherlock
Heather Pasfield	Matthew Hooker	Tisha Berker
Bethany Robinson	Jack Hunt	Jacob Butler
	Ryan Osborn	Charlotte Hooker
	Beth Pasfield	Nick Roberts
	Hannah Robinson	Oliver Sainsbury
	Ryan Strudwick	Leanne Strudwick
	Martha Thompson	Harriet Thorpe
	Lucy Vince	Verity Wainwright
	Alice Weller	Barnes Wheeler
		Jodie Allen
		Hannah Blowey
		Charlotte Hodges
		Jessica Lee
		Abbie Osborn
		Alex Skelton
		Rory Thompson

FROM THE SCHOOL OFFICE

The importance a school plays in the life of a village cannot be over emphasised.

St Mark's C E P school has successfully served the children and families in the local community since the middle of the last century, it has already ushered in the turn of the present century and, as it responds to current educational demands, is also enthusiastically preparing itself for whatever changes the new century brings. With the approach of the new millennium there is an opportunity to focus more clearly on the school as an integral part of the life of Hadlow Down. The part it has played in cementing village life up to the present time is unchallenged. In its present context it is also looking outwards with a wider educational view, as it responds to national initiatives on the educational front. It is against this background that it is important to share with the reader a vision of the way in which the school will again move forward into another century.

St Mark's will continue to be committed to providing positive learning experiences which, in addition to meeting modern educational requirements, will also draw on the strength of it's local history. Within it's christian ethos the school will continue such development and will enter the new century with a well developed corporate identity, enhanced facilities in terms of it's buildings and accommodation, and a strong sense of the important role it plays in partnership with parents in the lives of the children and their families.

The school therefore will continue to see itself not as a self contained entity appended to the local community, but one that is firmly rooted in it. It is within this vision that St Mark's will face the next millennium and will continue to respond positively to whatever challenges the future may bring.

At any stage in the life of a school the children will always hold their own, unique views on what their school means to them. What follows is a selection of views about their school held by current pupils of various ages.

Verity Poole   October 1999

Class 1 (the youngest children) revealed their future hopes for a more lavish school environment

The parents will have a car park.

We will all have a computer.

There will be a swimming pool in the school.

In the playground there will be lots of swings.

*The children from Class 2 (7–8 year olds)
were much more informative but perhaps
expecting rather too much*

St. Mark's in the 21st. century.

In 2100 there will be a bouncy castle outside the school with bouncy spikes and bouncy twirls.

*One very ambitious child suggested that there
would be a "mountain school" at St. Mark's
with a dry ski slope, karati classes, a full sized
football pitch and a very large kitchen to prepare
very large meals.*

Another wrote:

"St. Mark's School in the Future.
The uniform will be dark shirt white jumpers and navy blue trousers. The equipment in the playground will be a tenniss court and pich.
Inside the school a 12 foot long fish tank and canteen. There would be easier maths."

Another child obviously with a fixation regarding robots believes there will be robotic teachers, teaching the children and offering chewing gum for a correct answer

The ideal school was clearly identified by one of the girls:

We will wear black clothes to school

We get to bring pets to school

We get to do what ever we want

We get a swimming pool in the school

We get a bouncy castle in the school

We wear black coats at school

We have Mrs. Pool as our P.E. teacher

We have a teacher with snakes for her hair

We have 9000 children in the school

Amongst the other contributions, apart from the on-going theme of swimming pools and bouncy castles, children believed there would be easy space travel, opportunities to travel in an aeroplane whilst doing lessons and televisions helping to teach all the children.

The Futuristic Visit by Donna

"Hey Jack I wonder if everythings changed" I said.
"You'll see when we get there. Be patient, I'm trying to drive," Jack warned.
Jack is my big brother. we used to live in Hadlow Down for a long time. Since then we have been at our cousin's in London. Before I left I had made some predictions about what it would be like when we returned. "Look! There's the first sign. It says...Hadlow Down!" yes we're nearly there" I screamed.
"Are you going to rabbit on all the way there Billy?" Jack warned.
"Turn on the music mouth." I couldn't really be bothered but when I did, my favourite song came on. It was......

Here we are at St. Mark's school I can still remember my first day. I was"....
"Don't start that story again. You've told me a million times!"
"No look, I missed the turn. Oh well, how about we stop at the pub first?" "O.K. but you know it won't've changed, I blabbered on cockily!
"How about you put your money where your mouth is?"
"Don't be daft I'm broke."

"Ah here we are. How about we pop in and see how its going?" But the pub hadn't changed at all. Rotten old wooden doors, shabby falling down toilets (outside).
"Just as I remember!"
"Shut up. Well that hasn't changed much. Shall we stay or move

on?" "Move on"

"Right where next?"

"How about the shop".

"Don't be silly didn't you read the "Save the shop" Dad sent?

"Oh. yea I forgot. How about we go to Wilderness Wood?"

"Fine lets go. Get in the motor-mobil."

I was expecting just a little sign with Wilderness Wood on it, but I was shocked at what I saw. Big colourful flashing bulbs it read **If your tired and its a long drive home stop in at our 5 star MOTEL.**

"Hey Jack get a load of this, pull over" I pleaded "This I've got see!"

"We're not there yet!" As we pulled in down the smooth tar-marked curvy path.

"What's happened? Wheres the stony bumpy 2 way drive down to the car parks?" The car park had been moved to where the play area was, it was huge and nearly full.

"How long do you intend to stay here?" Jack questioned "Because we must move on."

"Right let's go then." Next to the school. The school had grown to 250 children. There are 6 new classrooms. The church had improved grelely. "Juck, could we stop at Marlow House because Dad's there isnt he?"

"Yes he is. O.K., but only for 30 mins, right?" Dad has his own bungalow. There was a public swimming pool (in and out) for everyone. Outings were planned every fortnight.

"WOW! Can I move in too Jack?"

"When you're older and retired"

"Never I'll work till I die!"

"We'll see, I very much doubt it. Come on let's go home"

"Can we come and visit again?"

"The next time you come back it will be to put you in that home! Let's get back to Tunbridge Wells before it gets dark."

"Bye Dad" I shouted.

St. Mark's C.E. School
Hadlow Down

CLASS 3

(9 – 11 years old)

St. Mark's C.E. School
Hadlow Down

*Gazing into a crystal ball Olly had
the following predictions to make:*

The cars are soler paneled and go 300mph. They can be
red, yellow, black, green pink and blue. The school is a
sports and casino school and 100m² big. The school casino
is for the children 7 to 11 years old. The sports are
football, Tennis, basketball, netball, hockey and rugby.
The houses are funny and the wizzy windows come in
these colours blue, red, yellow, green and silver.

The Old Book of 1999 by Alex

"Grandma we're bored"   "Go and play on your hover
board"
"Done that!"   "Go and read on the story screen"
"Done that!"   "I know, go exploring"
"Where?"   "In the attic"
"But its dark and scary up there!"   "Use a torch"
"But grandma whats a torch?"   "A light with a
button on it"
Grandma gave a sigh and remembered when she was
young in 1999 and how she used to walk down the
lanes by torchlight. Meanwhile Dan and Kate were
hovering on their hover boards up the stairs.
They crawled cautiously into the attic and swithed on
the torch.
"Cor its dusty up here"

"Ow I think I've tripped over something its its a book of some sort."
"Come on let's reads it"
"O.K."

Chapter 1 The New Inn Pub
The New Inn pub will always be the same as long as it stays built, though the loos will probably be put indoors not outside.

Chapter 2 St. Mark's School
St. Mark's school will probably grow larger than 56 children and I don't think it will be closed down for a very long time. The main sports in St. Mark's school will be football, netball and rounders. One thing is certain that St. Mark's is as enjoyable to the children as it is work.

Chapter 3 Wilderness Wood
Wilderness Wood is 48 acres of very impressive deer, bird, mice, and snakes. If you would like to sace their homes join our campain to save The WOOD.

Chapter 4 St. Mark's Church
Over 150 years old St. mark's Church is very old and I think it will become famous and go down in history.

P.S. To future readers try to write a book about the time you are in --- and you know that's what they did.

CLASS 3

(9 – 11 years old)

Things Were Much Different Back Then
by
Verity

Emma ran in-to school. She was late again! She typed in 106728
that was the secret code the door opened. The teacher Mrs. Davis said
"why are you late"? Emma racked her brains for an excuse then she
said "my bike had a flat tyre" Mrs Davis smiled. "Come on Emma I'll
help you set up your computer" Emma sighed phew! She believed me
she thought. Emma looked at her comuter screen. It was history. The
title was "What it was like to live in Hadlow Down in 1999 Emma
started reading. This is what it said.

The School
The school was made up of 3 main buildings 2 prefabs and a main
building that was built by the Victorians. The two prefabs had a boy
and girls toilet and a staff room and two class rooms. The main
building had a boy and girls toilet and a staff toilet. In that
building also there was a kitchen, reception class, and Hall There
were only 56 children in the whole school

The Wood
The wood had a play park and a shop that held events like the Easter
bunny hunt. At Christmas time you could go and dig up your own
Christmas tree there was a bluebell walk and lots more. Wilderness
Wood was run by Ann Yarrow and her husband. The bell rang Emma
walked outside. She sat on the electric swing. She pushed the blue
button so the swing would go slowly. Emma started to think about the
school 50 years ago so much had changed. She wondered where the

two prefabs had been. Maybe they had been where the family of squirrels live. She went to were the packed lunches were. They were allowed to eat out side. She picked up her packed lunch box in it there was a sandwich, packet of prawn cocktail crips and a blackcurrent drink she gobbled it up yum she thought. She finished her lesson and sooner than she knew it it was home time. She rode to her grandmother's house, when Emma got there she asked her grandmother "were things Different when you were my age?" and her grandmother said "yes" things were much different back then.

Jessica wrote about the year 2050. Her fictitious character Anna has a very particular view of school life in the future

In the year 2050 there was a girl named Anna. She went through her usual routine. Her alarm went of and out of the seiling came a machine that got Anna dressed. Along came a chair that could take Anna into school. Her uniform was a silck shirt and a silck top and her shoes were flipflops. The boys wore white suits and a whit shirts and a white jacket and if the boys got it muddy the headteacher would give the boys a electric shock. But if the girls got it muddy the headteacher would come with a towle and make them clean. The day was three hours long , lessons were two minutes and the rest of the day was art and play time. Anna loved playing Beanie Baby Club and all her frends snd all her frends and Anna made member ship cards. The best thing was play time. It was very long, well that's what Anna says I dont know.

St. Mark's C.E. School
Hadlow Down

CLASS 3
(9 – 11 years old)

St. Mark's C.E. School
Hadlow Down

Rory, who is a year 4 pupil, wakes up to a very new world

I woke up I had a look at my alarm clock the time was 1,o clock Am 15th. of march 2050. I was 9 a month a go and my granddad was 90. He had a small wrinkled face and a thin body I had woken up becouse I thought I heard a noise. There it was a gain a big rumbling sound. It must be thunder. I loved storms so did grand dad. I was staying with him for the night. Grand dad was awake. I heard him calling "come on Sam come into my room and watch the storm" OK I said so I walked into the room where granddad was. He was standing on the balcony and watching the sky. I went and did the same. Then ther was a flash of light. And granddad's house got struck by lightning. Luckily me and my granddad were wearing our slippers. And all shoes nowadays are Rocket powered and can travel up to speeds of 50 m.p.s. so we hopped out of the way just in time as the balcony cllapsed beneath us. We did a circle of the village. We passed an old pub cald THE NEW INN and we landed in Wilderness wood. We searched around for a suitable place to spend the night. My granddad went to scouts when he was a boy so he knew how to lasc sticks to-gether and in adout 10 minutes we had built a good place to spend the night. In the morning I went home to get some clothes for me and some clothes for granddad. When I came back we put them on. I had to go to school so grandad promised that he woud bild a hut to live in while I was at school. So I flew to school and in 10

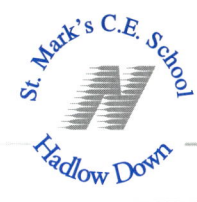

seconds I was there I pushed my card in to a slot in the gate and dor opened I flew into my class room and I switched on my computer and it said to days lesson is history. After our history lesson it was brake time. The play ground was huge and it had climing frames and slides and all the things an excellent play ground should have. Just then it started to rain and the roof started to close over it. Then we went home.

THE END

Hannah obviously believes that the role of teachers
will become redundant

Some Things never Change.

It was Friday 9th. November, the year 2050. The day dawned
bright and sunny. It was eight thirty in the morning. 8.30!
I had to take my Grandaughter Emily to school. Well, it was
my old school really I used to go there when I was young. It
was so much fun. You could go to school and play with your
friends and when the bell rang you'd line up a class at a
time and when the teacher called your class, you'd go in.

Emily is in year 6 now and doing extremely well, with
Geography, History, (she asked me about what the Millenium
Dome looked like before it had an extension) Science and
especially Maths.

The school was not like it used to be. Teachers were
replaced by computers. They didn't walk like we used to. They
had Hoverboards instead. The playground had swings,
slides and a roundabout, not just plain ordinary tarmac,
with coloured lines.

They didn't have a canteen, where you sat and talked
to your friends and ate your lunch. They had a social room
where there were comfy chairs, sofas and a little machine in
the corner which was like a computer. You tapped in what
you wanted to eat, waited for two minutes, and then, your
dinner came through a little slot at the front of the
computer.

Emily had soup for first course, Sunday roast for
second course, and Gypsy tart for pudding. Then she asked
me to have a go. At first I thought I'd refuse, then I thought
"why not? There's no harm in it," so I did and guess what? It
tasted lovely (Mmm somethings haven't changed) I even
went back for seconds!!!!

St. Mark's C.E. School
Hadlow Down

CLASS 3

(9 – 11 years old)

St. Mark's C.E. School
Hadlow Down

Many of the ideas that the children must have talked about are drawn together in this last story by Nick.

The School In 2050

One day James woke up and went down-stairs to have his microflakes. That was his favourite breakfast. Judy, his mum, asked how he had slept. James replied "Not very well. My new digital Time clock went off every 5 hours".

When he had finished breakfast he went back to his room to get dressed for school. He really liked his uniform it was a black suit and trousers with a white shirt.

It was now eight o'clock, time for school. James went back down, said bye to Judy, and got on his hoverboard. He travelled along the special path.

The big black gate automatically opened and he hovered to his class-mates. They were called Nick, Ben, Barnes and Jacob. They were talking about the new Robotic cyber pets and Barnes was going to get one. The ear buzzer went off. That was an ear piece that buzzed when it was the end of a lesson or beginning of play.

The whole school hovered to class in a long line. When they got in class they turned on their computers. James' computer told him it was History of St. Mark's school. His computer told him all about it.

There was the time when they planted some daffodils, and when you had to work on paper.

There were only 56 children then.

After that he had his lunch. He always had a packed lunch which was some chewing gum which you chew and it feels like you are eating a 3 course meal.

After lunch he went back to play cyber football which was a special ball which when you kicked it went extra fast.
The ear buzzer went off. It was back to work on History again.

At the end of school he went back home on his hoverboard. On the way back he passed the pub called The New Inn. A nice pub with an old fashioned snooker table and dart board.
Another attraction he went passed was Wilderness Wood. It is quite small now but it used to be very big.
When he got back he told his mum all about the school in 1999.

What a fitting ending it has been to this book to read about our future.

Thank you to the children of St. Mark's School Hadlow Down for their interesting ideas and stories. Maybe, just maybe in the future someone will find a copy of this book and determine just how accurate these predictions have been.